The Media and Peace

Also by Graham Spencer

DISTURBING THE PEACE? POLITICS, TELEVISION NEWS AND THE NORTHERN
IRELAND PEACE PROCESS

The Media and Peace

From Vietnam to the 'War on Terror'

Graham Spencer
School of Creative Arts, Film and Media,
University of Portsmouth, UK

First published 2005 by
PALGRAVE MACMILLAN
Houndmills, Basingstoke, Hampshire RG21 6XS and
175 Fifth Avenue, New York, N.Y. 10010
Companies and representatives throughout the world

PALGRAVE MACMILLAN is the global academic imprint of the Palgrave
Macmillan division of St. Martin's Press, LLC and of Palgrave Macmillan
Ltd. Macmillan® is a registered trademark in the United States, United
Kingdom and other countries. Palgrave is a registered trademark in the
European Union and other countries.

ISBN-13: 978–1–4039–2180–2 hardback
ISBN-10: 1–4039–2180–6   hardback

This book is printed on paper suitable for recycling and made from fully
managed and sustained forest sources.

A catalogue record for this book is available from the British Library.

Library of Congress Cataloging-in-Publication Data
Spencer, Graham
      The media and peace : from Vietnam to the 'War on terror' / by
Graham Spencer.
         p.   cm.
      Includes bibliographical references and index.
      ISBN 1–4039–2180–6 (cloth)
      1. War – Press coverage – United States.   2. War – Press coverage –
Great Britain.   3. Peace – Press coverage – United States.   4. Peace –
coverage – Great Britain.   5. Television broadcasting of news – United
Press States.   6. Television broadcasting of news – Great Britain.
I. Title.

PN4784.W37S665   2005
070.4'333'0973 – dc22

                                                          2005047242

10   9   8   7   6   5   4   3
14   13   12   11   10   09   08   07   06

Printed and bound in Great Britain by
Antony Rowe Ltd. Chippenham and Eastbourne

For my mother, Pamela Spencer and my brother,
Kevin Spencer

Every journalist who is not too stupid or too full of himself to notice what is going on knows that what he does is morally indefensible.

Janet Malcolm (*The Journalist and the Murderer*,
London: Granta, 1997)

Stand too close to horror, and you get fixation, paralysis, engulfment; stand too far, and you get voyeurism or forgetting. Distance matters.

Eva Hoffman (*After Such Knowledge*,
London: Secker & Warburg, 2004)

Contents

Acknowledgements

This study owes thanks to the many politicians and journalists I have spoken to in Northern Ireland over recent years who led me to believe that the media's problematic relationship with peace warranted a book. I would also like to thank the K. Blundell Trust for financial assistance towards this project and the University of Portsmouth who granted me teaching relief to complete it. Thanks to Victor Evans and the family of Nicholas Evans for kind permission to use his beautiful painting *Aberfan* for the cover. It goes without saying that my gratitude goes to colleagues Keith Tester and Chris Shilling at the University of Portsmouth. Special thanks to Jill Lake at Palgrave and to Penny Simmons for editorial support and advice. Most importantly, I want to thank my family and friends for warmth, kindness and support.

Introduction

The news media is not well disposed to peace. The war correspondent has no equivalent peace correspondent and extensive analysis about the media and war (Taylor 1998; Carruthers 2000; Thussu and Freedman 2003; Allan and Zelizer 2004) finds no comparative interest with the media and peace. Why is this? One obvious answer is that if the media is not concerned with peace, then there is little point in examining what is largely ignored or overlooked. However, in response to this position, one might also argue that it is precisely this absence of interest which raises important moral and social questions about what journalistic responsibility means. If the drama of conflict is given precedence over the undramatic but socially more desirable condition of peace, then what does this tell us about journalism and is this the kind of journalism that best serves society? This book attempts to address such questions by examining the role of the news media in a range of international conflict situations and highlights how a news obsessiveness with conflicts between dominant extremes tends to reinforce rather than challenge the path to violent conflict. If the news media tend to exacerbate political confrontation, whilst marginalizing non-confrontational discourse which seeks to de-escalate or prevent violent conflict, then this surely poses problems not just for the idea of journalistic objectivity, but society itself. The implications for society are clear. Peace depends on tolerance, which depends on understanding, which depends on information, which depends on the media. Although we can debate the degrees of influence which each provides within this continuum, there is enough evidence to tell us that tolerance has a greater chance of disappearing if we have no understanding of the 'Other' or see that 'Other' in terms of simplistic and crude stereotypes. The role of responsible journalism then is surely to try and produce information about other cultures and societies which contributes to a deeper understanding of each so that judgements made about those cultures and societies can be drawn on the basis of detailed information and interpretation rather than from emotive and sensationalized positions. Unfortunately, as the studies in this book reveal, news coverage is all too often concerned with entertainment and drama at the expense of detailed analysis and deconstruction. This has negative consequences for public understanding about how others are perceived, which provides the main point of focus for this book.

In order to interrogate such issues, I examine television news coverage (particularly US and British) from conflicts around the world and refer to examples of that coverage in order to develop discussion about the media's attention to peace and peace discourse. The role of television is particularly important for expansive communications and its global reach indicates its considerable power as a platform for politicians seeking to shape and influence national and international audiences. In relation to the media's potential impact on political policy and its role in political diplomacy, it is evident that television performs a more crucial function than the press and it is for that reason that I am more interested in it. Television news coverage of Vietnam, Rwanda, Bosnia, the Middle East, Northern Ireland and Iraq, reveals a notable lack of attention to voices of moderation and conflict prevention, as elite positions determine the parameters of debate and policy direction. Without access to counter-arguments which challenge dominant parties, news discourse not only legitimizes that discourse, but renders alternative articulations incidental, even worthless. This means, in turn, that the competitive zero-sum exchanges of mainstream politics determine the possibilities for action, but in terms of specific political rather than moral interests. The idea of a journalism which is peace oriented begins to look at this situation from the other way around. It puts moral questions and issues before the narrow concerns of party politics and actively seeks to stop violent conflict rather than merely supervise its development. Peace journalism, in other words, encourages us to think about the consequences of reporting and the human responsibility of trying to avert violent conflict whenever possible.

To interrogate the problem of reporting and peace this book consists of ten chapters. Chapter 1 is an outline of the conventions and processes which inform and sustain news culture. It introduces key contributions to understanding the constructs of journalistic practice and considers how the notion of objectivity influences understanding of journalistic responsibility. In Chapter 2, I look at the growing body of literature which examines the 'CNN effect' and the ability of television news to influence the foreign policy-making process. Instantaneous real-time news has produced a new set of pressures for policy-making which centre on the speed of communications. Although this chapter acknowledges growing speed in news output as a factor which necessitates close attention and respect by politicians, it also questions the ability of news to change or redefine political policy because of the pressure produced. If there are instances of news reports about suffering which fail to pressure governments into action, then what does this tell us about the ability of the media to move governments in directions they don't want to go in? And if it is politicians who determine policy rather than the media, just how much of a pressure is news coverage anyway? These issues will be dealt with in this chapter. Chapter 3 addresses the relationship between news and diplomacy and examines the process of 'diplomatic signalling' used by politicians and diplomats. The television news media is increasingly being absorbed into the diplomatic process and this has consequences for how diplomacy is practised and conveyed. The power of visual messages and non-verbal commuication are instruments of political communication which allow leaders to address a range of international audiences and leaders simultaneously. As a 'theatre of power' (Cohen 1987), television becomes the stage where leadership is played out and where the constant experience of threat and reassurance is managed to acquire public suport for policy. Although television has the potential to open up diplomacy to a range of protagonists who would be denied access if diplomatic exchanges were to be conducted behind closed doors, the media rarely introduce protagonists to the diplomatic process who deviate from the narrow concerns of elites. Reports may provide an opportunity for a broader range of non-governmental actors to engage in the diplomactic process, but the fulfilment of this opportunity is rarely realized.

Having assessed in the first three chapters the relationship between politics and news and how news might influence politics, I move on to investigate news coverage of Vietnam in Chapter 4. In particular, this chapter is concerned with the way the news media portrayed the peace movements in America who were opposed to the war, and considers the negative representations of the peace movements which were perpetuated in reports. These representations tended to depict peace organizations as a potential threat to social order by way of reference to left-wing elements, and thereby constructed the motivations of peace groups as antagonistic to authority and control. Such images provoked fear and disregard amongst audiences towards the peace movements, and contributed to making them even more unpopular than an already unpopular American government, whose Vietnam policy lacked credibility and cohesion. The American media's propensity to construct the peace movements as a potential destabilizing force within society reflected a lack of receptiveness to peace discourse and a concern for the more conflictive and emotive aspects of a story.

Chapter 5 considers news coverage of the Rwandan genocide and highlights Western indifference to intervention. This indifference indicates problems with news analysis of the genocide and refers to a range of stereotypical representations of African victims which serve to obscure underlying reasons for the violence. Western inaction to prevent the genocide was masked by a 'humanitarian response' to a refugee crisis created by victims trying to flee from perpetrators. The inability of news to properly distinguish victims from perpetrators is perhaps also further reflective of an inability by the Western media to examine the foundations of conflict and to highlight the need for preventative action to stop it. The genocide of Bosnia during the early 1990s provides a comparative assessment of 'humanitarian intervention' coverage which is addressed in Chapter 6. Once more we can observe a Western reluctance to act against a co-ordinated and concerted campaign of ethnic cleansing, but because of more intense pressure through coverage, we can also observe political efforts to confuse action and inaction, and to play up the genocide as a civil conflict in order to create confusion and disagreement about the purpose of intervention. The Balkan wars during the 1990s, which finally resulted in Western involvement in Kosovo to halt Serbian expansionism, demonstrate a containment policy by the West which ignored the complexities of conflict and failed to engage with the possibility of a credibly constructed peace.

Chapters 7 and 8 look at news coverage of peace processes in the Middle East and Northern Ireland respectively. Here I consider the problematic relationship which exists between confidentiality and publicity when societies are trying to move from conflict to fragile peace. Although the news media adopted a more sympathetic approach to peace in Northern Ireland compared to the Middle East, it remains noticeable that news has difficulties being receptive to more constructive articulations about peace, preferring to concentrate on power struggles and images of winning and losing. This impacts negatively on trust and confidence between parties and often contributes to intransigence rather than movement. How parties try to communicate their positions under the pressure of media scrunity, and the media's tendency to reduce the complexities of peace to a simplistic sequence of crises and breakthroughs are issues which are examined in these two chapters.

In Chapter 9, I consider the news media's role in relation to the first Gulf War, the 'War on Terror' and the Iraq war of 2003. Here, I am interested in the media's (in)ability to critically examine proposals for war and to look at the way propaganda was used by America and the UK in order to pursue an aggressive foreign policy agenda. This chapter charts a worrying propensity for the news media to complement government agendas in the 'war on terror' and the Iraq war highlights support for aggressive foreign policy aims in a post-9-11 world. The news media's lack of critical engagement with the 'war on terror' thesis promoted by the Bush administration reveals a new phase of reporting which makes use of 'non-information' by promoting speculation and threat as the foundation for public interest. In the new climate of fear, it is the reporting of *possible* rather than *actual* events which preoccupies much media attention and which constructs the 'war on terror' on a number of imaginary levels. But in the event of the 'war on terror' being a media war, where the 'enemy' is both everywhere and nowhere at the same time, we might well ask how is peace now possible? If news is the space where war is now being waged, what are the chances of news using that space to try and create peace, and indeed, what does peace mean in this context? These are the kinds of concerns which permeate analysis of the conflicts in this chapter and which build towards suggestions for a more peace-oriented media which are outlined in Chapter 10.

This chapter introduces developing themes and debates which have emerged in recent years in relation to peace journalism. This small but significant body of work attempts to connect with moral and ethical questions about journalistic responsibility and proposes a need for reporters to draw from conflict analysis theory in order to better assist the de-escalation or prevention of violent conflict. What is noticeable about some of the arguments which have contributed to the peace journalism debate is that journalists are viewed as humans first and journalists second. Because of this, human responsibility is expressed over the notion of detached observer and contributors tentatively try to make the case for moral duty as a key element within journalistic practice. In short, the premise of much of the literature starts from the position that it is more morally desirable to try and stop war rather than pretend that one has a professional responsibility to not try, and therefore not change the course of political action which is moving in that direction. The peace journalism debate is an important contribution to understanding the role of the news media in violent conflict, and considered in relation to the conventions of reporting conflict in this book, presents a valid and necessary critique of how the journalists report such conflict.

Throughout the book, there is considerable reference to conflict and there exists a certain amount of interchangeability in how this term is used. Although I hope that the distinctions will be self-evident, perhaps it is worth pointing out that I refer either to violent (physical) conflict on the one hand, or verbal or dialogue-based conflict on the other, but that I am essentially interested in the relationship between the two. With regard to the violent conflicts or wars analysed here, there is par-ticular attention given to how the media construct violence, and how they use conflict to inform structure and narratives about victims and perpetrators. Such representations are normally contextualized within a framework of conflictive discourse which is conducted between politi-cians and dominant parties and it is how the communications of those politicians and dominant parties are used by the news which particu-larly interests me in this book. My concern, by way of reference to a variety of case study conflicts, is to consider how news might try and prevent violent conflict rather than exacerbate it. This means approach-ing political discourse differently, and, by association, allowing different perspectives to be put forward about the likeliness or unlikeliness of violent conflict developing which, in the process, also contest the legit-imacy and credibility of such an outome. By allowing dominant pro-tagonists to control the emphasis of coverage, the perception is often created that no real credible alternatives are available to forge a diffe-rent (hopefully more positive) line of action.

In relation to the possibility of violent conflict, this raises a number of questions. Would more alternative positions in news help to open up 'constructive' discourse (seeking to avert conflict) and further illuminate the lack of imagination by those advocating 'negative' discourse (seeking to promote or create violence)? Would a news media which is more inclined to view the world as 'grey', rather than 'black and white', play a more expansive role with regards to situations which may have grave social consequences, and would the media fulfil its social respon-sibilites better if it became receptive to the voices of peace as well as the voices of war? These are the kind of issues and concerns which frame the arguments in this book.

1
News Culture

Journalism as field and practice

In his best-selling work *On Television and Journalism*, Pierre Bourdieu outlines the limitations and conventions of newsgathering by concentrating his discussion on the routines and practices of reporting in relation to what he calls the 'journalistic field'. For Bourdieu, the journalistic field is a space of cultural production which is created and sustained by the constraints, priorities and occupational routines of journalistic practice, and it is this space which 'produces and imposes on the public a very particular vision of the political field, a vision that is grounded in the very structure of the journalistic field and in journalists' specific interests produced in and by that field' (Bourdieu 1998: 2). The proposition that journalism is constructed through and within a 'field', offers a framework by which to interrogate reporting as a specific form of practice, which relies on organizational procedures and considerations that impact on the development and flow of public information and communication. As an assessment of news culture, Bourdieu's work is highly critical, yet offers us an interesting starting point from which to think about the methods of news production and some of the social and political consequences which news can have. It also offers us a reference point by which to develop a broader discussion of news culture and the practice of journalism generally. What is particularly noticeable with Bourdieu's critique, is that he is unhappy with the role that journalism performs in public life; a role which he believes justifies criticism because of a predisposition to market imperatives which contribute to 'produce a general effect of depoliticization' (ibid: 6). Bourdieu views the commercial and economic determinants of news production as inconsistent with intelligent discussion and dissemination of political debate, and argues for the need to rethink the relationship between journalism and power, if a growing trivialization of politics is to be averted. The consequences of a journalistic field which emphasizes entertainment and the individualization of political life over critical deconstruction of political life and its relation to social conditions appear to raise serious questions about what journalism is, and invite us to further examine such criticisms as well as assess their importance in the light of other studies which investigate journalistic culture and practice in a more detailed fashion.

Rather than journalism functioning as a process which contributes to an informed public sphere and which seeks to communicate debate about issues of social and political significance, Bourdieu considers news to be more concerned with confrontation between individuals (ibid: 3–4) and strategies of presentation between politicians who take part in spectacles of entertainment (ibid: 6). Journalism, he argues, is 'more interested in the tactics of politics than in the substance, and more concerned with the political effect of speeches and politicians' manoeverings within the political field (in terms of coalitions, alliances or individual conflicts) than the meaning of these' (ibid: 4). A tendency for journalism to construct politics as a series of antagonistic relations, for Bourdieu, means that 'events are reduced to the level of the absurd' and in turn, are 'cut off from their antecedents and consequences' (ibid: 6–7). Presented as a series of formulaic response and counter-response scenarios, where politicians are obliged to act out predictable gestures which complement the theatre of conflict provided by news narratives, politics is invariably reduced to a series of tragic and emotive charaterizations, which, in turn, contribute to the dramatization and trivialization of debate. Although this categorization of politics omits to take account of the presentational possibilities which politicians seek to exploit for reasons of political and ideological advantage, Bourdieu nevertheless raises important questions about the propensity of news to operate in a formulaic and repetitive fashion, which, he also contends, 'leads to a sort of leveling, a homogenization of standards' (ibid: 26). For Bourdieu, this process arises because of standards and expectations which are cultivated and sustained by the organization and routinized practices of the journalistic field itself, and it is the intensification of these standards and priorities which Bourdieu wants us to be particularly concerned about.

This routinized process of reporting, which is reinforced by journalistic competition (ibid: 22), is seen by Bourdieu to occur as an inevitable result of recurring pressures and limitations imposed on reporting by the nature of the field. Bourdieu's assessment of broadcast journalism returns to the theme of cultural constraint, which is brought to bear by the internal mechanisms and practices of the news industry. Those mechanisms and practices, which are responses to the competitive demands of the market, also shape the political world in relation to those demands. The implication of this environment for social life is clear: television journalism has become 'fast food' and presents politics as a product of entertainment in order to maximize audiences (ibid: 29). Rather than broadcast news being a platform for serious discussion and analysis of political initiatives and proposals, it has absorbed the market ethos of competition to the extent where contestation (both as process and practice) itself exists as the key determinant of the journalistic field. Here Bourdieu's critique presents us with a view of the journalistic field which is little different from other industries attempting to maximize audience consumption. The conventions and practices of the field reinforce the ethos of competition and by so doing, inhibit the deconstruction and investigation of politics for the public good. Although politicians have contibuted to this predicament, it would appear, for Bourdieu at least, that television news bears considerable responsibility for reducing politics to game-show entertainment.

Bourdieu's criticisms of news and its propensity to promote celebrity and superficiality bears some comparsion to Daniel Boorstin's classic work *The Image,* published in the early 1960s. For Boorstin, the construction of celebrity in politics is assisted by the manufacture of 'psuedo-events', which are events that exist only because of the news interest they generate. Within this context, a person is well known not so much for his importance within politics, but because of his well-knowness itself; an image which is sustained through an ongoing series of pseudo-events (1961). The basis of the pseudo-event is the interview, where the politician avoids specific details but works to create a positive impression. Uncertainty about the truth (because of the ambiguity created by a lack of substance) helps to maintain journalistic intrigue and ensures future coverage. Intrigue is supported by leaks which continue to hold journalistic attention and help give rise to other pseudo-events as a result. As the term 'pseudo-event' suggests, much political coverage is of no real social significance, but exists to keep politicians and political agendas public. By being made public the pseudo-event is imbued with an importance which in reality it lacks, but which it is given by its presence as news. What Boorstin observes is that pseudo-events have an accumulative impact which 'spawn other pseudo-events in geometric progression', and this happens because 'every kind of pseudo-event (being planned) tends to become ritualized, with a protocol and a rigidity all its own' (ibid: 33). Elaborating further on this point, he goes on, 'as each type of pseudo-event acquires this rigidity, pressures arise to produce other, derivative, forms of pseudo-event which are more fluid, more tantilizing, and more ambiguous' (ibid.). The press conference, which Boorstin considers to be another clear example of a pseudo-event, provides the opportunity to make news with little actual social or political relevance, but is devised and used to feed the newsgathering machine and maintain the illusion of importance. What Boorstin points towards is the inconsequentiality of much political news, which gains attention and significance solely because it exists as a product deemed newsworthy. In essence, the pseudo-event is a non-event which is transformed into an event because the news industry provides it with the significance and meaning which in reality it lacks.

Boorstin observes how there are certain elements which tend to characterize a pseudo-event. The pseudo-event must be dramatic, for this increases its chances of becoming newsworthy. It must have the potential to be repeated, for this helps reinforce the idea of importance. It must acquire financing to create the necessary presentational appeal. It needs to be effective in terms of performance. It should be conversational and personable in style. It should be staged to create the illusion of being informative. And it must provide the opportunity to create other pseudo-events by facilitating reaction, counter-reaction and leaks (ibid: 39–40). Leaks provide the 'dark information' (ibid: 34) which fascinate journalists and provide them the means to create exclusive stories and so remain ahead of their competitors. The greater the impression of exclusivity the more newsworthy the story. However, a consequence of prioritizing such information is that this is the way scandal and sleaze start to take priority over discussion, and it tends to feed subsequent pseudo-events and compound the absence of political analysis (news coverage of Bill Clinton's affair with Monica Lewinsky illustrates this trend). Like Bourdieu, Boorstin outlines a growing obsession with personalization and superficiality within reporting, which may be entertaining and may keep politicians within the public gaze, but which ultimately does a disservice to the prospect of a politically informed and intelligent public sphere.

The argument that television news uses entertainment (and specifically contestation) in order to try and maximize audience interest is also taken up by Epstein in his study *News from Nowhere* (2000 edn). Epstein asserts that the main intention of television news is not to inform viewers, but to keep them excited enough to keep watching. To achieve this, the networks resort to the use of story formats 'that are presumed most capable of holding the attention of viewers, regardless of their subject or content' (2000: 240). This technique of maintaining audience interest is, he notes, quite different from that used by newspapers since television news 'allows its audience no respite or selectivity in the flow of news it is watching', thus, 'in theory every news report must continually interest the audience' (ibid.). Furthermore, continues Epstein, 'since television is regarded a medium for the "transmission of experience" rather than "information," complex issues are represented in terms of human experience' (ibid: 262), and constructed in terms of conflictive differences between people. The importance of this narrative is that it adopts simplified formats and plots to keep audiences interested, and uses simplification and predictability because 'viewers' interest is most likely to be maintained through easily recognizable and palpable images, and conversely, most likely to be distracted by unfamiliar or confusing images' (ibid.). Associated with this use of immediately recognizable imagery is the casting of characters 'in the form of the fictive story, with narrative closure' (ibid: 263), which sustains the dramatic emphasis and informational order of reports. Finding agreement with Bourdieu, Epstein identifies the organization and routines of production as the basis of journalistic practice, and concludes that journalists 'avoid rational arguments not because they are politically committed to supporting "the system," but because they do not satisfy the audience requisites of network news' (ibid: 271). Like Bourdieu, Epstein acknowledges the inability of television news to analyse the causes and consequences of the events and scenarios reported, and considers this to be a direct consequence of the occupational priorities which shape news culture. The processes of event selection and story construction, in other words, are devised to complement and reinforce working practices which are themselves consistent with the imperatives of the journalistic field. It would appear that for both Bourdieu and Epstein, the bias of news stories is controlled more by the organizational priorities and conventions of newsmaking than a commitment to the values and principles of democratic life and an informed public sphere (ibid: 270).

This emphasis, which portrays news as entertainment that depoliticizes the political process (even though news clearly has political consequences) noticeably suggests negative implications for the production of 'public knowledge' (Schudson 1995: 3). The production of such knowledge is particularly limited when news has a tendency to present politics in terms of 'political technique rather than policy outcome' (ibid: 10), and considers political decision-making by way of its mechanical rather than ideological dimensions. Schudson's analysis of news, power views reporting as a process of operations structured 'within a cultural system, a reservoir of stored cultural meanings and patterns of discourse' (ibid: 14). The function of this process (echoing Boorstin) is to gain public attention by amplifying the social and political significance of events and capturing interest because of this amplification (ibid: 19). For Schudson, the formulaic narrativization and distribution of 'public knowledge' rather interferes with the notion of an informed public sphere, and exposes considerable shortcomings in how the news serves public life (ibid: 28–9). Here, once more, we return to the argument that restraints placed on news construction are underpinned by the cultural values which journalists share and that such values are constitutive of the journalistic field.

These values and the conceptualization which sustain them, are carefully deconstructed in Gans's seminal work *Deciding What's News* (1980). Here, Gans identifies a series of key values in the production of news which both determine journalistic output and obstruct the possibilty of objectivity (ibid: 42). He explains how story selection can be understood by thinking about the newsgathering process in terms of being journalist centred, organization centred and event centred. That is: (1) where stories are decided by way of professional judgements; (2) given the routine and organizational requirements of networks; and (3) events which exhibit characteristics that capture journalistic interest (ibid: 78–9). To maintain the emotive emphasis which stories are expected to have in order to capture audience interest, journalists need to stress appeal and adopt an interpretive approach through a line of questioning which works to magnify the drama (ibid: 307). Notably, events become newsworthy only when they display qualities which are consistent with journalistic values (Galtung and Ruge 1965; Gans 1980: 42) which complement the procedures and imperatives of journalistic practice.

For Bennett, a range of factors inhibit journalistic objectivity:

1 There are the values which make political events inherently newsworthy.
2 Newsmakers deceive themselves in the belief that objectivity is a prerequisite of good reporting.
3 The problem of attaining a point of view which is neutral.
4 The impossibility of reporting all facts combined with all possible interpretive contexts for those facts.
5 The pressure to meet deadlines, which restricts the space for comprehensive analysis (Bennett 2003: 192).

Considered in relation to these points, objectivity is illusive because of affiliations to political power, organizational constraints, the predictability of report construction, and the limited scope of news frames. It is precisely because of the interdependency between institutions of political power and organizational restrictions that journalistic objectivity is not only evasive, but unattainable. In looking closer at this problem, Bennett recognizes how 'maintaining the illusion of news objectivity depends on a narrow range of perspectives admitted into the news and by the heavy reliance on official views to certify those perspectives as credible and valid' (ibid: 199–200). The notion of objectivity, therefore, tends to be articulated within a series of procedures which prioritize 'mainstream political perspectives while underreporting competing views' (ibid.). Interestingly, this perspective suggests that the concept of objectivity as a measurement of quality journalism ignores the restrictive nature of the practice which shapes it, as well as the bias of values which determine the order and content of reports. But such bias, according to Bennett, is reflective of a standardization in reporting which reinforces rather than exposes the illusion of objectivity. For Bennett, the bias and order of information comes from a preoccupation with human interest stories (personalization), the emphasis on drama and crisis over continuity (dramatization), the dislocation of stories from each other and the broader context in which they are situated (fragmentation), and the tensions between authority and disorder (authority–disorder bias) (ibid: 44–50). Constructing reports through an informational bias highlights the formulaic nature of report construction and the homogenization of story-telling; a homogenization which is also sustained by journalists confirming the legitimacy and accuracy of reports by comparing and corroborating approaches to stories (ibid: 175).

What consequences might the journalistic field have for democracy given the conventions of practice? Gans argues that the potential for news to more substantively deal with issues of social and political concern could be realized if there was a shift towards what he calls 'multiperspectival news'. Here, Gans envisages a model of alternative news reporting which would provide a bottom–up rather than the current top–down approach. This approach, he argues, would help create more output, aim to be more representative, and emphasize the 'service' function of news (providing detailed information for sectors and roles that people see as important to their lives) (Gans 1980: 313–14). To make the news media engage more specifically with demands and concerns of public and social life, Schudson provides a list of points which elaborate the need for: a wider range of information, coherent frameworks for making sense of politics, news which reflects the interests of varied social groups, a wider range of news which provides the quantity and quality that people want, more media involvement in forcing government accountability, a wider empathy for other citizens in the world, and a forum for dialogue that more widely informs the processes of political decision-making (Schudson 1995: 28–9). This list is an attempt to confront what Schudson sees as clear deficiences in the way news communicates social and political issues and highlights how journalistic responsibility is oriented towards concepts of professionalism rather than contributing to an informed citizenry.

News economy

One cannot properly understand the functions and operations of the journalistic field without assessing how commercial pressures shape the processes of news production and affect the existence of news organizations. For Bourdieu, the pressures created by the market must be comprehended if one is to understand why television journalism functions as it does. The competitive environment of the market, which increases the pressure on journalists and news networks to compete with each other over audience ratings, creates a struggle for popularity and favours uniformity over diversity because of demand for this popularity (Bourdieu 1998: 72). Homogenization is a response to pressures created by the need to try and appeal to as many audiences as possible and is achieved through news agendas which conform to similiar production processes, routines among agencies, pressure to repeat the coverage of other agencies, and the use of repeating frames to make sense of events (Paterson 1998: 84–5). Collectively, such influences reinforce the tendency of news to produce 'an ideologically distinctive and homogenous view of the world' (ibid: 82) which remains consistent with market imperatives. But, with news, as with the global media system in general, the trend has been towards increased concentration of ownership and control, which has meant significant changes to the competitive environment in which networks operate. As Paterson highlights, in response to the changing economic climate of commercialism, news networks have now become ostensibly 'wholesalers' and 'packagers' of visuals, sound and text information (ibid: 80), where news is exchanged and retailed to the market. By operating in this way, news networks 'can be seen as simply adding value to existing information, and reselling it' (ibid: 81), and journalists' decisions must complement the commercial expectations which drive this process (ibid: 94).

The communications industries have played a key role in the move towards increased concentration by exercising influence 'over national legislation and government agencies' to an extent, argues Bagdikian, which 'would have been considered scandalous or illegal twenty years ago' (1999: 148). Assisted by advances in digitial technology and the market ethos which has facilitated corporate acquisitions, the communications industry has succeeded in easing government regulatory involvement in relation to ownership and news output (ibid.). Global news networks reflect the conservative and economic values which have helped shape the conditions of the market environment, and have played a necessary part in the development of subsidiaries which reflect business interests (ibid: 149). News, in other words, has become central to the consolidation of media power and the corporate needs of global media conglomerates (McChesney 1999: 16–22).

The impact of media conglomerates seeking to dominate output as much as possible in their own area (horizontal integration), as well as acquiring further channels of distribution for other products (vertical integration), has helped to shape a climate which has had a number of potentially damaging effects on the processing and distribution of information:

1 There is a propensity for smaller independent outlets to be squeezed out of the market because of advertising revenue being taken by the dominant organizations.
2 Corporate promotion encourages journalistic self-censorship and erodes diversity of content further.
3 News is pulled towards entertainment formats and human interest themes in order to capture audience interest.
4 As the public service ethos diminshes, it is increasingly being replaced by the profit motive.
5 Packaging and branding become more important than content and information (Bennett 2003: 97).

For the communication industries, concentration and privatization have produced other important consequences which can be summarized as the denationalization, liberalization, and commercialization of the public sector, which have led to regulations being eased in order to assist the consolidation of each (Murdock 1990: 10). Denationalization has led to a position where the power of the communications industry is strengthened by lack of global control over the concentration of media ownership; liberalization has injected a competitive ethos into markets which were previously dedicated to serving public service interests (ibid: 11); and a reduction in regulatory controls by governments has helped the information industries to further exploit market opportunities (ibid: 13). Such changes raise 'important questions both of government regulation of monopoly power in national and international markets, and of government policy, with respect to access by the public, to traditional types of public information' (Melody 1990: 28). Or, to put it another way, 'the global information and communication industries may have outgrown the national institutional mechanisms for ensuring that the public interest is seriously considered in their policies and practices' (ibid: 31).

Although, as Herman and McChesney note, national contexts differ in their relation to the global media market because of differing national policies and approaches (1999), it is evident that the global trend towards media concentration is funtioning as a considerable external pressure on national differences, to the point where 'all media firms are responding to a general market situation that is *forcing* them to move toward being much larger, global, vertically integrated conglomerates' (ibid: 189). News networks are but one means of cultural production for conglomerates which operate as 'synergies', using links between different media companies within the conglomeration to exploit economic opportunities and support broader commerical interests (Golding and Murdock 1999: 160). This philosophy of appealing to market demand and economic imperatives has corresponded with a reduction of news distributors and supported shifts in news selection and output, which has eroded representational diversity. As Paterson describes this development: 'Despite the increasing number of news services, ownership is highly concentrated, and broadcasters are becoming increasingly dependent upon a few news providers to supply the international images they use on air: the images that shape our global reality' (1998: 96). One result of this homogenization has been the reinforcement of a Western hegemonic position towards developing nations, and promotion of cultural preferences which diminish the significance of non-Western cultures (ibid: 95). News outlets have increasingly become marketplaces of ideas, which insulate the dominance of Western values and isolate non-Western values as incidental or threatening to the Western model. This insularity has been further strengthened by the reduction of network foreign news bureaux (Bagdikian 1999: 152), and by commercial priorities over issues of public citizenship and debate (ibid: 150).

News politics

For Bourdieu, political status has become inextricably linked to the journalistic field and news has become the main arena in which political reputations are made (1998: 5). It is because of this, he contends, that journalism creates for politicians 'vital symbolic support that they can't get for themselves' (ibid: 4). It is the representational power of news and its public consumption which therefore make journalism central to modern political life. However, this dynamic is also complex and multidimensional, and it is the complexity of this relationship which remains understated by Bourdieu. The interaction between politics and news is a symbiotic one, where journalism functions not just as an extension of political power (Hall 1978), but as a potentially disruptive influence on that power. The role of news, to put it another way, is not merely to reproduce political activity, but to interpret and influence the contestations which underpin that activity. As McNair defines this relationship: 'Not only do the media *report* politics, they are a crucial part of the environment in which politics is pursued. They contribute to policy discussion and resolution, not only in so far as they set public agendas, or provide platforms for politicians to make their views known to the public, but also in judging and critiquing the variety of political viewpoints in circulation' (1995: 73). In prioritizing a series of actions and reactions (ibid: 47), news packages politics into stories based on the perfomance of political actors (ibid: 208), and therefore presents politics as dramatic theatre. This theatre is absorbed into processes of reportage, interpretation and interrogation (McNair 2000: 105), which enable the performances to be scrutinized and assessed, before being presented as political stories (ibid.). In contemporary society, political journalism has, according to McNair 'entered a meta-discursive phase, in which coverage of political affairs is inseparable from that of policy-substance' (ibid: 171). For McNair, in contrast to the position taken by Bourdieu, by becoming more analytical in approach, journalism has taken on an increasingly interventionist role within the political decision-making process, which itself has responded by adopting sophisticated public relations and news management strategies in order to deal with the media's widening political role (ibid.).

The basis of the news media's importance in the political process lies in its ability to operate as an intermediary between politicians and the audience, with news outlets providing a platform able to deliver audiences to politicians in ways unavailable by other means (Blumler and Gurevitch 1995: 13). But, within this interaction, a range of other processes are going on which serve functions of political legitimacy, articulation, mobilization and conflict management (ibid: 19). Consensual and conflicting relations which are inherent to politics become amplified by the news media, highlighting both the supportive and obstructive impact which reporting may have on political life and the media's role as advocates of social control and change (ibid: 57). Although, as McNair observes, such influences indicate 'a rigorous test of ability and character for those who would wield political power' (2000: 175), it remains evident that problems that news may create for the political process is tolerated largely because of the mutual dependency culture which exists between the two (Blumler and Gurevitch 1995: 42).

Developing this analysis further, Wolfsfeld observes how 'the best approach for understanding the role of the press in political conflicts is to look at the competition over the news media as part of a more general contest for political control', where 'the flow of influence between antagonists and the news media can only be understood by the *relative* power of each side' (1997: 197). Providing five key points for considering the interplay between the news media and politics, Wolfsfeld's analysis is an attempt to engage with the problem of how relations between news and politics rise and fall with levels of contestation within the political field. He notes:

1 'the political process is more likely to have an influence on the news media than the news media are on the political process' (ibid: 215).
2 'the authorities' level of control over the political environment is one of the key variables that determine the role of the news media in political conflicts' (ibid: 216).
3 'the role of the news media in political conflicts varies over time and circumstance' (ibid: 217).
4 'those who hope to understand variations in the role of the news media must look at the competition among antagonists along two dimensions: one structural and the other cultural' (ibid.).
5 'while authorities have tremendous advantages over challengers in the quantity and quality of media coverage they receive, many challengers can overcome these obstacles and use the news media as a tool for political influence' (ibid: 218).

Looking at the role of news in the Middle East (which is considered in greater depth in Chapter 7), Wolfsfeld considers the relationship between news and politics during the first Gulf War, the Intifada and the Oslo Accords. Highlighting how political influence over the media changes with the conflict being covered, he identifies how the media were dominated by the authorities during the Gulf War; how reporting adopted a more independent stance, acting as a broker of power between the Palestinians and Israelis during the Intifada; and how coverage challenged the varying perspectives of those involved with the Oslo Accords process. Examination of these conflicts highlight how political control of the news process is the key determinant on news influence (ibid: 210), and how the tighter political control is over conflict, the more likely news is to reinforce that control. On the other hand, when control becomes weakened or destabilized by competing voices, the media subsequently reflects this antagonism, and its disruptive potential is increased.

Two important features of political influence over the news media indicate the representational power of news and its role as an environment for political life and diplomacy. First, the construction of what Elderman calls the 'political spectacle', and second, what Dayan and Katz term 'media events'. For Elderman, the political spectacle is a process of construction which negotiates and manipulates the flow of news in order to exploit its potential for the presentation of political meaning. Identifying how news tends to confirm rather than unsettle common values and beliefs, where 'If news stories challenge deeply held assumptions, they can be ignored; and if they point in no clear direction, they can be interpreted to conform to prior assumptions' (1988: 91), Elderman views the political spectacle as a device where ambiguity and subjectivity are used and exploited to 'constitute the political world' (ibid: 95). The political spectacle is not intended to assist public understanding or contribute to intelligent debate, but instead to make use of the dramatic emphasis which news provides by creating stories which produce 'a drama that objectifies hopes and fears' (ibid: 96). Such stories are designed to give definitional power to social situations through a spectacle that 'normally rationalizes those conditions' (ibid: 103) by the use of conflicts and antagonisms. The political spectacle Elderman continues, uses political language to manage a range of problems and challenges, and manages meaning through conflict in order to achieve political credibility (since without conflict 'the issue is not political, by definition' (ibid: 104)) and legitimacy. Elderman considers conflict as vital for effective political control since it maintains movement and prevents the rigidity of static consensus, which is itself problematic because it interferes with the idea of political power being dependent on 'the persistence of unresolved meanings' (ibid: 19).

For Elderman, uncertainty and ambiguity is the basis of the political spectacle, and he suggests that it is how such conditions are controlled which should concern us most of all. Certainty and consensus, he notes, are not flexible, but inherently unstable compared to ambiguity, which is fluid and difficult to pin down. Ambiguity gives politicians more room for manoeuvre and enables problems to be presented as solutions (ibid: 21–3), as well as allowing problems to be flexibly used in order to divert public attention from potentially more threatening issues of concern (ibid: 27). Within a political field of conflict, it is uncertainty and ambiguity which provides the space for movement and which allows conflict itself to be more effectively integrated into political action. Unlike the rigidity of certainty, ambiguous language 'is a sign and facilitator of bargaining', and it is ambiguous language which tends to keep participants engaged during moments of intense disagreement (ibid: 25). The political spectacle therefore provides opportunities for diplomacy and interaction precisely because it evades specificity.

Though news tends to reinforce power relations and a hegemonic approach to politics and political ideas, it is evident that its ability to amplify meaning corresponds with a propensity to amplify ambiguity, as well as preferred and dominant ways of doing things. For the role of peace, this ambiguity is particularly important, and the promotion of media events are useful indicators of how such meanings may be used for the development of diplomatic interaction (as Negrine puts it: 'The imagery and ceremony contained in "media events" can also be extremely powerful and politically useful ways of signalling dramatic change' (1996: 171)). Media events which are usually large scale and staged to reach international audiences 'are imbued with important symbolic, political, social and other properties which set them apart from the coverage of more 'ordinary events' (ibid: 170), but it is the imagery which they promote that most strongly intimates the clues 'to changing relationships' (ibid: 171).

The most comprehensive analysis of what media events do and mean, is found in the work of Dayan and Katz who, as part of their analysis, identify some of the key political implications of the media event as diplomacy. Because media events tend to be broadcast live, they 'can integrate nations' (1992: 204) and 'breed the expectation of openness in politics and diplomacy' (ibid: 203). Media events, Dayan and Katz maintain, 'create a new resource for diplomacy', where 'the diplomacy of gesture may have the power to create a favourable climate for a contract or to seal a bargain' (ibid: 205). Further highlighting the importance of the media event as a platform for diplomatic activity, they note how 'public exhortations pressure negotiators into not slamming doors. Losing face consists in failing to emerge with a positive statement. The drama of diplomatic media events is one of overcoming differences. When all else has failed, media events may succeed in breaking diplomatic deadlocks or in surmounting stalemates by creating a climate conducive to negotiation, one in which the public signals its anticipation of reconciliation' (ibid: 204–5).

The ability of the news media to convey messages to a wide range of audiences also demonstrates its expansive power and brings into view once more the significance of ambiguity as part of the diplomatic process (which Dayan and Katz consider to be central to effective diplomatic communications). The openness of negotiation through the media event presents the negotiator 'with the impossible task of addressing his own constituency back home, his partner's constituency, and, last but not least, world public opinion – all at the same time' (ibid: 205). And yet, they observe: 'it can be done; the fact is that media events manage to deliver different messages simultaneously. Their power in difficult or blocked situations derives from what diplomats call constructive ambiguity; that is, from the paradoxical framing of elusive content in strong declarations of intent' (ibid.).

The media event has a number of effects on public opinion and political institutions (ibid: 199–202) which: help to reinforce the status of participants and issues involved; make evident the personalization of power; create expectations of openness; remove the need for intermediaries; and reconfigure social relations (ibid: 213–14). Along with the political spectacle, what the media event helps us to realize, is that news coverage can provide a range of communicative imissing for politics which are largely drawn from the political arena, which itself influences the organization, planning and management of journalistic interest. But, what this also indicates is that the routine and predictable nature of news coverage augments the communicative power of the event by showing it repeatedly. Homogenized coverage which applies similar patterns of interpretation also serves to exaggerate the perceived significance of the event, and thereby increases its diplomatic importance. However, it is important to bear in mind that news diplomacy is complex and that 'it can include bringing information to light, contributing new information, and persuading "public opinion", rather than simply bringing about dramatic change in policies' (Negrine 1996: 175). Since the media have the power to magnify mistakes as well as successes, it is evident that the relationship between news and politics shifts and changes, but that such shifts and changes are primarily brought about by politics rather than news.

Conclusion

The relationship between news culture, news economy and news politics, indicates three core elements of influence which impact on the journalistic field. The idea that news culture constructs politics through narratives which trivialize and dramatize issues and debates that are of social and public significance points us towards the realization that news depoliticizes politics by concentrating on the entertainment of conflict. Moreover, as Bourdieu implies, because of its emphasis on celebrity, style and individuality, news has contributed to making politics barely distinguishable from other forms of popular culture (here, too, the emphasis is on celebrity, style and individuality) and helped the demise of an informed and politicized public sphere as a result. Bourdieu's argument may be seen as a dramatization itself, however, for although he is surely correct to point out the tendency of news to prioritize entertainment over debate, he neglects to scrutinize the involvement of politics itself in this game or assess how modern politics has transformed its delivery of messages and comments to accommodate the growing range of presentational possibilities which news now affords. Nevertheless, perhaps for Bourdieu, this is largely irrelevant since however news constructs and represents politics, and however politics responds to such constructions and representations, the overriding problem remains of narratives which trivialize and situate issues in the realms of the personal rather than the public.

But although Bourdieu's assertions may have credibility, there is also a tendency to generalize the processes of newsmaking and the relationship between politics and news. Yes, we might argue that one only has to watch the news to see that it takes a largely homogenized approach to stories and analysis, but we should also note that different political circumstances require different political responses and reactions, and it is obvious that political reaction to a sex scandal is not going to be the same as to a serious foreign policy dilemma. One cannot help but note that Clinton's affair with Monika Lewinsky seems to have received more media scrutiny than his policies towards Afghanistan, Bosnia, Rwanda and the Middle East (we probably feel more familiar and 'informed' about his affair anyway), and that Boorstin raises a very important point when he suggests that the performance or the illusion of politics seems to have replaced politics itself. However, this should not distract us from the range of uses which political communications perform, depending on the issue or problem which arises at any one point in time. Nor should it disguise the complexity of relations between politics and news and the varying consequences of political stories (domestic stories differ markedly from foreign policy stories which address different audiences and different cultural/political concerns). The economic and cultural influences on newsmaking may well be restrictive and predictable in terms of effecting output, and it is difficult to deny that news exaggerates the more dramatic and sensational aspects of an event or situation at the expense of debate and reasoned argument. However, we need to remember that ultimately it is politicians who shape the contours of communications rather than news. The political spectacle and the media event are but two examples where the communication of politics takes on a presentational sophistication which has major implications for diplomacy and conciliatory politics and it is this area in particular with which I am concerned in this book. What I want to explore more closely in the next chapter is the relationship between news and politics in regard to policy, and to try and identify the influences and impacts which coverage might bring to bear on political intervention in humanitarian crises. This, I think, will demonstrate the complexity of news–politics relations, and help to facilitate further discussion about how reporting interacts with political action.

2
The Impact of News on Foreign Policy

The CNN effect

The ability of news reporting to instantaneously cover unfolding political situations and events has raised questions about the impact of news
on political decision-making and policy formation. Much analysis
which has addressed this problem is concerned with the pressures which
news coverage can bring to bear on politicians, and whether political
policy can be shaped by the influences of news through what has
become known as the 'CNN effect'. According to Gowing, the CNN
effect is a process which derives from real-time reporting, where instantaneous reporting of conflicts and diplomatic crises can create expectations which challenge foreign policy aims (1994a: 1). For Bell, the
substance of the CNN-effect debate centres on 'the tendency of governments to adjust their policies to cope with the something-must-
be-done demands generated by TV coverage of a humanitarian crisis'
(2003: 37). The ability of news to move policy in this way is a result of
television news images which 'compress transmission and policy
response times', which, in turn, 'puts pressure on choice and priorities
in crisis management' (Gowing 1994a: 1). The basis of the CNN effect,
then, is speed, since it is speed of coverage which is able to create problems for politicians by demanding a quick response, and it is speed
which is able to reveal policy uncertainty and highlight political
incompetence in the light of an emerging conflict or diplomatic
crisis. Without a coherent, thought-through policy agenda, real-time
coverage, it would appear, is able to expose weaknesses which can have
political repercussions.

One notable problem with the CNN-effect debate, however (as
Robinson rightly points out (1999)), is that it remains rather unspecific
about the extent of television's relationship with policymaking in the

24

real-time news environment, and has difficulty pinpointing the influences which coverage actually has. Gowing's work, for example, makes a number of claims which appear to mystify more than clarify the effects of television news on foreign policy, and which indeed seem somewhat contradictory. Thus, 'real-time television coverage serves to highlight the policy dilemma but does not resolve it' (Gowing 1994a: 12). Or, 'Television coverage' is 'a powerful influence in problem recognition, which in turn helps to shape the foreign policy agenda. But television does not necessarily dictate policy responses' (ibid: 18). Or, although 'there is no doubt that for some policy makers the real-time TV coverage does have a defining role in policy' (ibid: 84), overall 'future real-time television coverage of the proliferation of regional conflicts will create emotions but ultimately make no difference to the fundamentals in foreign policy making' (ibid: 87). Paradoxically, Gowing's analysis seems to suggest that real-time news makes both a difference and no difference to political policy. Expectations for actions can be created which politicians may be forced to react to (making a difference), but this pressure rarely translates into a policy shift (making no difference). Thus, in Croatia and Bosnia, television may have 'highlighted the West's impotence and failure to find enough of a diplomatic consensus to prevent or pre-empt war', but its coverage 'did not force crisis prevention' (ibid: 7). Similarly, coverage of the Serbian bombardment of the UN Safe Area of Gorazde in April 1994, or the 200,000 people slaughtered in Rwanda during the same month, proved unable to pressure Western governments into actions which departed from existing policy goals (ibid: 7). Indeed, notes Gowing, in the case of Rwanda, what coverage did do was merely provide opportunities for a Western response which 'illustrated the new pragmatism and reluctance' to engage in humanitarian disasters (ibid: 86).

Further indicating difficulties with ascertaining the extent of influence which real-time television news images can have on politics, Gowing argues that television images have 'nuisance value' which, by working in contradiction to the slow, systematic and reflective processes of policy formation (Gowing 1996: 83), can increase the likelihood that something will be done. But this something which may, or may not be done, needs to be considered in the context of what he calls 'pseudo-decisions', such as 'statements of concern or condemnation', or 'expressions of outrage', which act as responses to the pressures of instantaneous coverage (ibid: 84). The scope of reaction, Gowing tells us, 'can be anything from a UN Resolution to sending a press spokesman out' (ibid.). Though Gowing points us towards the realization that it is politics rather than news which determines approaches to conflicts and crises, the confusion arises because his discussion relates the *possible* rather than *actual* effects of coverage to policy. To illustrate once more the potential for inconsistency, Gowing asserts that coverage can have *tactical* significance, with 'localized, immediate impact' and *strategic* relevance, which produces 'medium-to-long term' impact on government policy-making (ibid: 85). Morever, such impact can contribute to periods of 'policy panic', undermining 'a government's ability to maintain its iron will for minimalist engagement' (ibid: 86). But, even given the power of real-time coverage to incite such developments, we are stlll left with the conclusion that 'only rarely is there a change to overall strategy' (ibid: 88). What Gowing fails to evidence is how images of horror translate into political action which deviates from a policy line drawn up at the start of a humanitarian crisis (1994b: 47).

According to Strobel, the CNN effect is said to exert an 'inordinate influence on policy' by way of producing 'temporary emotional responses', which 'conflict with the more considered judgement of foreign policy officials, forcing them to take action that will soon have to be reversed or modified' (1996: 357). Strobel then goes on to contend that 'the CNN effect does not exist in many places where it is said to be found, and even where its traces can be detected, they are exaggerated, working only in combination with other factors' (ibid: 359). Importantly, the pressures of television news 'hold no power to force US policymakers to intervene in a civil conflict where there's no clear national interest' (ibid: 358), and if television does seem to have an influence, this is seen to occur because of political actors framing and inciting coverage to begin with. Indeed, instead of news images acting as a lever to promote a need for involvement and intervention in ways which politicians would prefer to avoid, 'pictures and other news media products can help explain the need for intervention to the public, making officials' task of persuasion that much easier' (1997: 162). What this suggests is that the power of television news images to influence policy is misleading since it points towards a cause and effect argument which lacks evidence of a clearly identifiable cause and effect process. A more realistic explanation is that the potential impact which such images may or may not have to disrupt policy is determined to a large extent by how politicians deal with those images, and how they use that significance in the context of existing policy aims. The immediacy of real-time news may unsettle politics, but this tendency to unsettle also highlights the need for politicians to reassert control over the situation and clarify their approach to it (Hoge 1994: 136–7). The argument that 'In the absence of persuasive government strategy, the media will be catalytic' (ibid: 138), merely reaffirms the findings of Hallin, who, in conducting analysis of news during the Vietnam War, noticed how strong political consensus tends to be reinforced by the news media, whereas lack of consensus and disorganization tends to be amplified (either way, it is politics which creates the conditions which the media draw from) with potentially destabilizing consequences (Hallin 1994). The political consequences of media communication are therefore inextricably linked to political pervasiveness (Hoge 1994).

Within the CNN climate, the instantaneity of real-time communications allows for a corresponding immediacy of exchanges between parties which enable 'bypassing the entire apparatus of intelligence, diplomacy and national security' (Stech 1994: 38). The immediacy of real-time coverage has political significance not just because it may allow politicians to become aware of conflicts and crises, and force them to respond to those problems within a context which television has initially determined, but because the presentation of such conflicts and crises is made available to the wider public at the same time, thus making it difficult for politicians to refute or ignore the importance of the situation which unfolds (ibid: 39). Pressure on politicians is created, then, because on the one hand news can demand reaction which might magnify positions of uncertainty or weakness and, on the other, because that weakness is witnessed publicly on an international stage, providing opponents and other actors with an opportunity to capitalize on the visible uncertainty. For politicians to successfully manage the CNN climate, it is clear that they must be seen to be reflexive, adaptive and prepared to utilize the persuasive signs and symbols necessary to support public perceptions of political strength and certainty (ibid: 45). The creation of such perceptions is dependent on politicians being able to transfer the effect of real-time news pressures on to opponents and to make evident that, under those pressures themselves, they have been able to show leadership and strength. In other words, just as the impact of real-time news can create problems, so it can provide opportunities for those problems to be overcome (or managed), and for public profiles to be improved. Moreover, the speed of exchanges which real-time television news creates, and which has become a key consideration in modern political communications, provides a platform for gestures and signs which have diplomatic significance (McNulty 1993). This speed offers political leaders the opportunity to reach global audiences and individual leaders simultaneously, and in the process offers a reflexivity of exchange which traditional forms of diplomatic activity lack (ibid:

82). The potential for reporting to be either a help or a hindrance to political policy is therefore determined by the relationship between speed of coverage and the organizational and presentational skills of policymakers.

The CNN effect and Somalia

The argument that the CNN effect can be both an accelerant and an impediment to policy aims (Livingston 1997: 293) has been extensively assessed in relation to American involvment in Somalia in 1992, when a 'consensual humanitarian intervention' moved to become an 'imposed humanitarian intervention', before becoming a 'peacemaking operation' in 1993 (ibid: 313). The question of whether television news acted as an accelerant or impediment to these policy changes reveals some interesting findings about the extent of pressure exerted by coverage, which again brings us to the realization that media influence needs to be seen in relation to a broader range of political factors. If news coverage cannot push policy in the direction where officials do not want it to go, then its role becomes concomitant to official goals, to a greater or lesser extent (even coverage which appears to challenge policy aims, as I have argued, does not in itself reverse those aims, but may become part of a clarification process, or a shift in emphasis which is politically advantageous). It is important to bear in mind that news is perpetually shaped by official actors and that changes to the news agenda occur because of those actors (Livingston and Eachus 1995: 416). In turn, those who are most effective at influencing news agendas will also be more successful at using coverage to assist policy aims (ibid: 427). In the case of Somalia, where coverage is considered to have become 'part of the policymaking process' (ibid.), the overall conclusion about the relationship between reporting and policy is that 'media content came in response to official initiatives, and not the other way around' (ibid.). The problem of political policy appearing to be out of official control may well offer the media a greater opportunity to further destabilize that situation, but this destabilization does not amount to demands for an alternative policy direction. The pressure which real-time coverage creates is a pressure for dealing better with that coverage and for using the space afforded by reporting to create a sharper focus for policy aims.

Merin is clear that in the case of Somalia, the idea that the media drove foreign policy (Bell 2003: 37) is a myth. He argues that only when Washington had brought Somalia to the media's attention did it become news, and that coverage 'did not originate in the independent actions of journalists but in the interaction of journalists engaged in routine newsgathering practices and sources in Washington who made efforts to get Somalia onto the foreign policy agenda' (1997: 386). Further, continues Merin, 'journalists worked closely with governmental sources in deciding when to cover Somalia, how to frame the story, and how much coverage it deserved' (ibid: 389). Stories which emerged from Somalia highlighted potential problems for the Bush administration if there was a failure to act, but those problems were being initiated and promoted by Democrats and not the media (ibid: 402). Merin goes on to point out that the political difficulties which coverage might have caused Republicans arose first from 'outspoken allies in Washington, whose efforts to get Somalia onto the news in the first place appear to have been indispensable' (ibid: 403), and it is because of this influence that he concludes in relation to Somalia: 'television turns out not to be the independent, driving force that much of the commentary or its influences would lead one to believe' (ibid.).

The observation that 'framing of the crisis in Somalia as a humanitarian disaster *the United States could do something about* does not appear on television until it had appeared in Washington first' (Merin 1999: 131) raises questions about whether the CNN effect is pressure or influence, whether it moves policy or merely produces change in how policy is presented. Although if it had decided to do nothing to confront the humanitarian crisis in Somalia this could have negatively impacted on the White House, Merin contends that 'CNN stories had no discernible impact on American policy' and that 'plans to increase the U.N. presence in Somalia continued to stall' because 'the call for intervention was not echoed in Washington' (ibid: 132). Summing up his analysis, Merin notes that 'The case of U.S. intervention in Somalia, in sum, is not at heart evidence of the power of television to move governments; it is evidence of the power of governments to move television' (ibid: 137).

For Gowing, it was television news images of a dead US soldier being dragged around the streets of Mogadishu which contributed to a change in policy by the United States, but he also acknowledges that this change was influenced by a shift in political attitude which had developed in response to the possibility that involvement in Somalia might be lengthy and unlikely to sustain public support (1994b: 54). Levels of reporting from Somalia 'tended to follow administration actions, rather than precede them' (Strobel 1996: 360), and coverage which was critical of the Bush administration was elicited by minor policy actors rather than reporters who set out to challenge the US approach (ibid: 364). For

Strobel, the Bush administration's decision to intervene in Somalia was not a decision based on humanitarian motives, but one based on political strategy. Intervention was perceived as necessary to diffuse mounting pressure to engage with the developing crisis in Bosnia, and seen as an 'easier' option to demonstrate a commitment to world order, rather than dealing with the complex and potentially more dangerous conflict in the Balkans. Unlike Bosnia, Somalia offered the possibilty of a quick response to a humanitarian crisis and appeared to present a test case for dealing with such disasters. It also provided a model for future approaches to humanitarian crises in that it highlighted the importance of having an exit strategy as the basis of intervention (Stobel 1997: 146). What Somalia appears to demonstrate, then, is that even though television has changed the way in which foreign policy is devised and expressed, at best it can only make pronounced the political factors which exist to begin with (Sharkey 1993: 18), and it is a tool to be used either effectively or badly by governments (Livingston and Eachus 1995: 427).

Problems with the CNN effect

Perhaps the most extensive examination and critique of the CNN effect and the anomalies it throws up can be found in the work of Robinson (2002). Robinson acknowledges that news coverage can have both a 'strong' and a 'weak' effect on intervention policy, but argues that both positions are linked to political control. A 'strong effect' is created when 'politicians feel compelled to act or else face a public relations disaster', and in this instance 'media coverage is a sufficient or necessary condition for policymakers to intervene in a humanitarian crisis' (2001: 942). In contrast, a 'weak effect' occurs when coverage 'might incline policymakers to act rather than create a political imperative to act' (ibid.). Yet taking into account that there may be situations where the media's influence can be more or less, depending on policy goals and political conviction, Robinson also notes that CNN influence exists because journalists are able to exert pressure on policymakers to respond to issues which they might otherwise prefer to avoid (ibid: 941). But even here a further problem now comes into play because although coverage has been connected with interventions, it has also been connected with avoiding interventions, such as in Rwanda in 1994 (ibid: 947). What does this tell us? It seems to tell us that if pressure from coverage can assist intervention in certain circumstances and not others, then this happens because of political conviction and not because of coverage.

Returning once more to how politics rather than reporting determined intervention politics in Somalia, we should bear in mind Robinson's observation that 'only low levels of media coverage occurred prior to the decision to intervene and that substantial media attention actually followed that decision. Moreover media coverage was 'broadly supportive of Bush's intervention policy' (ibid: 941). Overall, Robinson contends that 'rather than helping the Bush administration to intervene in Somalia, media coverage actually turns out to have helped build support for the policy of intervention' (ibid: 952).

It is hard to explain political action and inaction towards humanitarian crises with the proposition that by critically focusing on political uncertainty the media can influence policy (as Rwanda indicates) (Robinson 2000: 614). To try and address this notable problem and the contradictions of the CNN-effect argument, Robinson adopts what he calls a 'policy–media interaction model', which attempts to combine the CNN-effect argument with Manufacturing Consent Theory (a position which seeks to explain the media's role as an extension of elite ideology and power). Here it appears that Robinson is attempting to straddle two posts, one which takes account of political influences over news coverage, and the other which identifies how news coverage has the ability to effect politics (1999). But once more we encounter a confusing attempt to try and reconcile two apparently contradictory positions, where the media, on the one hand, are seen to make a difference to policy and, on the other, seen to make little or no difference. To try and get around this, Robinson brings another factor into the equation, which is empathy with those seen to be suffering. Thus there is 'media influence on policy when there exists: (1) policy uncertainty and (2) critically framed media coverage that empathises with suffering people' (ibid: 614). But the argument that coverage which incites empathy is able to bring pressure on the policy process is tenuous to say the least. Coverage of Rwanda failed to shift an unwillingness in the West to intervene, even though images of suffering were broadcast. More importantly, there is the intimation here that reporting is able to produce a moral imperative to act, when perhaps no such moral recommendation can be offered by television news (Tester 2001). Furthermore, we should bear in mind that compassion fatigue (Moeller 1999) and repetitive coverage of humanitarian crises may facilitate inaction and indifference rather than initiate intervention (Tester 1997). The issue of empathy is certainly problematical with regard to television news coverage of suffering, and is worth pondering a little further if we are to reach some understanding about its potentiality in news terms.

Although an examination of empathy does not feature to any real extent in Robinson's discussion, it becomes an important point to address because the power of television news to understand and enter into the feelings of others is contentious. This notion of empathy becomes especially dubious if we consider that television news uses and objectifies suffering as a condition to complement the imperatives of newsgathering, but rarely seeks to understand or engage with the feelings of sufferers themselves, who are largely reduced to voiceless objects of misery. More importantly, we can come back to the problem of Rwanda and ask, if we saw images of suffering there and did nothing (Polman 2003), then what does this tell us about the ability of news to create empathy? Without getting too bogged down in a theoretical analysis of empathy, we must bear in mind that news prioritizes suffering (it chooses to look at certain types of suffering and ignores others) and this casts doubt on the idea that the media creates empathy in any general sense (also, a true moral position on suffering requires a non-discriminatory approach to suffering).

The minimal coverage given to the conflicts in Sierra Leone and Chechnya in recent years may not tell us that the suffering in those places is any less significant than anywhere else, but what it does seem to tell us is that such suffering is less significant in news terms. This selectivity highlights the point that since real empathy to suffering is dependent on being non-discriminatory towards it, then news must have problems creating a true sense of empathy because it discriminates between suffering constantly. Television news picks and chooses what suffering to cover, and it is this picking and choosing which should remind us that news empathy with suffering may not be as direct or obvious as one might think. If empathy in news terms is questionable, then this has consequences for Robinson's argument which views news empathy as a key element in the policy–media interaction model and a determining factor in the CNN effect (Robinson 2000: 614). I am not saying that it is impossible for news to facilitate empathy, since as BBC reports from Ethiopia in the early 1980s indicate, this may be possible (Boltanski 1999), but what seems important to note here is that consideration of empathy needs to be carried out in relation to specific instances of suffering and humanitarian crisis, and not seen as an inevitable result of coverage which is critical, and of suffering people.

According to Robinson, media coverage can produce a '*potential* negative public reaction to government inaction' (Robinson 2000: 614), which can provide a pressure for action. This suggests that in a situation where political policy is uncertain, news coverage can operate outside of elite opinion and in doing so, 'play a key role in causing policy change' (2000: 615). But here we should also bear in mind that pressure to intervene in humanitarian crises can have negative as well as positive effect. News coverage invariably depicts conflicts and crises in terms of perpetrators and victims, and this representation can elicit expectations and demands for revenge just as it can elicit a constructive humanitarian response. A sense of outrage about images of suffering can also be used by protagonists to accelerate a conflict or crisis, thus making a possible resolution more difficult. Equally, the emotive and dramatic emphasis of reports can distort or simplify a problem and encourage a response that may be ill-informed and counter-productive, hindering an effective political response and heightening the need for immediate reaction, which may compound the very situation it seeks to resolve. Though once more these issues are not assessed in Robinson's analysis, they nevertheless highlight the complex range of conditions and situations which may impact on news coverage of humanitarian crises, and which require careful examination as variable influences. Taking Robinson's theoretical model into account (where the news media and politics have intersecting influences), it appears that aside from the technological developments which underpin news reporting and which demand quicker responses from politicians, analysis of the CNN effect fails to adequately examine differing levels of influence, or how reporting initiates degrees of movement and adjustment in political policy. Nor, indeed, does it seem to advance much beyond the work of Hallin (1994), which appears to offer a more coherent and convincing case about the possibilities of media influence on policy.

In his study of how news reporting impacted on the politics of the Vietnam War, Hallin makes conclusions which have a bearing on the CNN-effect argument, since he too points out that media influence is inextricably linked to political control (or lack of it). Hallin could quite reasonably be talking about the CNN effect, for example, when he notes that change in news coverage of the Vietnam War 'seems best explained as a reflection of and a response to a collapse of consensus – especially of elite consensus – on foreign policy' (1994: 53). Charting how news coverage of Vietnam shifted from reinforcing the political consensus, to reinforcing the dissensus which developed as the war went on, Hallin explains this shift through transitions in reporting which depend on three interconnected spheres. These spheres indicate conditions of 'consensus reporting', where coverage tends to reiterate political consensus, to 'legitimately controversial' reporting, where disruptive or critical coverage takes place within the bounds of what is seen to constitute objective journalism, to a third sphere, where coverage is seen to become a distortion of acceptable political debate by drawing from sources and actors considered to be beyond the pale of legitimate comment (ibid: 53–4). Drawing from these spheres in order to explain the changes in reporting the Vietnam conflict, Hallin comes to a conclusion which finds notable consistency with the findings of those writing about the CNN effect when he argues that 'whether the media tend to be supporting or critical of government policies depends on the degree of consensus those policies enjoy, particularly within the political establishment' (ibid: 55). And that 'news content may not mirror the facts, but the media, as institutions, do reflect the prevailing pattern of political debate: when consensus is strong, they tend to stay within the limits of the political discussion it defines; when it begins to break down, coverage becomes increasingly critical and diverse in the viewpoints it represents, and increasingly difficult to control' (ibid.). Because of this, Hallin argues, the media 'strengthen prevailing political trends, serving in a time of consensus as consensus-maintaining institutions and contributing, when consensus breaks down to a certain point, to an accelerating expansion of the bounds of political debate' (ibid.). It is clear, then, that for Hallin media influence is closely tied to political consensus, and that the ability of the media to act as an intervention within political discussion is shaped, to a considerable extent, by the emerging contestations or differences which arise.

Yet we cannot ignore that additional pressures are brought to modern political communications by the speed of real-time coverage which was largely absent during the Vietnam War. According to O'Heffernan, there are three important areas of impact which need recognition in the media–policy relationship debate. First, television coverage is able to expand the range of participants in international policy events, and in doing so is able to increase the range of variable influences as a result: as O'Heffernan puts it, 'Television complicates policy making by opening the door to new, usually nongovernmental players', and it is this introduction which also brings 'more unpredictable variables into an already complex diplomatic world, and dilutes agreements, customs and alliances that have been built up over decades' (1991: 75). Second, television is able to speed up the momentum of policy, and this can result in considerations and decisions about policy being made more quickly (ibid.). Third, O'Heffernan believes that television is a key determinant in policy agendas. His justification for this view comes from the observation that television invites a 'reduction of central control over diplomatic and political activities', and that television produces infor-

mation which is difficult for policy officials and diplomats to incorpo-
rate into policy-planning, such as signals and gestures which depend on
visibility and access (ibid.). However, although it is the instant visibility and access to political communications which can generate information that is lacking in traditional diplomatic relations and exchanges,
we should also note that this visible and instantaneous communication
can invite responses which may be counter-productive to policy. Immediate communication tends to demand immediate reaction, which, if
not thought through, can hinder policy goals and induce misguided
action. It is important to remember that news simplifications inevitably
overlook the complexities of policy (Seib 1997: 139), and that 'superficial coverage is likely to be met with superficial policy' (ibid: 143), with
crisis management emphasized over crisis prevention (ibid: 149). A
further problem exists for governments which fail to provide reporters
with adequate responses and information, which is that reporters will
fill that void with information and responses from elsewhere, allowing
alternative sources the opportunity to shape the agenda and provide
governments with questions they might have avoided if responses were
comprehensive and consistent. Or, to look at it from the other way
around, 'strong foreign policy leadership will not leave an opinion
vacuum that the news media will fill' (ibid: 150).

In relation to complex emergencies, Natsios is quite clear that the
CNN effect is secondary to political motivation, which he considers the
key factor in approaches to humanitarian crises. His argument, which
looks primarily at the United States, is based on three propositions about
intervention. First, a humanitarian response tends to take place if the
geopolitical interests of the United States are under threat, and in this
instance, media coverage is peripheral to action (1996: 153). Second, in
an instance where a crisis occurs in a place of incidental geopolitical
interest, aid will depend on resources made available, but coverage may
help to shape the expectation that funding for such resources should
continue (ibid: 157). And third, that US engagement in a humanitarian
crisis which is tangential to geopolitical interest will be resisted if military action is required, the UN Security Council needs to be involved,
or diplomatic efforts will need to be made in order to harness the
support of other nations (ibid: 159). Simply put, Natsios asserts that in
a pre-intervention phase, media pressure will be largely ineffective if US
government interests are not served, or if diplomatic actions are needed
which remain incompatible with such interests, but that once intervention takes place, pressure is potentially increased because opportunities for critical coverage are intensified. What this (along with other

studies referred to here) throws up is a need for studies which analyse not just intervention in humanitarian crises, but non-intervention, and it is this latter category which presents particular problems for the CNN-effect debate. If engagement with humanitarian disasters is made more probable because of news coverage, then how is non-intervention explained in cases where comparable coverage of suffering and misery exist which are not followed by action? And can't the only realistic explanation be that non-intervention demonstrates how it is political rather than moral motivation which forms the basis of action? Gowing's suggestion that US withdrawal from Somalia was influenced by images of dead American soldiers being broadcast may, on the one hand, high-light the media's ability to magnify what is going wrong, and point towards the possible negative political consequences of this magnifica-tion, but as suggested earlier, withdrawal is more convincingly explained by looking at US apprehensions about commiting to Somalia in the first place and that the images, rather than challenging American involve-ment, helped to support expectations of disengagement which was always the politically preferrable option. It therefore seems more likely that although news may be a significant influence on the speed of reaction to questions about policy, it is a less significant influence on how that policy is initiated and executed. The CNN effect may con-tribute to how policy is presented, but it does not define policy itself.

Although it is politics rather than news which decide policy, it is the ability of news to circumvent closed-door diplomacy (Gilboa 2000) and provide a platform for wider diplomatic communications which perhaps more specifically illustrates its political importance. Within a global public sphere, real-time news has changed the scope and imme-diacy of interaction and exchange and impacted on the discussion of political issues (Volkmer 1999). The implications of this development for diplomacy are both transformative and pervasive. As McNulty points out, by accelerating diplomatic interactions and conveying information to a wider range of players, participants and spectators, news constructs tensions which require careful handling (1993: 68). The problem for policymakers and politicians, is that television news can amplify or understate the importance of situations and in so doing distort their actual relevance. It is this potential distortion which also increases or diminshes the perceived standing of such situations, but which neces-sitates response and reaction to meet the raising or lowering of interest. This propensity to deal with issues and events in ways which are inconsistent with the substance of policy or political engagement underlines the communicative power of television, and it is this power which becomes a key consideration in diplomatic affairs. There is, as McNulty argues 'a special impact when they [policymakers] see a state leader go on television to explain his or her message to the world community or to a specific leader' (ibid: 77), which excedes the impact of communications made away from the cameras. It is this tendency of television news to exaggerate the successes and failures of governments, and the fact that representatives are denied the 'luxury of time', which perhaps most appropiately sums up the impact of the CNN effect.

Conclusion

The CNN debate highlights the pervasive power of television and its real-time potential to amplify inconsistencies and uncertainties within the political arena. Through the compression of transmission and response time, pressure can be applied on politicians to respond quickly to news stories in ways which they might prefer to avoid. Clearly, given this pressure, television is able to make life uncomfortable for politicians, and may reveal cracks or inconsistencies in statements which can be taken as evidence of unclear policy and lead to questioning which further unsettles the prospects of a congruent policy position, or impacts on the room for manoeuvre which politicians may have. But the possibility of news disrupting or destabilizing policy by amplifying incoherent responses and approaches to conflict exists not because of an inherent subversiveness within the journalistic community, but because of a political community who are more or less competent in articulating positions and courses of action. If political thinking is disrupted through a lack of agreed or thought-through policy, then the media will magnify this condition. If political policy is agreed and there is a consensus about how policy should be presented, the media play a similiarly magnifying role. That news acts as an accelerant or impediment to policy aims therefore occurs not because of any moral responsibility which journalists may have, but because of political circumstances. The contention that news may create a 'something-must-be-done' attitude, comes about not because journalists have an agenda to move governments into action, but because politicians have not convincingly articulated a 'something-will-be-done' response. When governments fail to respond quickly to emerging crises, the news media are able to ask why (a question which suggests that something should be done), and this invites a reponse which must justify the current approach. In one sense this can be seen as active pressure which impacts on politics, but such pressure should not be seen as a determinant for the action which may, or may not follow. This relates more particularly to national interests and strategic concerns.

One cannot deny that real-time global news has opened up opportunities for an extended range of players to engage and interact with media–policy debates, and that this expansion also corresponds with an intensification of possible pressures and contested discourses. This has consequences in terms of widening the field of objections and counter-responses to communicated positions, but even here we should remember that significant though this development is, there is little evidence that for dominant Western powers at least, this intensification of potential pressures leads to a change in the course of policy or national goals. The potential effectiveness of the CNN effect does not derive from revelations of humanitarian disasters which demand immediate action, as Rwanda indicates. Rather, its impact is inextricably linked to the matter of national interest. Therefore, the power of news to interrupt or intervene in policy is enmeshed with its ability to incite debates which have direct ramifications for the course of policy being pursued. In this instance, news may start to have a bearing on questions about legitimacy and appropriateness. What this points towards is not only that news influence is largely determined by the political environment from which it draws, but that its level of impact is linked to how important the crisis is to the priorities and goals of that environment. From this position we can argue that news does not destabilize policy because of some moral imperative, but because of the perceived importance of that crisis in relation to a specific political project.

3
Diplomacy and Signalling

The politics of using the news media for purposes of diplomacy invites us to consider such diplomacy as a form of theatre. The gestures, presentations and language (both verbal and non-verbal) which communicate, with varying degrees of complexity, signals to recipients and audiences, point towards a multitude of meanings and potential messages which constitute diplomatic exchanges. Along with key contributions which address news and diplomacy, I want to consider this complexity by drawing on Elderman's discussion of the symbolic uses of politics, which concentrates on the relationship between meanings, emotions and symbols (1967), and Goffman's analysis about presentation of the self, which outlines the importance of theatrical performance as a basis for guiding and controlling impressions of the self (1969). The value of Elderman's work on politics and symbols is that it helps us to view political communications as a process which constantly uses symbols (for example around concerns of leadership, language, perceptions and settings) in order to arouse responses which act as a threat or a reassurance to audiences, and it is the production of responses around these two themes which are self-evidently imperative in diplomactic relations. Goffman's study, on the other hand, engages with behavioural aspects of communication, and considers how that behaviour underpins the formation of character as well as how impressions about character are managed. Clearly, in relation to both works there is an emphasis on emotion and reaction to presentations of the self which is relevant to diplomatic interactions, and which will enable us here to think about how politicians present themselves through the theatre of television news. However, I begin this chapter by referring to some of the core theories which have contributed to debates about the functions and techniques of diplomatic communication, and use these to help both introduce and contextualize the arguments made by Elderman and Goffman.

The realization that television operates as a theatre of power which provides a space for diplomatic communications has been well argued by Cohen, who notes how television performs a vital role in helping 'to achieve an identity of intended and perceived meanings' in the diplomatic setting (1987: 1). The visibility of television allows for non-verbal forms of expression to support conventional linguistic forms of communication and should be seen, insists Cohen, as 'not a spasmodic, anomalous activity but a continuous, purposive instrument of foreign policy' (ibid: 3). In that television creates an immediacy, it is seen as comparable to direct experience, and because those who communicate through it use a range of visual signals and codes that recipients react to, it produces emotional impact which is constitutive of its theatrical power. What we can further deduce from this, is that if television is theatre, then those who appear on it are necessarily actors who adopt performance techniques which suitably characterize their intentions and potential actions. The role of television in politics has, according to Cohen, transformed the parameters and demands of presentation since politicians have to be not just communicators, but performers. As he puts it: 'Those qualities of reticence formerly associated with the ideal diplomat are completely unsuited to the television screen. The image is the message. It is the visual impression even more than what is said that counts for the viewer. Whether he likes it or not the television performer is, by definition, on stage' (ibid: 7). And it is because of this theatricality, asserts Cohen, that words and gestures are scrutinized for signals which reveal an *'assumption of intentionality'* (ibid: 212) that disclose potential diplomatic moves.

For Cohen, the power of television as a medium of communication is sustained not only by its ability to broadcast words, but by its ability to show non-verbal signs. In this instance, expressions of anger, concern, friendliness, consternation and so on become essential parts of diplomatic representation and allow for a performance which 'personalizes and hence renders comprehensible otherwise obtuse aspects of state policy' (ibid: 215). Since 'posture, gesture, facial expression, body movement, dress and so on equally pass on important clues about such things as status, role, identity and feeling' (ibid: 2), it is apparent that the medium of television offers the potential to communicate in ways which transcend the limitations of national linguistic boundaries. Television, in other words, 'has transformed formerly intimate mannerisms into signals of public import' (ibid.) and it is precisely because such signals are examined and considered in detail by recipients, that non-verbal communication has become 'a crucial instrument of diplomacy in its own right' (ibid: 224). Significantly, the message of television encapsulates performance politics to the extent where the gesture is the underpinning of diplomatic intention and where it is often the case that 'acts carry more conviction than words' (ibid: 213).

Non-verbal signs, though an essential part of diplomatic language, form only part of the communicative repertoire available to the official who transmits through television news, however. For Cohen, diplomatic language 'should say neither too much nor too little because every word, nuance and omission will be meticulously studied for any possible shade of meaning. Nor is the convention of tact and politeness in the wording of diplomatic communications just an anachronistic tradition, but refers back to the same principle of non-redundancy: rudeness or abruptness would in itself be assumed to carry an important aspect of the message' (1981: 32). Both what is included and excluded are therefore features of diplomatic language, which communicate perceived intention or non-intention that affects those engaged within the diplomatic exchange. But even here, other factors need taking into account. Cohen identifies communicative effects which are 'tools' of the television diplomat that broaden the potential for negotiating the diplomatic space.

First, there is *constructive ambiguity* which occurs when the communicator seeks to leave options open 'by formulating a position which can be accepted with equal satisfaction by both sides as a point of departure for negotiations or at least to avoid deadlock and a breakdown of talks' (Ibid: 33). The point of constructive ambiguity is to provide scope for manoeuvre and so reduce the potential for being 'boxed in' by decisions and set positions. By interacting with the principle of change, constructive ambiguity allows for engagement and consideration without compromising party goals or intentions. It is based on the recognition that each side must be prepared to concede something in order to gain something, but that clarity would weaken each side's negotiating position and a favourable outcome.

Second, *loaded omission* 'is a linguistic device used by diplomats permitting unpleasant and embarrasing points to be made without their being articulated in so many words' (ibid: 33). In such a case, parties can refuse to engage with a development by referring to treaties or policies which counter the course of action being promoted, and so appear to support the decision of non-action.

Third, there is *periphrasis*, which 'is a form of diplomatic expression which permits controversial things to be said in a way understood by all but without needless provocation' (ibid: 34). Explicit language can sometimes destabilize sensitive negotiations. In this instance, a position must be articulated which indicates reasonableness, but also highlights unease and general disagreement with the position being taken.

And fourth, there is the lingusitic device of *diplomatic understatement*, where firm decisions are made without apparent eagernesss or emotive support. Through the use of diplomatic understatement and 'by separating tone from content this stylized form of communication permits precision without enthusiasm. A "frank" exchange of views describes a conversation in which both sides put forward their positions without reaching agreement'. Thus '"agreement in principle" may be a tactful way of postponing, perhaps indefinitely, a firm commitment' (ibid: 34).

The cumulative significance of these visual and verbal signals points us towards the importance of television news as an arena for diplomacy and negotiation. It also demonstrates the potential for television to play an active role in the choreography of communications and related moves. Underpinning the choreography of diplomatic communication lie the use of visual signals and cues which provide 'the transmission of *intrinsic signals*'. These signals 'visually relate to that which they signify, and 'their distingushing feature is not that they resemble their significant; they *are* their significant' (ibid: 39). Alongside the extrinsic code 'in which the act signifies or stands for something else, and the coding may be arbitrary or iconic' (ibid.), parties who use television to communicate diplomacy therefore construct positions through signals which impact directly on the processes of diplomatic exchange and bargaining.

The problem of meaning

The ambiguity which arises from diplomatic signalling is also a problem of meaning and its interpretation. Since negotiating advantage tends to rest with those who have the most flexible approach, and it is ambiguity which contributes to such flexibility, it is clear that ambiguity is a basis of negotiating strength (Jonsson 1990: 32). However, the success of ambiguity depends on how the message is received as much as the message itself, and this is where problems can develop; especially in relation to international bargaining, where differing 'metaphorical understandings of the international relations and the issue at stake' can become obstructive to communicative aims (ibid: 35). Cultural perceptions of negotiating may differ between states and this can hinder the successful use of ambiguity in exchanges. To illustrate how differences in negotiating strategy need to be taken into consideration when addressing the ambiguity of signals, Jonsson points out how 'historically Persia, India, Byzantium, the Arab domain and Russia have conceived of diplomacy as a quasi-military activity which has entailed a view of negotiation as 'a strategic device, designed to lead to victory rather than to compromise or mutual understanding' (ibid: 39). Whereas, in contrast, 'American negotiators, for their part, tend to see negotiating sessions as *problem-solving exercises*', reacting against what they determine to be lack of flexibility (ibid: 40). As Jonsson goes on to make clear when providing a further example of cultural disparity over negotiating strategy and the metaphorical implications of language and gesture, 'diplomatic relations between the United States and Egypt have suffered over the years from misunderstandings due to cultural antinomies, as American propensities for directness, understatement, honesty and impersonalism clashed with Egyptian indirectness, hyperbole, concern with social desirability and personalism' (ibid: 42). Or, to put it another way, the US tendency to view negotiations as problem-solving exercise 'stands in marked contrast to the tendency of collectivistic cultures to distinguish between "normal" distributive bargaining and negotiation that entails a challenge to identity or test of honor' (Cohen 1996: 494). What is apparent from this perspective is that 'culturally conditioned codes' (ibid.) are important if gestures and signals are to be understood and reciprocated in ways favourable to the diplomatic process, and that careful development of verbal and non-verbal language has to evolve in order to minimize misunderstandings, and overcome cultural differences about language. What is needed in relation to diplomacy across cultures is a continued working and reworking of communications to address the problem of signals being interpreted as more or less than their intended meaning. This process of confusion and attempted clarification is an inevitable part of the diplomatic dynamic and highlights that bargaining consists of both 'cooperative and conflictual elements' (ibid: 64).

For Jervis, the use of signals, which he argues 'can be thought of as promissory notes' and indices, which he defines as 'statements or actions that carry some inherent evidence that the image projected is correct because they are believed to be inextricably linked to the actor's capabilities or intentions' (1970: 18), is constitutive of the diplomatic apparatus which officials use. However, entwined with the application of both, is the strategy of ambiguity. Jervis's analysis of ambiguity is more complex in detail than that of Cohen and Jonsson, and for that reason deserves examination if we are to more comprehensively understand the importance of the relationship between signals and ambiguity. Significantly, Jervis highlights two central themes in the diplomatic exchange: developing a position of strength and not deviating from key goals. Both are best achieved by maintaining a coherent line of communication which does not create potentially inconsistent signals, since this can signify uncertainty, increase pressures and lead to unwanted concessions. Furthermore, the sender must seek to protect the desired image being projected and minimize the chance of others drawing possible meanings which may disadvantage the sender, or allow recipients to read possible weaknesses which can be exploited (ibid: 119). Crucially, ambiguity is a protective device at this stage because if the recipient is unsure of what it being said, then this makes exploitation of communications that much more difficult to achieve (ibid: 120). During the formative moments in the diplomatic process, Jervis notes: 'It is the noise and ambiguity in the signaling system that provide flexibility and protection by reducing the danger and damage to an actor's reputation when he undertakes probes and initiatives' (ibid: 123). Furthermore, 'Many times, especially at the start of negotiations or informal soundings, an actor will wish to put out feelers that can be denied if the response is not appropriate' (ibid.). Although the use of ambiguity may reflect a tentativeness and non-commitment to engagement, it is precisely this non-commitment which helps interaction to take place, since recipients cannot be certain about ambiguous steps until they have reciprocated with similar steps (ibid: 125).

What Jervis also brings to our attention with the ambiguity of signs is the potential for misinterpretation of the image they are designed to project. If the main intention of ambiguity is to minimize the scope for certainty, then a necessary correlation of this has to be greater uncertainty, which can further interrupt or unsettle the interactive process (ibid: 126). This uncertainty, which protects the image being sent from being interpreted as a definite position, is particularly evident in the case of indirect communication channels like television, which lends itself to the construction of ambiguity more easily than direct communications. In comparison to the ambiguity of television diplomacy: 'An actor who agrees to meet his adversary in private may find himself pressed to clarify his values, priorities and demands. And premature attempts by third parties or one side to get the actors to take clear positions may only make future compromises more difficult' (ibid: 129–30). And yet ambiguity must not be so ambiguous that it fails to make evident the possibilities for bargaining and movement (ibid.). If images and messages do not show some indication of change, there is little point of reciprocation. Effective ambiguity in the context of diplomacy must therefore suggest movement, but movement which corresponds with the course of action desired by the sender rather than the receiver. Knowing what image to project and what not to project is clearly a matter of careful political judgement, making the ambiguity of signals necessarily dependent on the possibilites and conditions of engagement between the parties at any one point in time.

Although it is important to point out that diplomatic solutions ultimately rely on detailed, complex and laborious meetings, conducted in private through face-to-face discussion and negotiation, it is also necessary to realize that indirect communications are needed to help facilitate this outcome. Indeed, for Cohen, the relationship between what he calls 'high-context' and 'low-context' communication, is central to effective negotiating across different cultures. In the case of low-context interaction, the emphasis is on explicit statements and little attention is given to the context within which communication takes place. Whereas, for high-context communication meaning is implicit and suggestive rather than direct. Here 'the surrounding nonverbal cues and nuances of meaning' are as significant as the message being conveyed, and the environment of communication carries additional influence which impacts on the perceptions of those involved (1996: 490). Notably, television operates as an instrument of high-context communication and uses the symbolism of images to avoid precise positions. It also achieves a greater socializing function in terms of communication than low-context exchanges, which, by concentrating on language and its potential meanings, tend to perform an informational role (ibid.). Because of the socializing function which high-context communication produces, it is argued that interactions within this frame seem to find agreement easier than through the low-context model. The priorty with high-context communication is to 'avoid an abrupt and abrasive presentation, to maintain harmony, and to save the face of the interlocutor. Meaning is imparted by hints and nuances' (ibid: 492). Meaning, in other words, is suggested through the symbolism of images and signals.

Symbolism and politics

The relationship between symbolism and political power is convincingly interrogated by Elderman in his classic text *The Symbolic Uses of*

Politics. For Elderman the important political act is embodied within a symbolic framework which 'evokes a quiescent or an aroused mass response because it symbolizes a threat or reassurance' (1967: 7). Ideally, the basis of such a response is constructed through the use of symbols which have little to do with reality, but which meet public expectations and desire for gratification (ibid: 9). However, gratification is increased if psychological distance is maintained between symbols and the perceptions they evoke. Emotions are intensified through distance and distance is created by dramatic emphasis which the symbol encapsulates (ibid: 11). But, argues Elderman, meanings are not instrinsic to symbols themselves, rather they are in society and people, and they 'bring out in concentrated form those particular meanings and emotions which the members of a group create and reinforce in each other' (ibid: 11). What is being stressed here is that reactions and meanings derive from symbols which emphasize drama, and that responses occur in relation to symbols precisely because they provoke an emotional reaction which inspires action. 'For the spectators of the political scene', notes Elderman, 'every act contributes to a pattern of ongoing events that spells threat or reassurance' (ibid: 13). The duality of theat and reassurance underpins the need for engagement because the threat is always present, so requiring vigilance from those groups with perceived interest. But, the extent of interest can hardly manifest into direct political involvement for the mass audiences who consume symbols. Instead, their involvement is reduced to emotional reaction and not engaging with the shifts and turns of policy formation (ibid: 15). In relation to politics, it is evident, contends Elderman, that the institutions of democracy 'are largely symbolic and expressive in function' (ibid: 19), and it is clear that for such symbols to be communicated, the media are vital.

The communicative possibilities which might be carried by the symbolic moment are given potency by the ambiguity of symbols (allowing people to inject their own interpretations) and the emotions which they elicit (which derive from such interpretations) (ibid: 30). Symbols and their potential ambiguity also allow oversimplifications and distortions in their reading, and tend to support the desire of audiences to see the world in stereotypical and personalized terms (ibid: 31). Furthermore, since 'emotional commitment to a symbol is associated with contentment and quiescence regarding problems that would otherwise arouse concern' (ibid: 32), it emerges that symbols are integral to perceptions of order and threats to that order. What underscores Elderman's understanding of symbols is the threat which exists when symbols appear, because however symbols are represented, they are inevitably represented in relation to something else which stands in tension and exerts a threat to the symbol itself. The symbol of leadership, for example, is automatically threatened when it arises in relation to something for which leadership is required. Or, to put it another way, when a situation develops which leadership must address, then leadership must also be threatened in the process of dealing with that situation (in order to appear as leadership, the action which a leader carries out must invariably overcome a threat). It is within this tension that the possibility of both threat and reassurance are realized, and it is through this tension that political use of symbols is exercised. The symbol of leadership can be seen another way, which is that leadership exists because of how others react to it, and where 'If they respond favorably and follow, there is leadership; if they do not, there is not' (ibid: 75). Attempting to reduce anxieties about chance, uncertainty, insecurity and inability to confront problems, the symbol of leadership strives to create the impression that each can be dealt with, and does so by 'personifying and reifying the processes', so that the leader 'can be praised and blamed and given "responsibility" in a way that processes cannot' (ibid: 78). Those in positions of leadership 'therefore become objects of acclaim for the satisfied, scapegoats for the unsatisfied, and symbols of aspirations of whatever is opposed' (ibid.).

Elderman offers a key distinction between the television appearance of leaders and those who engage in direct communication with reporters, trying to deal with questions as they arise, and that distinction is performance. Focusing on the symbolic power of setting, Elderman observes that 'the television screen, presenting a live performance, creates not close contact but a semblance of close contact', and unlike the official who deals with reporters, the television appearance makes the words of a leader 'unchallengeable and unchangeable' (ibid: 101). 'Like every dramatic performance', Elderman continues, 'this one concentrates impressions and evocations, becoming its own justification. Instead of a channel of information, we have an instrument for influencing opinion and response. The setting, and how the mass audience respond to it, define the situation and the action' (ibid.). Crucially, 'in the continuous interaction between official actor and mass public, setting supplies both the norms and justification for the action and the limits beyond which mass restiveness and disaffection become increasingly probable' (ibid.). What Eldeman here offers us in his examination of the relationship between leadership and setting is a sophisticated understanding of the symbolism which underpins political power and its communication. His proposition is that both 'background' and 'ground' are mutually reinforcing characteristics of symbolic meaning (ibid: 102), and that the performance political leaders give invites concerned reaction because of its symbolic orientation and the social recognition which (re)constructs that which is communicated on the basis of threat or reassurance. This has particular validity for political diplomacy where change (and so threat) is particularly heightened. Here the symbolic power of politics is pronounced and the television performance which leaders provide can take on notable significance precisely because it is unchallengable and unchangable as Elderman identifies. Moreover, since the television performance may be taken as a public declaration of intent, it thus acquires a communicative power which cannot be reached elsewhere.

The setting within which the leadership performance is contained, is more than a combination of physical elements and 'includes any assumptions about basic causation or motivation that are generally accepted' (ibid: 103). Crucially, the setting provides a context for performance and that context acts as a key determinant for audience reactions about that which is being communicated. The setting therefore creates the perfomance environment and provides a symbolism of its own which helps further activate the symbolic significance of leadership. As Elderman defines it: 'settings not only condition political acts. They mold the very personalities of the actors' (ibid: 108). Yet the communication of political symbolism relies ostensibly on language as the expression of reassurance or threat. It is language which gives the political act its power, its potency. Whereas settings provide 'only impressions yet to be interpreted' (ibid: 196), the complexities and nuances of rhetoric help to simplify and make emotive what is being articulated in order to try and gain public acceptance. But alongside this must be taken into account a range of groups seeking to contest the flow of meanings by similiarly adopting their own rhetoric and frame of references as a counter-response. This contestation highlights the potential instability of meanings which circulate, and indicates competing alternative perspectives which contribute to the reflexivity of the political environment and the construction of threat and reassurance which arise from it.

What Elderman points towards in his study is that political communication is more to do with performance than politics, and that the act of communication acquires meaning though the symbolic capital which is brought into the performance. More specifically, Eldeman analyses the language, meaning, action, conditions and self-definition which constitute impressions and reactions, and situtates his findings within the realms of social pyschology. By looking at the symbolism of the meanings produced, Elderman also refers us to the social setting where those meanings are conveyed and by so doing introduces us to the power of effective performance. It is how performance is communicated and how it uses the symbolism of meaning which also shapes the perceived extent of threat or reassurance and influences subsequent political action.

Presentation of the self

What emerges with certainty at the beginning of Goffman's book *The Presentation of the Self in Everyday Life*, is the unpredictability of communication. However deliberate one may try to be when communicating, there is always the possibility that the message communicated may not be understood as intended, creating complication around the notion of intention. For intention to be successful, it is clear that whoever receives the message must be predisposed to the meanings inherent within it, but in that the communicator seeks to convey a favourable impression of himself, there is also scepticism in the reception (1969: 18). Once more we return to the communication and perception of threat and reassurance, and the realization that communication is performance. There is, to put it another way a dramaturgical emphasis to how self presentation is conducted and for this to be effective it is apparent that considerable stage-management is called for (ibid: 26). What is particularly central to Goffman's study is the simple premise that 'when an individual appears before others he will have many motives for trying to control the impression they receive of the situation' (ibid.), and that in order to unravel how this is achieved, we need to examine some of the techniques used which support this aim. This has obvious consequences for thinking about how political performance is communicated and interpreted through the media and provides a necessary extension of the discussion outlined by Elderman.

For Goffman, the performance which individuals produce when they interact relates to expectations which are socially defined. Performance, in other words, tends to connect with a role which is already loaded with socially recognizable meanings and probable interpretations (ibid: 37). Although situations change and the context of the perfomance continuously shifts, it remains the case that understanding of the performance rests on having seen the performance before, and therefore understanding what it (potentially) means. But what gives the performance particular impact is what Goffman calls 'Dramatic Realization'. Here, the process of interaction becomes more convincing when 'the individual typically infuses his activity with signs which dramatically highlight and portray confirmatory facts that might otherwise remain unapparent or obscure' (ibid: 40). As part of the performance, then, the performer is not only projecting words but expressing them, and through that expression, using emotion and drama to create a desired emphasis. But, performances can be misunderstood and viewed as more or less significant, depending on how audiences interpret and react to the cues and signals being communicated. This brings us back to the ambiguity of communication and the interesting observation made by Goffman that just as audiences have a tendency to accept signs, so that tendency to accept can produce a misreading of situations if not presented in the expected context. The potential for misreading is especially accentuated if audiences are sceptical or unhappy about what is being communicated to them. This heightens the need for careful expressive control and indicates why careful consideration of audience reception is necessary (ibid: 59). It also underlines why the communicator must seek to engage or involve the audience, by minimizing opportunies which may aggravate or incite disagreeable reaction. By avoiding a performance which contributes to unpredictability in the audience, the performer is more likely to gain audience support, but for this 'a certain bureaucratization of the spirit is expected so that we can be relied upon to give a perfectly homogeneous performance at every appointed time' (ibid: 64). This, it would appear, is central to the socialization process which includes rather than excludes audiences.

The characteristics of performance which contribute to its success must not be made obvious, however. In other words, the audience must not be aware of how the performance is influencing them if it is to be convincing. As Goffman notes, 'if a performance is to be effective it will be likely that the extent and character of the cooperation which makes this possible will be concealed and kept secret' (ibid: 108). The reason for this is relatively straightforward: if an audience is made aware of how the performance is trying to influence them, they will resist, thus diminishing the power of the performance. The success of the performance, then, is dependent on those watching it not realizing that it is a performance, but seeing it as an interaction to be involved in. The paradox here, though, is that power is given to those who perform rather than those who receive the performance. For audiences, passivity is more likely than active engagement. If the audience is made aware of the mechanics of performance, then the power of the performance is lost, since such power depends on the techniques and conventions of performance being unnoticed. Once critical attention is given to how the performance is constructed it is viewed very differently, thus for those engaged within the political/diplomatic process attention given to the performance of opponents is quite different to those who have little or no interest in the techniques of political persuasion or performance. Here, another kind of viewing takes place, which is attentive to the details and nuances of expression as well as the ambiguities, symbols, settings and the like which are constitutive of the performance.

That which is not said can be as important as that which is said. The effective performance must be economical in relation to what is said and not overplay or dilute meaning with unnecessary elaboration. The performance, to put it another way, is weakened by overacting. The importance of restrained expression is also stressed by Goffman, who observes: 'The image that one status grouping is able to maintain in the eyes of an audience of other status groupings will depend upon the performers' capacity to restrict communicative contact with the audience' (ibid: 234). Goffman points out how distance is required between performer and audience in order for the dramatic significance to take effect. But, although closeness erodes the emotive and dramaturgical impact of the performance because it suggests knowledge and information which might render the performance useless, it is also apparent that the performance offers the possibility of closeness precisely because the audience would expect to gain something which they did not know before. In the realm of political communications and diplomacy, the performance is crucial for acquiring a sense of the opponent and his intentions. Indeed, in the absence of full information about his opponent 'cues, tests, hints, expressive gestures, status symbols etc.' become 'predictive devices'.

Morever, continues Goffman 'since the reality that the individual is concerned with is unperceivable at the moment, appearances must be relied upon instead. And, paradoxically, the more the individual is concerned with the reality that is not available to perception, the more he must concentrate his attention on appearances' (ibid: 241–2). Such appearances will also determine future experiences and be taken as evidence of how interaction should be conducted and played out; as well as how reactions might be made and acted upon. Or as Goffman puts it, 'The impressions that the others give tend to be treated as claims and promises they have implicitly made, and claims and promises tend to have a moral character' (ibid: 242). It is because appearances have the ability to be taken as indications of morality that the performance is given such power within political diplomacy, and why interaction 'is enmeshed in moral lines of discrimination' (ibid.). By establishing impressions by which they are judged, politicians seek to create the perception that moral standards are realizable, and by so doing, they perform as 'merchants of morality' (ibid: 243). The basis of just how convincing they are is the performance they give and without television they would be without a stage to give that performance.

Conclusion

It is worth summarizing some of the key points raised in this chapter and discussing how those points might be useful for thinking about political uses of television news. To begin with, what this chapter has set out to do is to indicate the complexity which exists in the world of political communications, and to introduce some of the problems which underscore diplomacy through news. To do this, I have highlighted the importance of television as theatre, looked at the cultural differences which impact on communications, outlined the role of ambiguity and symbolism in diplomacy, indicated the relationship between threat and assurance, and emphasized the power of performance as a process which draws the other areas together. As a starting point, Cohen's consideration of television as being a 'theatre of power' shows that what takes place within that theatre is performative in function, and that television is central for providing visual impressons which have emotional impact. Cohen also identifies how television gives us the prospect of intentionality and links that possibility to the development of both non-verbal communications and ambiguity of language. By establishing television as a space for performance, Cohen illustrates how instrumental television is in the development of foreign policy. For those engaged in diplomatic communications, television becomes the place where each tries to assess the credibility and intentions of the other, using the signs and signals conveyed to gauge positions and test intentions. Each must be careful not to promote the wrong message or impression, making the planning and execution of the performance vital. Critically, the use of ambiguity within the exchanges provides space for wider exploration and negotiation of issues, and minimizes the chances of being 'cornered'; a situation made more likely by precise statements. The visual impressions carried by posture, body language and so on present the recipients of communication with information which is then absorbed into the process of counter-reponse, and subsequently helps to shape the atmosphere and direction of diplomacy.

Perceptions of meaning and how they are interpreted and negotiated are culturally defined. But different cultures interpret meanings differently and may view negotiations from a vantage point of alternative perspectives. Visual impressions, in other words, though important, may not be received and recognized as intended, raising the possibility of misreading or reacting negatively to what senders may determine to be positive. Jonsson points out how the logic of images must be considered within a framework of co-operative and conflictual elements, and that negotiations are essentially contestations which must negotiate across these two opposites. What allows interaction to continue throughout this tension is ambiguity. By shrouding signals, messages and statements with ambiguity, politicians widen rather than restrict communicative space, augmenting the scope for increased contestations between parties in the process.

The presentation of leadership, and the reactions leadership provokes, is closely aligned with the constant and shifting dynamic which exists between threat (and the fears which threat incites) and reassurance (which aspires to alleviate threat). Leadership only matters in relation to circumstances which have the potential to disrupt and destabilize, and in such circumstances it is called for. The image of leadership depends on using the symbolism associated with leadership and the leader is expected to say or appear to do something which will remove the threat. Since effective leadership requires leading rather then being led, it is vital that leaders also construct the threat which they set out to address. The relationship between threat and reassurance is one of mutual interdependency (there is no reassurance without threat and no threat without reassurance), but we must also bear in mind that both are largely symbolic, relying on emotional rather than intellectual response. The perception of threat and reassurance is ostensibly an emotional perception. It therefore requires not close scruntiny, but the use of oversimplifications and stereotypes which routinely draw from myths and subjective histories (most of the case studies in this book highlight the media's role within this process of mythmaking and the fears which can be inflamed by amplifying the threat/reassurance duality). Television news uses leadership to inform us about what we should be concerned about and allows leaders to tell us how they intend to deal with that concern. It therefore reinforces the need for threat and reassurance and has a responsibility for how both are communicated. Indeed, since television news functions to exaggerate threat and reassurance by allowing other parties the opportunity to try and turn the reassurance offered by a leader into a further threat, we can see that it amplifies the field of contestation and presents the tension between these two opposites as the symbolism of democratic debate.

What the first three chapters of this book have set out to do is to discuss the relationship between news and politics and highlight some of the tendencies which exist within this relationship. Cultural, economic and political influences on news indicate the pressures which limit the possibilities of coverage, but we also need to recognize that news interacts with the political process and in so doing has political consequences. The potential impact of news on politics and policy is shaped and contained by the political environment which news draws from, but it is the political climate which provides news with stories which can reinforce or challenge political aims and objectives. How news responds to political representations of conflict and the role it plays in examining that conflict is the question which sustains the next six chapters as we look at reporting and conflict around the world. What interests me in relation to these conflicts is how reporters responded to dominant discourses about conflict, and whether they challenged the legitimacy of conflict by looking at possible ways to help de-escalate or prevent it. Conceptualizations about news objectivity (however defined) clearly come up against problems if debates about proposals for peace are ignored in favour of debates about war. Similarly, the notion of impartiality dissolves if an equal measure of argument is denied to those who oppose war compared to those who promote it. How the symbolism of conflict is communicated and the role played by news within this communication is a complex and multi-dimensional process. Politicians are able to convey intentions and reactions through news, but this conveyance is also about what information news chooses to include. It is news which provides the space and coverage for communication to be made public and it is news that selects which responses and counter-responses are shown. Journalism clearly has a political responsibility in how it reports politics and it is the consequences of this responsibility which permeate the case-study conflicts which now follow.

4
Vietnam

Approximately one year after the start of the American-led invasion of Iraq in 2003, the British newspaper *The Independent* published an image of coffins covered in the US flag being returned to Delaware, America. Under the title 'The image turning America against Bush', the coffins are being unloaded from a transport plane by 12 troops. The accompanying article informs us how the White House is trying to prevent the release of such images, because of 'their potential to inflict political damage on Mr Bush as he campaigns for re-election' (24 April 2004). This reaction is not merely concerned with the future as suggested, however. It is concerned with the past and more specifically is rooted in fears and anxieties which evolved during the Vietnam War. In a real sense, the Vietnam War was the test case for how future governments need to deal with news media during a period of military conflict. For successive American governments (remembering that US involvement in Indochina lasted over six elections (Kattenburg 1980: 315)), the 'Vietnam Syndrome' has become a condition without end, where political fears about the news media representing wars in ways which are likely to jeopadize public support is ever present. Embedded within the consciousness of America, and particularly American governments, the Vietnam Syndrome is an indication of uneasy relations between the media and foreign policy and its ability to amplify the failures of state conflict. It is also seen in political circles as a key reason why America lost the war in Vietnam (lost because it did not win) and for that reason it is a condition which has become a burden of history which symbolizes a failure of foreign policy. The Bush administration's reaction to images of dead soldiers returning home is testimony to the historical influence of Vietnam and tells us about the tense relationship which often exists between the media and governments during times of war.

As the first television news war, Vietnam also presents an important case study by which to assess the media's role in relation to conflict and disputations about that conflict.

The political background

The Vietnam War developed as part of America's obsession with the threat of communism and the politics of the Cold War. The possibility of North Vietnam annexing the South was seen by America as a major threat to other states in the region, as well as damaging to American geopolitical interests and its global position (Hall 2000: 13). As part of a strategy to contain the possible dangers of communism, American policy was concerned primarily with supporting the Saigon regime in South Vietnam and using this relationship as justification for prosecuting a military campaign against the North. The initial decision to commit forces to Vietnam, made by Kennedy at the beginning of the 1960s (and which occupied the administrations of Johnson and Nixon afterwards), was taken because it was believed that 'A Victory by the Vietnamese communists would only encourage . . . revolutionary movements elsewhere in the world', and provide 'an advantage for the Soviets and Chinese' (ibid: 10). Vietnam itself was therefore seen as important in the sense that 'its control by a communist regime threatened all of Southeast Asia' and 'the economic needs of the Western alliance and Japan' (ibid: 81). A military campaign was seen to be the most effective way to confront the communist threat, but proved to be a major miscalculation in terms of America underestimating the communist resistance. Confidence that military superiority would quickly dispel the insurgents from the North proved misplaced, and indeed contributed to the quagmire which consumed and ultimately defeated successive American administrations. The strategy of pursuing a war of 'attrition to wear the enemy down and force them to negotiate a settlement favourable to the United States' (ibid: 31) was ultimately misguided, and based on a flawed sense of superiority (Karnow 1994: 15). Flawed because America was forced to concede a stalemate situation in its war against communism, and indeed needed such a stalemate 'in order to continue to avoid the dreaded consequences of defeat or the appearance of defeat' (Kattenburg 1980: 315). Justification for continuing its presence in Vietnam depended on perpetuating 'theories of worldwide interlinkage of national liberation wars and the credibility of U.S. commitments' (ibid.), which took on a moral imperative in an attempt to contain and ultimately defeat communism. However, as the war went on in a stalemate position, it became increasingly evident to the American public that there was a discrepancy between the costs of war (both militarily and economically) and the optimistic propaganda promoted by successive administrations (ibid.). Lasting until 1975 (after close involvement with Indochina since the mid-1950s), when American troops were finally withdrawn and communist forces captured Saigon (Karnow 1994: 700–1), the Vietnam War became associated with a traumatic history (Kattenburg 1980: 314–25), remembered more as a failure of military and diplomatic strategy (Hall 2000: 86). As such, the burden of Vietnam became a key consideration and perceived fear in future military planning and foreign policy activities.

Vietnam and the media

As the first 'Living Room War' (Arlen 1969), Vietnam became a news spectacle without precedent. Although news reports lacked the instantaneity of today, with dispatches taking on average 30 hours and more to reach the networks (ibid: 7), the prospect of conflict becoming a 'continuous floating variety show' (ibid; 113) was relatively unexpected and produced a number of influences which politicians were somewhat unprepared for. Efforts to blame the media for a lack of political control over the course, direction and justification of the war were routine at the time. As Pach points out, President Lyndon B. Johnson in 1967 'considered the news media in general – and TV news in particular – a major adversary in his efforts to show that the United States was making progress in meeting aggression and sustaining self-determination in South Vietnam' (2002: 451). Even though television journalists had given support to Johnson's policies (ibid: 452), the developing conflict exposed problems with the administration's approach. In an attempt to deal with growing negative coverage and the belief perpetuated within journalistic circles that bombing should give way to peace talks (ibid: 454), Johnson 'blamed his difficulties on slanted and hostile media coverage' (ibid: 456) and sought to intensify public relations initiatives to demonstrate that the war was proceeding as planned (ibid: 458). Although this campaign provided some relief from a growing unease about the purpose of war, this relief was short-lived and effectively collapsed when a wave of assaults carried out in South Vietnam by Northern communists in 1968, which became known as the 'Tet Offensive', took place (ibid: 461–2). So called because the attacks corresponded with the lunar new year and Vietnam's most important holiday, the offensive took the US by surprise and countered dominant articulations that the conflict was progressing in ways consistent with American goals (Hall 2000: 47–51). Unable to comprehend that returning images from Vietnam were undermining the perception that the conflict was succeeding, Johnson was convinced 'the television was somehow responsible for the collapse of popular support for his administration's war policies' (ibid: 463). Even though Johnson had tried to adapt policy to meet the growing difficulties caused by critical coverage, it emerged that he 'had failed to win the war on television' (ibid: 464).

It is important to recognize that television did not influence the Tet Offensive, as Johnson claimed, even if coverage was a consideration in policy planning. Prior to Tet, reporting had largely conveyed the impression that the war was proceeding well (Pach 1998: 58). But the questioning of US military activity, which developed in 1966, intensified in 1967 when journalists 'complained about the gap between Johnson's rhetoric and the realities of war' (ibid: 61). Government efforts to depict the conflict in a more positive light were supported by efforts to instigate closer relations between public officials, editors, reporters and military commanders (ibid: 59), but this campaign became impossible to sustain after the images of horror and destruction associated with Tet. As a key turning-point in the war, Tet effectively collapsed the argument that progress was ongoing and led to a situation where even news anchors began to dispute official explanations of the conflict (ibid: 69). Tet became the moment when the broader ramifications of the war became subject to closer scrunity (ibid: 74), and when reports 'widened the Johnson administration's credibiity gap' (ibid: 76). Unable to maintain public confidence in the legitimacy of the war and undermining the public relations drive which had sought to undercut calls for disengagement, 'television coverage of the Tet Offensive affected public policy and influenced popular attitudes – changing minds, confirming prejudices, sowing controversy' (ibid: 81).

Television news coverage increasingly magnified problems of leadership and policy direction as the war progressed, but most noticeably after Tet (Pach 1994: 92). Then a change of emphasis highlighted a more critical frame of analysis by television reporters, who had previously tended to uncritically accept official explanations and government briefings (ibid: 91). Nevertheless, even though the images of Tet had contributed to the perception that the American offensive was failing (ibid.), it also remained evident that 'television's war was a series of disconnected episodes of combat' (ibid: 107), which reflected the fragmented and disorganized pattern of the war itself. This fragmentation appeared to parallel a similarly disjointed policy approach, which served to intensify doubts about American purpose and brought pressures to bear on an administration, increasingly concerned about growing public unease (ibid: 106). The impact of Tet, more specifically, had been 'to deepen doubts about the war and destroy confidence in the Johnson administration's handling of it' (ibid: 109). Johnson's withdrawal from the presidential race two months after Tet indicated his inability to effectively shape the news agenda and counter the growing sense that the public has been misled on questions of policy, progress and moral responsibility. From Tet onwards, 'television presented a war that was puzzling and incoherent – a series of disjointed military operations that were often individually successful but collectively disasterous. Night after night, television slowly exposed the illogic of attrition' (ibid: 112). This moment had became a turning-point in the war by bringing to question the dominant perception that the American effort was succeeding, which the media had previously sustained (ibid: 98), and countered assertions that bombardment was having positive impact (ibid: 99). The pro-war stance that the television media had taken, which derived from a broad 'acceptance of the cold war outlook that was responsible for U.S. intervention in Vietnam' (ibid: 100), now shifted in the wake of changing political circumstances.

We should not assume that such a change was exacerbated by journalists who had been given an opportunity to be much more critical of the US administration, however. Even after Tet, as Knightley points out, 'the correspondents were not questioning the American intervention itself, but only its effectiveness. Most correspondents, despite what Washington thought about them, were just as interested in seeing the United States win the war as the Pentagon. What the correspondents questioned was not American policy, but the tactics used to implement that policy' (2000: 417). Importantly, as Knightley notes, the administration's policy of providing practically any journalist with access to the war zone contributed to problems of information control and further destabilized attempts to promote a unified political agenda (ibid: 419). By not controlling news access effectively, it became increasingly difficult for the US administration to shape news agendas in line with the optimism and propaganda campaigns which were needed to help legitimize strategy and policy goals (ibid: 423).

Although it should be acknowledged that post-Tet, the news media did not become more receptive to an anti-war agenda, it is also the case that a broader questioning of political policy failed to materialize into any systematic interrogation of the opposition and its motives (Taylor 1997: 112). Criticisms of the media's approach by the administration was an indication, asserts Taylor, not of journalists trying to undermine the war effort, but 'doing their job more efficiently than they had been before 1968, when they had been uncritically supportive' (ibid.). Images of body bags returning to the US appeared to counter arguments that the war was proceeding in accordance with government lines, and particularly from 1969 onwards (during the Nixon administration) began to undermine public support for the war, at the same time helping to facilitate the growing anti-war movement. The contention that the media were the main reason for a decline in public confidence was an attempt to divert criticism from the administration which was itself responsible for the uncertainty (ibid: 114). The media amplified an emerging dissensus about policy and so reflected rather than initiated the political ambiguity which resulted in dwindling public support. Significantly, though, there does not appear to have been a specific moment when reporting shifted its focus from a submissive to a more critical perspective. As Taylor observes, it was the cumulative impact of horrific imagery over a period of time which shifted perceptions and led to pressures which impacted negatively on the credibility of official explanations (ibid: 115).

That 'Vietnam was a failure of political leadership' (Neuman 1996: 174) was denied by Johnson, who believed that reporting had drained any desire to confront communism, contaminated public opinion and ultimately condemned his presidency (ibid: 171). Johnson could not seem to fully comprehend the evident inconsistency between his optimistic statements and the images being broadcast (ibid: 177), just as he could not seem to appreciate the contradiction of proposing a limited war, but calling for more troops, or talking about negotiations whilst bombing intensified. As Neuman observes: 'This dissonance between words and actions doomed him. They called it the credibility gap' (ibid: 176). Whilst it became increasingly obvious that the war was being lost in Washington (ibid: 183), it was also obvious that television news had developed an ability to undermine official viewpoints. The presentation of images which served to challenge government assertions 'hinted at the immense subversive potential of the medium' (Cummings 1992: 84) and exposed gaps in political versions of progress and legitimacy. The broader effect of such coverage is now seen to be connected to a growing public dissatisfaction with the war and developing unease within Washington (Carruthers 2000: 108) and the emerging realisation that 'a war which was nightly screened on television could not be won' (ibid: 109).

Nevertheless, it is also important to understand that a critical para-digm of reporting did not occur because journalists took on a more con-flictive role in relation to official discourse, but rather because 'their sources radically reappraised the war, triggering an adjustment in re-portorial mode to accommodate dissent' (ibid: 147). As Carruthers summarizes this development, 'media coverage of the Vietnam War demonstrates, then, how precisely media are attuned to the fluctuations of their sources, and within what narrow boundaries they operate their balancing mechanisms so that the very practices of "objectivity" operate to inscribe a routine bias in favour of power elites' (ibid: 150). This reliance on the comments and reactions of official representa-tives and agents occurred, as Hallin notes, because conceptions of objective journalism tend to resist the notion of an oppositional jour-nalism (1994: 43). Critical coverage developed, Hallin continues, because journalists became increasingly interested in dissent as a devel-oping story. Moreover, dissent was broadly framed within limits of official discourse thereby preventing 'any real opportunity to present alternative interpretations of the news' (ibid: 49). In the case of oppo-sitional viewpoints existing in reports, it became noticeable that 'opponents of administration policy would appear in these stories to explain and justify themselves, not to discuss the war in Vietnam' (ibid.).

Given this propensity for journalists to exclude, and so delegitimize oppositional positions, it also became increasingly apparent that 'what-ever tendency there may have been for journalists to become more skep-tical of administration policy, it does not seem to have translated into sympathetic coverage of the opposition' (ibid: 51). Indeed, concludes Hallin, 'as a forum for political debate, television remained open pri-marily to official Washington, despite the rise in political protest' (1989: 201). Critical coverage was therefore restrained within a frame of refer-ence which sought to protect rather than unsettle the political legiti-macy of conflict. Even 'on those rare occasions when the underlying reasons for American intervention were discussed explicitly, what jour-nalists did was to defend the honorableness of American motives' (ibid: 208). Unsurprisingly given this emphasis, the anti-war protests and posi-tions which advocated peace were presented 'not as a participant in political debate', but as 'a threat to "internal security"' (ibid: 193). Able to undermine the credibility of anti-war discourse by focusing 'primarily on the movement itself as an issue, not on what it had to say about the war' (ibid: 199), reporting remained ostensibly unreceptive to the nuances and constructiveness of anti-war discourse.

Reporting the anti-war movement

The effect of anti-war discourse on US policy towards Vietnam high-lights an interesting relationship between the media, public opinion and politics, and reveals a general negative representation of peace campaigning by the media at this time. The interaction of public opinion with the planning of political policy towards Vietnam developed particularly after 1965, and coincided with a growing undercurrent of dissent about the course and legitimacy of the war (Small 1987: 186). This dissent was reflective of growing critical articulations about the war which became an active consideration in the policy intiatives of successive administrations through to 1972 (ibid.). The impact of the anti-war movement on American society generally was problematic, however, and failed to harness expected levels of support from a public dissatisfied with how the war was progressing. Significantly, 'many Americans who were distressed by the war were more distressed by the anti-war movement and what they perceived to be its rowdy and un-patriotic activities' (ibid.). Such activities were amplified by media interest which focused on confrontations between protesters and the police, and juxtaposed images of domestic unrest with footage from the war itself (Mandelbaum 1982: 164). Because of representations which undermined the articulation of any unified or coherent anti-war discourse, along with images which depicted styles of dress, patterns of behaviour and sexual conduct which appeared to challenge dominant values and norms, it has been argued that the anti-war movement may have helped prolong American engagement in Vietnam (ibid: 165). But, a more credible explanation would be that the anti-war movement made little or no difference to the length of time America was engaged in conflict. As Schreiber notes, the impact of anti-war demonstrations on public opinion was 'linked to changes in the Vietnam-related views expressed by the news media', rather than demonstrations which were seen as 'largely irrelevant to Vietnam-related opinions' (1976: 232). For Schreiber, 'demonstrations had no measurable effect on the decline in favourable public opinion', therefore making it 'unlikely that demonstrations could have served as "mediating links" between the war and the American public' (ibid: 225).

Schreiber's study tells us nothing about how the media 'constructed' such demonstrations, however, and for that reason offers little in the way of explanation as to why the unpopularity of the anti-war movement developed. Importantly, this is because Schreiber's analysis fails to relate media representations of the anti-war movement with a 'systematic denegration of the New Left', nor does he explain the recurring stereotypes which supported this emphasis. In a detailed study of how the media portrayed the anti-war movement, Gitlin identifies a series of categorizations which contributed to 'deprecatory themes' which 'began to emerge, then to recur and reverberate' in coverage from 1965 onwards (1980: 27). These themes that Gitlin refers to amount to a combination of news frames and narratives which reinforced negativity. Gitlin identifies:

1 'Trivialization', which is concerned with how coverage made light of the anti-war movement's language, sense of dress, values, aims and age.
2 A process of 'polarization', where the anti-war movement was considered in terms of extreme positions and elements within it, compared with far-right groups and thereby depicted as a combination of extremist factions.
3 The media emphasized antagonisms and dissensus within the movement itself, thus contributing to an image of it as being disorganized and chaotic.
4 Demonstrations were routinely shown to be subversive and unrepresentative of social norms and values.
5 There was a 'disparagement by numbers' tendency within reporting, where the amount of people involved in demonstrations was regularly underestimated.
6 There was a generally contemptuous attitude toward the movement's legitimacy and effectiveness (ibid: 27–8).

For Gitlin, the net impact of such representations combined to portray the movement as uncoordinated, extremist and part of a New Left conspiracy that presented a threat to social order (ibid: 29). This negative representation was then used by the government to criticize and undermine the movement. As Gitlin, describes this process: 'The media spotlight brought the incandescent light of social attention and then converted it to the heat of reification and judgement. The spotlight turned out to be a magnifying glass. The State used that glass to help point, and justify, its heavy hand of repression' (ibid: 246).

Gitlin's analysis of the anti-war movement is clearly seen as identifying external influences, where government objectives and the media's tendency to support elite viewpoints and discourse combined to construct the movement in negative terms. But, other reasons might also be considered for the anti-war movement's lack of success, which are internal to the movement itself and, indeed, reflective of peace movements generally. In his article which looks at why disarmament movements fail, Clotfelter identifies how peace movements have been the least effective of popular movements, unable to fulfil short-term goals and influence public policy. 'Wars have ended', contends Clotfelter, 'but not because of the work of peace movements' (1986: 98). The reasons he gives for this are numerous and indicate the complex range of factors which impact on the organization and influence of peace movements themselves. Challenging the nationalist sentiment which underpins most Western nations, is one key problem faced by peace movements. The suggestion that peace movements offer no real resistance to the threat of enemies helps to entrench the view that 'they are not seen as reflecting the basic values of society' and so inimical to shared values (ibid.).

A second reason for the failure of disarmament movements arises 'because they identify with such widely approved symbols and themes as to deny themselves a clear identity' (ibid: 99). To illustrate this point, Clotfelter looks at the threat of nuclear war and argues that the fear of war, which movements seek to amplify, tends to assist the case of 'leaders who promise security through increased military strength' rather than encourage wider support for peace groups (ibid.).

Third, disarmament movements fail 'because they become identified with threatening symbols unrelated to disarmament' (ibid.). This point picks up with themes which Gitlin highlights and is related to images which shock and offend, and which become the basis for broader social understanding.

A fourth reason offered by Clotfelter derives from the problematical relationship between peace and the social change which peace requires. As Clotfelter observes, 'Given the distance separating the unjust present from a just future, this would mean that disarmament must wait for a transformation of human beings and societies' (ibid: 100); indicating the need for peace organizations to recognize how a change in public consciousness is necessary for support about disarmament to take hold. A fifth problem arises for disarmament movements because 'they are unable, or unwilling, to convince people that wars hurt national economies' (ibid.), and therefore present a coherent case against the negative impact which war has on the economy; within disarmament discourse, Clotfelter identifies how the economic effects of war have been incidental to arguments about the case for peace (ibid.).

The final reason why disarmament movements fail relates to an inability 'to bridge class and ideological divisions' (ibid: 101). Since most peace activists come from the middle class, there is a tendency, Clot-felter argues, to exclude rather than involve the working classes, which obstructs development of a broader support base (ibid.). What this work underlines with regard to anti-war movements, is that there are prob-lems of presentation and legitimacy which are internal to those move-ments and which cannot be fully understood by looking at how they are depicted by the media (crucial though that obviously is). Clotfelter highlights problems of presentation which are largely the result of struc-tural inconsistencies within peace movements themselves, but even if these problems were resolved there is no guarantee that this would translate into greater media interest. Clearly, a positive representation of the anti-war position depends as much on the receptiveness of the media as it does on better organization and articulation of the anti-war case. In other words, just as Gitlin tends to ignore the internal defi-ciences of the anti-war movement, so Clotfelter tends to avoid the role of the media in the public communication of peace.

The problems of internal organization and external representation faced by peace movements were contributory factors to the demise of the Vietnam anti-war movement, leading to its inevitable decline as a point of media interest. As Small observes: 'after several years of spec-tacular and unprecedented mass marches and demonstrations, the media became bored. Media inattention was one of the reasons why the antiwar movement came to an apparent halt in 1971' (1987: 189). This boredom came about because activities which occurred almost daily in support of the anti-war movement, took on a certain predictability which was unable to sustain journalistic attention (Small 2002: 151). The scale and nature of the marches which proved vital in 'contribut-ing to success or failure in attracting the attention of the decision-makers, the media and the public' (ibid: 191) demonstrate the media's concern with the quantitative and visual aspects of the marches, and the potential of scale and visual presence to translate into political pres-sure and public concern. But as Gitlin has discovered, it was this narrow emphasis which served to reinforce negative perceptions and ultimately hinder the possibilties of anti-war dialogue emerging as a substantive counter-argument to the government's war policy. By focusing on the dramatic and more contentious elements of the marches, the media amplified 'activities that alienated some middle-class Americans watch-ing their evening newscasts' and 'disturbed parents, fearful that their own children would become radical protestors' (ibid.). Though such limitations inhibited articulation of the anti-war position, it never-theless seems that these pressures were used and absorbed by the US government in its policy decisionmaking (Small 1984: 16). A combination of media attention to issues of escalation and growing public disenchantment augmented political pressures and provided a climate which the anti-war movement tried to capitalize on, often with counterproductive effect.

The anti-war movement is seen to be relevant only because its motivations intersected with a broader public unease about the war which the media had played a key part in promoting. The problem for the anti-war movement was that although the Vietnam war was unpopular, the movement itself was even more unpopular (Mandelbaum 1982: 165), and this unpopularity, along with a lack of public credibility, provided the American administration with the opportunity to further maginalize and erode the movement's chances of acquiring public sympathy. Notably, the Nixon administration 'tried to equate dissent from its policies with disloyalty, or at least disreputability. Hostility to the counterculture and the antiwar movement were central themes in the Republican campaigns of 1970 and 1972' (ibid: 166). The administration, in other words, tried to use the unpopularity of the anti-war movement as a distraction from the direct pressure it faced, and sought to depict the aims of the movement as inimical to social order and political leadership. Significantly, the administration recognized that for 'the antiwar movement, the Vietnam War seemed a crime', whereas 'to the American public it was a blunder' (ibid.), and used this distinction to portray the movement as being driven by left-wing ambitions which jeopardized democratic norms and values. This stereotyping found resonance with the wider public, and supported the argument that the movement may have assisted, rather than obstructed, the war policy of American administrations (ibid: 165).

Taking into account problems with the unification of the anti-war movement and the lack of a single discourse able to clearly articulate a strategy for de-escalation, as well as additional problems faced by anti-war movements regarding organization and implementation of coherent messages which resonate with the public, it is evident that with regard to the Vietnam anti-war movement, the media played a key role in exacerbating these problems. This exacerbation tells us something about the media's receptiveness to state power, challenges to that power, and a concern with conflict rather than peace. But it is also difficult to conclude that the media would have been more sympathetic in its coverage of the anti-war movement had the movement been able to present its position more coherently and systematically, and this is because of the media's tendency to rely on elite political discourse and power. The anti-war movement's inability to offer a counter-strategy to the Nixon administration's demonization of its motives may hint at the movement's lack of co-ordination in terms of promoting a single message, but this problem also needs to be considered against negative representations and routine simplifications of anti-war discourse. The more extreme elements who used the anti-war movement as a platform to voice objections to state represssion, were given coverage by the media and used to provide a useful stereotype for government officials to use in relation to arguments about pacifism being a threat to social order (Small 2002: 25).

News images of demonstrations increasingly concentrated on symbols of left-wing resistance and reactionary youth, ignoring the less dramatic representations of peace which sought to connect most directly with middle-class audiences, and thus contributed to distrust rather than sympathy for the anti-war case (ibid: 35). Such images also tended to support government assertions that the movement was concerned not really with peace, but the merits of communism. Nixon thought it necessary to intensify criticism of the anti-war movement (partly because of fears about any advantages it might give the communist enemy in Vietnam) by repeating the assertion that the movement was concerned with a need to surrender to the communists because of its own communist intentions (ibid: 152). The protests and demonstrations were routinely seen by many in Washington as providing encouragement to the North Vietnamese, and therefore prolonging the war. For others, the anti-war movement was perceived as an obstruction to diplomacy and a possible peace settlement because it presented America in a position of weakness, forced to reach a settlement because of internal domestic difficulties and therefore disadvantaged in the diplomacy process (ibid: 161).

Interestingly, the media's propensity to routinely portray the anti-war movement through its most visually dramatic and more immediately recognizable symbols did not translate into an equally dramatic emphasis on the scale of demonstrations and protests, even though this was a key feature of the movements political significance. If 'crowd size became a key to success', and 'if the movement wanted to demonstrate to the administration that it was growing in potential influence, it had to attract ever-increasing crowds' (ibid: 27), with the consequences of underplaying the scale of demonstrations highlighting the disadvantageous political consequences which this representation can have. This also indicates the political bias of news coverage and its tendency to see opposition to state power in terms of a threat rather than public objection to policy, conducted within the realms of what may be seen as reasonable conflicting differences. The lack of positive coverage of the demonstrations seemed to both reinforce public suspicion and concern about the intentions of the movement, and discourage further participation in the protests themselves (ibid: 46). Far less concerned with the substance of the anti-war position and the legitimacy of the arguments it offered (ibid: 28), images of arrests carried out by police suggested that the movement was actually a threat to national security and that given this threat, should not be afforded the 'constitutional niceties' expected (ibid: 146). Repressive tactics by the Nixon administration which were magnified by the media, also acted as a deterent to other prospective supporters seeking to be part of the anti-war movement, and contributed to Nixon's election strategy of undercutting further support for demonstrations (ibid: 147).

Conclusion

What emerges from much of the literature about news coverage of the Vietnam War is a widespread receptiveness to government positions and a correspondingly widespread lack of receptiveness to the anti-war movement. Although coverage produced problems for successive administrations, this occurred largely because a coherent and co-ordinated strategy was lacking which the news media amplified. Inconsistencies between government statements and the development of the war demonstrated disparities in political policy which transpired into growing public unrest. However, we should not view these political difficulties as illustrative of any attempt by the media to subvert government policy. As Hallin's extensive study of the media and Vietnam makes clear (1989), although news coverage may have helped to exacerbate problems of credibility, this was overwhelmingly a situation of each government's making and the news media reflected that.

News coverage of resistance to the war by the anti-war movement demonstrates a notable absence of media interest in the substance of the argument which the movement sought to articulate. The possibilities of change which the movement represented were routinely represented as threats and contextualized within a framework which positioned the resistance in relation to themes and issues of social (dis)order. Rather than portraying the movement as an opposition, able to legitimately contest the policy of government and so offer a competing discourse operating within the bounds of democratic society, the movement was often portrayed as a dangerous challenge to social norms and values and therefore outside the bounds of respectable or responsible opposition. Picking up on government attempts to construct the movement as having communist sympathies (a process with McCarthyite associations), the media tended to reinforce perceptions that the movement had closer affiliations with the communist enemy by focusing on symbols and images which suggested unpatriotic, or left-wing tendencies. This interference was ostensibly a visual construct, where demonstrations were regularly covered by concentrating on the most obvious and extreme oppositions to the government position and, as argued, had negative impact on the potential support base which the movement sought to augment.

Given this emphasis, it is evident that the news media were largely unreceptive to debates and articulations presented by the anti-war movement and that the nuances of argument were ignored in favour of what the movement suggested or implied through its appearances. A trivialization of the movement's position occured through this visual emphasis, which succeeded in reducing the objections to an expression of subversion and potential danger. Significantly, this also demonstrates that at this time it became a priority for the media to construct the anti-war movement as the product of a broader cultural expression, where resistance had become fashionable and symptomatic of a growing social attitude which sought to articulate peace and community as a counter-position to government objectives which prioritized global interests and capitalist dominance. A consequence of this contextualization is that the details and substance of the anti-war movement's arguments were replaced by a series of codes and references which were connotive of change and so instability. Rather than constructing the movement's position as a necessary counterweight to political dominance, the rowdy and unpatriotic images served to underpin the importance of that dominance, and helped to establish a need for the government to reassert the social order which the movement appeared to disrupt and jeopardize.

Coverage of the anti-war movement offered a dramatic obstruction to the American government which had obvious news appeal, but this should not be construed as a product of critical reporting. Problems encountered by successive American administrations were ostensibly of their own making and a result of misplaced ideas, both about strategy towards the course of the war, and the ememy being fought. The anti-war movement compounded such problems, but overall, failed to achieve the goal of halting conflict. Part of the responsibility for this failure must, of course, reside with the movement itself, but we should not exclude the media from playing a part in this outcome. What the

Vietnam experience and news reporting at this time indicate is that articulations and messages about peace seem to interest journalists only when they exacerbate conflicts. Essentially, the news emphasis was not on the need to disengage from Vietnam, or de-escalate conflict, but on pressuring US governments to deal with war more effectively and manage news better.

5
Rwanda and Reporting Africa

The Rwandan genocide of 1994, where 800,000 people were slaughtered in 100 days, raises important questions about Western political indifference to conflicts which lack strategic interest and indicates problems with news reporting of Africa. What this chapter sets out to do is question the political background to the genocide, UN and US prevarications over intervention, and the role of news in relation to the genocide and how the West responded to it. Inside Rwanda, local radio played an important function in the planning and exacerbation of the genocide, and was used by the Hutu elite to encourage the systematic murder of the Tutsi minority. Radio broadcasts were a clear sign that genocide was being co-ordinated, yet failed to incite outside action or intervention. Western indifference to the developing genocide was barely challenged by the media, which failed to cover the slaughter until it had transmuted into a humanitarian disaster and a refugee crisis. This reaction by the news media to Rwanda is in keeping with a broader lack of concern with Africa, consistent with coverage which continues to view such conflicts as ethnic hatreds, and which fails to capture audience interest. Tribal differences, racial distinctions, civil wars and colonial histories are factors too complex for the requirements of simplistic news reports, and so do not merit careful deconstruction. As BBC correspondent Fergal Keane summarized this tendency in his book *Seasons of Blood* (about the Rwandan experience):

Where television is concerned, African news is generally only big news when it involves lots of dead bodies. The bigger the mound, the greater the possibility that the world will, however briefly, send its camera teams and correspondents. Once the story has gone 'stale', i.e. there are no new bodies and the refugees are down to a trickle,

the circus moves on. The powerful images leave us momentarily hor-
rified but largely ignorant, what somebody memorably described as
'compassion without understanding'.

(1995: 7)

This chapter seeks to argue that because stereotypical representations
depict distant Others like those in Rwanda as uncivilized and ultimately
inferior, so this helps rather than hinders the case for inaction (until,
that is, the story has become a humanitarian disaster) and does little to
help articulate the case for intervention, which is the starting point for
peace. It would be too much to suggest that media coverage of Rwanda
made the genocide worse, but pertinent, I think, to contend that negative coverage, along with Western intransigence, assisted those determined to carry out the genocide more than those trying to escape
from it.

Historical and political background

In the words of Alain Destexhe, 'the massacres in Rwanda are not the
result of a deep-rooted and ancient hatred between two ethnic groups.
In fact, the Hutu and Tutsi cannot even be correctly described as ethnic
groups for they both speak the same language and respect the same traditions and taboos'. Although there are noticeable social differences
between both groups, it is the case, argues Destexhe, that those differences are not of ethnic or racial origin. Such categorizations are largely
a product of colonial influence, where, 'by exaggerating such stereotypes and supporting one group against the other', the 'colonizers reinforced, consolidated and ultimately exacerbated such categorizing'
(Destexhe 1995: 36). It was, notes Destexhe, the German and Belgian
colonizers who developed the categorization of Hutu and Tutsi 'according to their degree of beauty, their pride, intelligence and political organization', and who 'established a distinction between those who did not
correspond to the stereotype of a negro (the Tutsi) and those who did
(the Hutu)' (ibid: 38). Through these differentiations, the colonizers sys-
tematized political and social organization based on Tutsi superiority
(ibid: 39). This separation evolved over time 'into an ethnic problem
with an overwhelmingly racist dimension', and created political disparities which 'were progressively transformed into racial ideologies and
repeated outbreaks of violence resulting from the colonial heritage
which was absorbed by local elites who then brought it into the political arena' (ibid: 47). The relationship of this colonial categorization to

the present is important, asserts Gestexhe, because 'the present gen-
eration has internalized this ethnological colonial model, with some
groups deliberately choosing to play the tribal card. The regimes that
have ruled Rwanda and Burundi since independence have shown that
they actually *need* ethnic divisions in order to reinforce and justify their
positions' (ibid.). Attitudes and feelings about group differences are
therefore a necessary component in the struggle for political, economic
and social power, and the process of killing is but one form of control
amongst others, including 'war, bribery, foreign diplomacy, constitutional manipulations and propaganda' (Prunier 1997: 141).

According to Prunier, the systematic co-ordination of murder in
Rwanda was facilitated by three causes:

1 because of an adherence within Rwandese society to authority;
2 because most of the population are illiterate and so tend to believe
the word of authorities;
3 because 'There was a "rural" banalisation of crime', where murder
was presented through a 'vocabulary of peasant-centred agricultural
development, which constructed conflict as a struggle for land and
animals, where enemies were expected to be rooted out like weeds,
and murdered if society was to exist and prosper (ibid; 141–2). Such
thinking prevented the development of democratic institutions,
encouraged group solidarity, and maintained underlying tensions so
they could be manipulated and co-ordinated through a 'sensibiliza-
tion' process, designed to manufacture an atmosphere which encouraged peasants to carry out massacres as if 'bush clearing' (ibid:
137–8). The genocide of 1994 was a clear example of Hutu power
being contained through manipulation of the peasant masses, and
to get the peasants to 'feel that they had no choice but to protect
themselves from an evil that was both facelessly abstract and embodied in the most ordinary person living next door' (ibid: 170).

This process accelerated after the Arusha Declaration for peace was
signed in 1993. The Arusha peace process was an attempt by nine
nations and two intergovernmental organizations to negotiate an end
to civil war between warring factions in Rwanda (Jones 1995: 240–1),
and to address relations between the Habyarimana government and the
Rwandan Patriotic Front (RPF), which represented Tutsi exiles who fled
after a Hutu takeover in 1959 (Clapham 1998: 198). Initial moderation
by the Habyarimana regime eventually came under threat from groups
close to the president and growing RPF opposition, which culminated

in an invasion of Rwanda in 1990. However, international support for different parties within this tension 'helped to exacerbate rather than moderate the conflict within Rwanda', and failed to identify the range of factions which permeated Rwandan society (ibid: 199). In recognition of growing unrest and possible destabilization, Habyarimana attempted to create the impression of a multi-party government, but in consisting almost entirely of Hutu elites, this move served to further separate groups dedicated to preserving Hutu power from the more moderate Hutu elements who might work with the RPF (ibid: 200). In response to growing violence and unrest, an African-backed peace process which followed a three-year campaign by international players, both state and non-state, to bring about conflict resolution in Rwanda (Jones 1995: 226), tried to mediate between the Habyarimana government and the RPF. In 1992, the Habyarimana government conceded to internal and external pressure and 'agreed to the establishment of a multi-party transitional government, as condition for which the internal opposition insisted on peace negotiations with the RPF' (Clapham 1998: 201). However, extremist groups more actively engaged in violence had not been involved in the negotiations, and the new dispensation consisted largely of minor parties with little in the way of political leverage or influence (ibid: 205).

These groups capitalized on a growing dissatisfaction with the Arusha deal and sought to mobilize resistance, which would underpin the genocide that followed. Hutu factions who had gained nothing from the Arusha accords, and viewed the process as one of concessions to the RPF, organized to exaggerate tensions and fears, and began to co-ordinate a campaign of extermination against the perceived Tutsi threat. The Arusha accords thus led to an intensification of extremist training and planning, and the genocide was a clear attempt to wreck any agreement which might contribute to a weakening of extremist positions. As Jones concludes: 'Though we cannot cogently argue that the intervention of Arusha provoked the genocide *per se*, we can certainly insist that the Arusha process had tragic *consequences*, even if they were unintentional' (1995: 243). Rather than help bring about a conflict resolution situation in Rwanda, the involvement of national and international communities in Arusha brought about a transformation of conflict by reinforcing a sense of urgency and desperation, which extremists used in order to further co-ordinate and accelerate the genocide. This failure by those at Arusha to produce a settlement which would hold and find wider resonance amongst the more extremist factions inside Rwanda was not helped by the exclusion of those factions from talks, just as it was not helped by the pursuit of exclusive agendas by those involved in the mediation. A weakening of positions inside the talks was an inevitable result of debating concessions which further reinforced extremist assertions that a settlement would lead to a worsening situation for those the extremists claimed to represent (Clapham 1998: 209).

The planning and execution of genocide by the Hutu elites on Tutsis in 1994 produced a muted response from the international community, and has since provoked severe criticism of US and UN resistance to intervention (Power 2003; Melvern 2000 and 2004). Even though killing had been steadily increasing from August 1993 after Arusha and the official government radio station Radio Rwanda, along with the private station Radio Mille Collines, had been encouraging action against Tutsis, international reactions were largely evasive and muted (Burkhalter 1994: 45). On 6 April 1994 President Habyarimana (who was seen by extremists as having conceded too much at Arusha) was shot down in an airplane over Kigali and within 30 minutes of his murder the killing began (ibid: 46). The overriding response from the US administration at this time was either one of reticence, or to present the genocide as a product of tribal conflicts or civil war (ibid: 47). Resisting calls for intervention and wider UN engagement, the Clinton administration avoided describing the slaughter as genocide, which under UN law would have called for intervention, and worked hard to avert sending a force to Africa which might encounter the same response as the US had experienced in Somalia. By obstructing calls to commit troops, the US effectively undermined the support of other nations who would participate in an American-backed plan to stop the genocide and provide a peacekeeping presence (ibid: 49). Believing that another costly venture into Africa would be to no real political advantage, and that there would be no domestic repercussions by refusing to engage, the US decided to do nothing (Power 2003: 335). In discussion of Rwanda, there was a tendency to emphasize the genocide as a peacekeeping problem and to avoid talking about human rights action (Burkhalter 1994: 52).

This emphasis, as Burkhalter notes, meant that geoncide 'was treated, not as a human rights disaster requiring urgent response, but as a peacekeeping headache to be avoided' (ibid: 53). The language used routinely spoke about 'possible acts of genocide' in order to try and sidestep pressure for action (Destexhe 1994; 13), whilst the situation in Rwanda was referred to not as a comparison to the Holocaust, but the debacle of Somalia (Power 2003: 357). As Power summarized America at this time: 'The American public expressed no interest in Rwanda, and the crisis was treated as a civil war requiring a cease-fire or as a "peacekeeping problem" requiring a UN withdrawal. It was not treated as a genocide demanding instant action' (ibid: 373). Looking closely at elite opinion and the development of popular dissent about possible non-intervention, the Clinton administration concluded that there was 'no group or groups' that would make the 'decisionmakers feel or fear that they would pay a political price for doing nothing to save Rwandans. Indeed, all the signals told them to steer clear' (ibid: 373–4). By continuing to dispute the murders as symptomatic of genocide, the US resisted the obligation of engagement and demonstrated its indifference to what was happening (Prunier 1997: 274)

Radio and genocide

Within Rwanda itself, radio stations such as Radio Rwanda and Radio Mille Collines played a key role in the dissemination of fears and hatred and proved instrumental in helping to orchestrate the killing. UN officials and human rights groups had indentified the part played by radio in the escalation of tensions and the incitement to murder some time before the genocide began, and without success, had called for the US along with other countries to jam the broadcasts (Metzl 1997: 629). The Clinton administration chose not to jam the broadcasts because of cost, fear of being drawn further into the genocide, and problems with international law, which stressed the need to uphold free expression. Though issues with international law could no doubt have been circumvented in the case of genocide, this obstruction was used as a reason to avoid jamming and once more underlined the US position of non-action (ibid: 630). Refusing to help jam broadcasts was further evidence of the desire to remain peripheral to the genocide and avoid pressures to intervene.

Radio Rwanda, which 'was essentially the tool of Hutu extremists from the government, military and business communities' (ibid.), provided information and details about how massacres would be conducted, whilst Radio Mille Collines organized roadblocks, and named those who needed to be found and executed (ibid: 631). This information, which was known outside of Rwanda and given attention by CNN along with a section of the print media, failed to attract broader international interest or the pressure for a credible response (ibid: 632). The contention that radio jamming could have helped to save a considerable number of lives did not translate into any meaningful action (ibid: 636), and a fear for key protagonists like the US was that moves to jam broadcasts would indicate a commitment to action, which could lead to further involvement and operations which ran counter to foreign policy and domestic interests.

Radio Rwanda broadcast propaganda distorted the potential threat of the RPF by talking about massacres which had not occurred (Des Forges 2002: 239). The intention was to stoke up Hutu fears by accusing Tutsis of planning and committing genocide and thereby encourage a response of corresponding intensity and ferocity. By accusing Tutsis of the very activities which Hutus were themselves carrying out, Radio Rwanda was instrumental in orchestrating fears and anxieties which supported the campaign of murder (ibid.). Promoting orders from Hutu elites, radio contributed to the systematic and relentless demonization of the Tutsi enemy and heightened the 'kill or be killed' atmosphere necessary for pre-emptive murder. It also warned against any sympathies for the Tutsi and represented such sympathizers as the 'enemy within', who themselves warranted the same treatment as Tutsis (ibid: 246). This use of radio and its incitement to carry out genocide was, as argued, well known by the West, but received negligible concern, even though preventative action would have created a situation where 'jamming radio would have helped sap the authority of the regime and made Rwandans less ready to follow its orders' (ibid: 248).

Media coverage of Rwanda and reporting Africa

International media reporting of Rwanda adopted a range of conventional positions consistent with past simplifications of African conflicts, and routinely resorted to stereotypical portrayals of those involved. For BBC correspondent Fergal Keane, 'a well-planned campaign of politically and materially motivated slaughter' came 'to be explained away as an ancient tribal conflict', and reiterated colonial representations of internal hatreds without apparent external influences (1995: 8). Just as reporting neglected the preparations and controlling forces of genocide, so it failed to cover Rwanda when the slow process of rebuilding began (ibid: 186). Attention given to the humanitarian disaster of Rwandans fleeing Rwanda to neighbouring Zaire and the refugee exodus which brought predictable images of suffering and misery to television screens in the West highlighted the 'Ethiopian factor' as a 'recurring theme in much of the journalistic and academic analysis of the Tutsi/Hutu divide' (ibid: 14), and conveyed suffering as a problem of scale, without context or historical precedent. However, such images were not without political relevance to those engaged in the killing, since as McNulty reminds us: 'The net result of this media-driven agenda was a vicious circle – crisis, images, intervention, further crisis, more images, repeated intervention – that helped exacerbate the Rwandan crisis to the point of genocide, and then exported that crisis to neighbouring Zaire' (1999: 269).

McNulty contends that such reporting constructed a paradigm 'which generally fitted into the typical African mould of biblical catastrophes', and the 'mechanical ethnicization' which 'comforts us in the knowledge that the perpetrators are mad (driven by tribalism, ancient blood lust, etc.)', but that we, by association, are sane, able to act and deal with a situation which locals are evidently unable to stop themselves (ibid: 270). Proposals for intervention to help alleviate the humanitarian catastrophe which the genocide created may, on the face of it, be motivated by efforts to help, but the exclusion of important contextual explanation of how suffering came about also indicates a distortion in coverage which omits colonial dominance and a long history of control over Africa and its representations (ibid: 271). According to McNulty, colonial depictions of Hutu and Tutsi divisions served to obscure the overriding Rwandan ethnicity of both groups, and underscored the viewpoint of journalists, who used such a distorted analysis as a point of reference by which to comprehend the genocide (ibid: 277). Overall, purports McNulty, reporting suffered because of ignorance, minimal knowledge of Rwandan ethnicity, and an agenda shaped by past coverage of African conflicts (ibid: 279).

Explanations which emphasized tribal divisions as the basis of the slaughter and massacres, effectively obscured the differences between perpetrators and victims and confused responsibility for the genocide. This confusion served to help perpetrators more than victims and demonstrates how reporting, through ignorance and stereotypical interpretations, may have helped to exacerbate rather than help halt the genocide (ibid: 281). By imposing a Western neo-colonial agenda of reporting which ignored local reaction and comprehension of the genocide, international news reporting ostensibly paralleled the political indifference displayed in the US and UN, and only began to exert pressure when the genocide was seen to have developed into a clear humanitarian disaster. Though the pressure for humanitarian intervention suggests a level of influence by reporting on the actions of Western governments, it nevertheless remains the case that a reductionist tendency by the media to equate genocide and the refugee crisis as similar tragedies without political motivation or historical reason (Shaw 1996: 173) meant that coverage kept to predictable depictions of misery and suffering which had become synonomous with African news stories.

Before looking at some of the issues which might arise from the viewing of such suffering, perhaps it is worth saying something about the use of stereotypes in this context and how they shape perceptions. The propensity of reducing Rwanda (and Africa more typically) to a series of stereotypes about tribal hatreds, uncivilized attitudes and racial disputes indicates a point of view which interprets inferiority from a perspective of superiority. As Said notes in his study of Orientalism and the attitudes of the colonial West, this outcome depends on a 'flexible *positional* superiority, which puts the Westerner in a whole series of relationships with the Orient without ever losing him the upper hand' (2003: 7). This upper hand depends on 'reiterating European superiority over Oriental backwardness' (ibid.) and thus maintaining a dominance in how the Oriental is understood, interpreted and explained. But this interest is also overwhelmingly political in orientation and strives to create 'a distribution of geopolitical awareness' through a series of textual understandings, which are about power and values that intersect with that power (ibid: 12). Notably, this power is contrived through clear demarcations between 'we' and 'they', where 'they' are constructed not through the discourses of 'them', but the discourses of 'us'. The construction of representations, histories and discourses about 'them' is therefore also about 'us', and maintaining the narratives and associated beliefs of dominance which allows 'us' to control how 'we', as well as 'they', are seen. Such representations, therefore, are about authority and how that authority is perpetuated through the many forms of dissemination which help reinforce it (ibid: 19–20). This relationship may also be understood in terms of 'strong' and 'weak', where expectations of action are largely seen as the strong giving (or imposing their perception of help) on the weak, and where the weak are expected to be dependent on the strong to deal with situations which they cannot (or have no right to) cope with themselves. The notion of dependency is therefore inextricably linked with the legitimization of dominance and the dominant deciding courses of action which the weak must accept gratefully, whilst continuing in their state of powerlessness.

The notion of constraint is important in thinking about others in this way, for as Said observes: 'Orientalism is better grasped as a set of constraints upon and limitations of thought than it is simply as a positive doctrine' (ibid: 42). But the basis of such constraint is surely the circulation of myths and stereotypes which enable others to be characterized so narrowly and simplistically. Pickering's work in this area is particularly useful for thinking about news representations of Rwanda. The stereotype, he asserts, is constitutive of 'certain forms of behaviour, disposition or propensity', which 'are isolated, taken out of context and attributed to everyone associated with a particular group or category' (2001: 4). By homogenizing a group or category, and therefore making them recognizable as a particular stereotype, an 'element of order' is created based on 'an apparently settled hierarchy of relations'. This hierarchy works to sustain 'existing power relations' through 'a sense of certainty, regularity and continuity' (ibid.), and by so doing, enables a level of control which serves to reinforce dominant discourses and the perceptions they evoke. Within this process an inherent superiority is at work and necessarily so, since the construction of stereotypes is dependent on those being stereotyped also being unable to effectively challenge or resist the stereotype being imposed. Or, as Pickering describes this process: 'The evaluative ordering which stereotyping produces always occurs at a cost to those who are stereotyped, for they are then fixed into a marginal position or subordinate status and judged accordingly, regardless of the inaccuracies that are involved in the stereotypical description of them' (ibid: 5). Moreover, this imposition 'imparts a sense of fixedness to the homogenized images it disseminates', and 'attempts to establish an attributed characteristic as natural and given in ways inseparable from the relations of power and domination through which it operates' (ibid.).

What is important for effective streotyping is that 'we' do not identify with the 'they' being stereotyped. In other words, 'we' do not belong amongst 'them' and 'they' do not belong among 'us'. This politics of not belonging is dependent on those who do not belong being looked at not on their own terms, but on the terms of those outside, and 'by symbolic boundaries which contrastively identify them as inferior' to the we who define and represent them (ibid: 109). They are Others, who live in another world (in this case commonly referred to as the Third World), who cannot challenge or properly resist 'the profound, but unquestioned sense of superiority of those who produced the stereotypes and their profound, but unrecognized depth of ignorance of those who are so stereotyped' (ibid.).

Pickering takes the concept of 'race' as an example by which to think further about the stereotype and those who perpetuate it. 'Race', he contends, 'denotes a form of labelling imposed on certain groups by those who base their sense of difference from these groups on their self-arrogated superiority.' Ethnicity, on the other hand, 'provides a means by which certain groups create their own sense of identity, which they characterise and express in their own terms rather than those used to justify their marginalised status' (ibid: 114). Categorizations about race have a long history in the colonial representation of Africa which continue to influence how it is seen, comprehended and dealt with. Such categorizations also permeate news and impact on the definitional boundaries it uses to make sense of conflict and those involved within it.

At the time of writing, press reports have highlighted a campaign of ethnic cleansing in Sudan where over one million people have fled their homes ('There is no hunger says Sudan as children die', The *Guardian*, 25 June 2004). This crisis briefly appears on television news from time to time, but more as a potential refugee crisis and humanitarian disaster, without context or analysis of power struggles around ethnic differences. Using footage which is immediately identifiable as symbolic of the African experience, this story has now disappeared from view, and will no doubt not resume until a bigger disaster materializes, or the West decides this is a problem worthy of more serious attention. Similiarly, developing tensions which have grown in Ivory Coast since the death of its founding president have also yet to be acknowledged as a newsworthy problem by the media ('A last chance for peace', The *Guardian*, 8th July 2004), and remain in keeping with a general disinterest in the massacres and ethnic slaughter carried out over recent years in places such as Sierra Leone and the Democratic Republic of Congo.

The stereotype of reporting Africa as a place of racial hatreds and tribal savagery (Eltringham 2004: 63) has, it would appear, become so normalized it perhaps seems unnoticeable. But this normalization depends on certain procedures and characteristics in order for the illusion of normality to be created and maintained. As Pickering argues, although notions of normality change, the process of 'unifying diversity, resolving difference, or settling disagreement' remains constant (2001: 176). The presentation of what is normal must also be articulated, or is at least implied, through the representation of what is abnormal, therefore making normalization a dynamic of categorizations. As Pickering puts it: 'You are or are not normal in respect of a particular category. Normal is not something you can simply be' (ibid: 177).

For Pickering, the example of sickness or disease in relation to health demonstrates how the positive, reasonable and normal expectations of health, as opposed to the negative, unreasonable and abnormal expectations of sickness or disease, serve to present those in positions of health as effectively superior and necessarily dominant (ibid.); a position of power similiarly inferred and projected by television news stories where the power of observer (the journalist) over the observed (the suffering victim), demonstrates the normality/abnormality relationship. This relationship also brings into play a further duality, which is the familiar compared to the strange; or more specifically how we react to strangers. The stranger, notes Pickering, 'is inherently ambivalent', unlike 'us' who have clear notions of belonging, and it is because the stranger is neither 'here' nor 'there', that 'normative structures of assessment and censure' are disturbed (ibid: 204). The stranger is problematic because he or she stands somewhere between us and them, and therefore inflicts difficulty on the crude categorizations which are needed to maintain symbolic boundaries of normality (ibid.). The stranger is thus a threat, an unknown and a potential danger (and more so if immediate categorization is elusive), who 'exists in a continual contact zone between belonging and unbelonging' (ibid.), and who interrupts convenient notions of good and bad. This has some relevance for thinking about how television news images construct the starving and suffering victims of war and genocide, since the idea of good and bad in such a context is not only inappropriate, but quite useless (how, for example, could television news have effectively demarcated good and bad in the context of the refugee camps in Goma where perpetrators of the genocide were existing and moving alongside victims?). The African refugee who has come to represent the humanitarian crisis, is a stranger precisely because the concept of belonging is challenged (who can claim that the refugee belongs to the predicament he finds himself/herself in?), and because the suffering victim we are invited to watch is a stranger who falls outside of normative structures of compehension.

Convoluted arguments about compassion fatigue (Moeller 1999) and studies which look at how we react to suffering others (Cohen 2001) perhaps further confirm the difficulties of establishing a clear reference point on such issues. But what is important to recognize is the fleeting and ultimately superficial attention which television news brings to such moments. Television news may attempt to incite some empathy in the viewer by showing scenes of misery, but the victims of this misery are temporary objects of attention. Just as they appear without explanation (how often are underlying reasons for their condition explored?), they disappear without explanation, along with the news teams who move on to another story, only to return when similar circumstances allow the media to reconstruct what Benthall has termed 'parables of disaster' (1993). This does not mean that journalists do not have an impact on what is being reported here (humanitarian agencies depend on such interest to gain support (de Waal 1997)), but that by avoiding analysis of complex reasons which gave rise to the crisis they cover, reporters incite 'compassion without knowledge' (Seib 2002: 73); which produces actions that may be detrimental to the sociocultural norms and values of those being acted upon.

How is peace served by the media when it tends to operate in this way? With regard to Rwanda two themes are evident. First, the genocide was largely ignored, and second, its apparent consequences were not. What we might further deduce from this is that questions about the possibilities of peace were overlooked in favour of the more short-term appeal of compassion and perhaps it is here, in this disparity, where inconsistencies and difficulties about the media's role become most pronounced. The news media's inability to engage earlier in Rwanda, when plans for genocide were already known, is highlighted by Seib as an indication of selectivity in the reporting of Africa and a general obsession with images and narratives of disaster and relief, over the more complex issues which underpin violence:

> With a prejudice against stories from abroad – especially from little-known places of negligible strategic importance – getting news organizations to cover these stories is increasingly difficult, at least until the situation has become so horrible that it can no longer be ignored. The role of the news media as a sophisticated early warning system, alerting the public and policymakers to crises before they become tragedies, has become virtually obsolete.
>
> (Seib 2002: 76)

Interestingly, what Seib alludes to here is that the impression of compassion which reporting may generate is actually an institutional construct, a representative illusion, rather than a consequence of efforts by journalists to outrage those viewing. And this is so because, as Seib points out, news organizations tend to cover Africa when events 'can no longer be ignored' (ibid.). One possible extension of this argument, given the media's control over when, why and how to cover a humanitarian crisis, might contentiously be that under such circumstances the relationship becomes less about what journalism can do for those suffering, and more about what those suffering can do for journalism. As Ignatieff points out when discussing the self-serving motivations of news:

> In the mingling of heterogeneous stories, and in the enforcement of the regime of time, the news makes it impossible to attend to what

one has seen. In the end, one sees only the news, its personalities, its rules of selection and suppression, its authoritative voice. In the end, the subject of news is the news itself: what it depicts is a means to the reproduction of its own authoritativeness. In the worship of itself, of its speed, its immense news-gathering resources, its capacity to beat the clock, the news turns all reality into ninety-second exercises in its own style of representation.

(1999: 30)

It should be said here that the tendency to see Africa as little more than a recurring sequence of images about disaster and relief is not necessarily a reflection on the individual journalists who report from there, however. As we know, some of the most informative, sensitive and detailed interrogations of Rwanda have been made by journalists (Keane 1995; Neuffer 2001; Gourevtich 1998; Peterson 2000). But, what is most evident here is that these accounts are individual not institutional, and as such do not exist as merely a continuum of the reports which took place (although still no doubt influenced by the interpretive framework which shapes journalistic training and conceptualization of the events being looked at). Arguably, these accounts of Rwanda represent an attempt to construct a post-genocide compassion which is more instructive and useful precisely because they are not bound by the narrow and predictable responses which news reports demand. Perhaps the real advantage of such contributions is that they help us to comprehend the genocide more effectively and in the spirit of post-Holocaust meditations, help us 'to think not only about why groups hate each other but how such hatred is inflamed; and, if we are to be modestly hopeful, how, therefore, it can be contained' (Hoffman 2004: 216). But what is particularly crucial to this experience (and is perhaps lacking in a number of the accounts) is listening to local reactions and perceptions and trying to help facilitate the constructive interaction of oppositional groups by allowing those groups access and control over the discourses which shape perceptions of the self.

Simplistic news reports which depicted Rwanda as 'the latest bloody chapter in an age old conflict', and which routinely described the killing as 'tribal bloodletting that foreigners were powerless to prevent' (Melvern 2004: 231), merely served to reinforce international hesitation and confirmed rather than challenged US and UN resistance to engagement. Given that reporting tended to reinforce and so helped legitimize the stance of non-intervention, it is apparent that the news media were not helpful in pressuring moves towards peace, or helping to halt the genocide. Rather, any pressures which were created by news came about when the genocide had transformed into a humanitarian disaster. Then the need for help became focused on the immediate needs of those suffering (important though that was), and it was the desperation of circumstances at that time which appeared to justify the media presence.

Even in the wake of clear and mounting tensions and violence after the Arusha accords, the news media still did next to nothing to help instigate moves for peace, concentrating instead on disaster imagery. Using stereotypical images of the starving African, and instilling a sense of moral superority in those who viewed the unfolding misery through a lens which composed the crisis in ways consistent with what de Waal has descibed as 'disaster tourism' (1997: 82), coverage concentrated on the obvious and easily recognizable images of mass suffering in order to confirm 'exaggerated, dire predictions and stereotypes of pathetic dependency' (ibid.). This perception, which arises through a series of interlocking and overlapping characterizations that ignore local politics and division, has had to be challenged in the post-genocide period by Rwandans trying to come to terms with the slaughter. Indeed, as Eltringham contends, Rwandese have actively had to counter the racist paradigm running through much of the coverage, and resist the distortions perpetuated through reports in order to make sense of how the genocide was planned, developed and executed (2004: 181). By reinforcing perceptions of Western domination over Africa, the media's role in Rwanda reflected an indifference to understanding the complexities of the suffering there, and in so doing prevented the necessary interrogation with causes and reasons for the genocide. Because of this, news helped rather than hindered arguments for non-intervention.

Conclusion

What emerges from examination of the news media's role in Rwanda is a rather stereotypical response of disaster and relief which ignored the underlying complexities and reasons for genocide and failed to generate pressure or develop arguments for military intervention. Concerned primarily with images and narratives about the suffering and voiceless victims of genocide, news chose to ignore the part played by the West in this outrage (not only historically, but for knowing it was happening and deciding to do nothing to help stop it) and enabled potential responses to be debated within an atmosphere of general indifference. Much of the positional superiority adopted in news coverage reaffirmed the images of dependency which have become symbolic of the African experience. Reference to stereotypical portrayals of victims, and a failure to examine the motivating reasons for genocide inevitably meant a failure to distinguish between systematic mass murder and the humanitarian disaster that followed. This tendency to not interrogate and explain the extent and severity of the violence, but to focus on the consequences, relates to an interest in effects over causes and in the process helped to blur arguments about intervention.

Western indifference to engagement in Rwanda was reinforced by a reliance on images which confused ethnic differences and power struggles, and largely ignored political moves which had succeeded in orchestrating the murderous campaign. Reports concerned with numbers of deaths and images of refugees seeking help confirmed a predictable response from the Western media to African misery, constructing narratives of loss and helplessness which legitimized humanitarian responses and therefore assisted in moving criticisms about military intervention to the periphery. Having not fully engaged with the Rwandan crisis until the situation had become a humanitarian catastrophe, the media conveyed the dominant impression that the story was essentially about helpless victims and with that emphasis, notions of superiority and inferiority also came into play. Expectations about givers and receivers, the pitiful object of suffering and the civilized viewer in a position to grant assistance, draw associations from a history of news reporting which has contrived to present the starving and desperate of Africa as not of the civilized world inhabited by Westerners, but of another world inhabited by tribal savagery and misery (Carruthers 2004). Questions of how hatred developed, how it was controlled and exacerbated, and of Western complicity in the process through having known and having chosen not to intervene as the genocide progressed, were notably absent from much of the news coverage of Rwanda. This absence made it easier for governments to hide their indifference to intervention and to shift the argument on to humanitarian debates. Once the frame of humanitarianism came into play the image of non-action changed to apparent action and with that change, possible pressure for further intervention dissipated.

6
Bosnia and Kosovo

The dissolution of Yugoslavia after the fall of the Berlin Wall in 1989, and the struggle for independence amongst those states which comprised the federation, created a collapse in social and civil order which was incited by nationalist tendencies and the collapse of one-party political authority throughout Eastern Europe (Glenny 1992: 32). The struggle for dominance between Croatia under the leadership of Franjo Tudjman, and Serbia under the leadership of Slobodan Milosevic, effectively ended the possibility of an ethnically mixed federal state as Tudjman and Milosevic pursued expansionist policies in order to create 'ethnically homogeneous States' (Hartmann 1999: 51). The collapse of communist control in Yugoslavia in 1990, which led to multi-party elections but did not produce democratization, paved the way for the republics of Slovenia and Croatia to assert political autonomy and the right to self-determination, and also reignited Serbian nationalist aspirations, contributing to the struggle for political independence and accelerating the disintegration and chaos which came to reflect the Balkan tragedy (Woodward 1995: 143). Significantly, rather than producing transition to democratic reform, the elections provided a platform for the release of nationalist viewpoints, which sought to legitimize the struggle for territory, increased fears, escalated tensions, exacerbated conflict and pushed the protagonists towards war (a process not helped by external foreign influences seeking to exploit market opportunities and push through economic change at a time of growing fragmentation and chaos) (ibid: 145).

Discussions which took place between the six republics through 1990 and 1991, dealt with the question of moving Yugoslavia towards 'a loose association of soveriegn states'. But, for Milosevic, they became a means 'through which the country's disintegration could be regulated'

(Glenny 1992: 37), as Croation moves towards independence signalled moving the Serbian minority in Croatia out of Yugoslavia. Milosevic's refusal to recognize Croatian independence was motivated by a desire to forge a powerful Serbian state under his leadership, and to seek political control by orchestrating the chaos and devastation of Yugoslavia in the pursuit of Serb dominance (ibid: 37). In the struggle to strengthen political positions as Yugoslavia collapsed, social and economic aims were hidden within the smoke of ethnic conflict, which became the basis for campaigns of ethnic cleansing and genocide. Since Milosevic and Tudjman both displayed 'territorial ambitions in Bosnia' (Glenny 1999: 638), there was an inevitability that Bosnia would become absorbed into the war which was consuming the Balkans. Bosnia-Hercegovina's declaration of independence in 1992, which was supported by America, was rejected by the Bosnian Serbs and fighting began.

Atrocities carried out by Serbs against Muslims produced a shift in the focus of Western opinion, as the 'question of external intervention in the region revolved less around perceived strategic or economic issues than around humanitarianism' (ibid: 639). The international repercussions of the disintegration, which elicited a variety of external responses to the developing chaos relating to historical affiliations and political interests (ibid: 638–9), failed to play a constructive role in the developments which led to Yugoslavia's break-up (Woodward 1995: 270). Western reponses to the atrocities and massacres which took place in Bosnia were largely humanitarian gestures, as the outside world looked on for three and a half years whilst the genocide continued. Justifications for the non-intervention invariably centred on the tenuous argument that involvement would compromise and threaten the humanitarian activities (Rieff 1995: 15).

The perception that ethnic hatreds could explain the genocide that took place obscured the basis of the Balkan conflict. As Hartmann points out, ethnic differences were exploited by political leaders in order to incite conflict, maintain separations and destroy the transition to political independence (1999: 52). However, the representation of conflict as the resurgence of ancient ethnic hatred was a construction which also suited resistance to intervention by the West, who 'refused to identify the conflict as an international armed aggression and instead characterized it as a civil war' (ibid: 53). Depicting ethnic hatreds as the motivating factor of conflict obscured the 'geopolitical and institutional preconditions of sovereignty: obtaining the strategic and economic assets and borders of a secure future state, destroying those of one's enemies, and building (in the course of war) the armies and foreign alliances of a new defense' which supported war aims (Woodward 1995: 272). Such war aims meant that the ethnic mix of Serbs, Croats and Muslims inside Bosnia became increasingly polarized along with the radicalization of multi-culturalism, brought about by growing instability and fears about war (Glenny 1999: 644).

The Serbian policy of ethnic cleansing sought to expel the Muslim population and by the end of 1992 2 million Bosnians, mostly Muslim, had been forced to flee their homes (Naimark 2001: 160). In order to expand Croatian control, Bosnian Croats sought to expel Muslims and counter Serbian claims for territorial dominance (ibid.). Bosnian aspirations of a unified state were also at odds with the political aims of Croatia and the racist tendencies of Tudjman towards Muslims (Glenny 1999: 645). Croats obstructed aid supplies to Sarajevo as Muslims tried to resist the division of Bosnia along Croatian and Serbian lines (ibid: 646), and efforts to broker a peace plan chaired by Cyrus Vance and David Owen in 1993, which relied on carving Bosnia into three states, were rejected by Bosnian Serbs and ran counter to Muslim demands for a unified state (ibid: 640). The plan widened disagreements between Europe and America, and indicated a dissensus which aided Milosevic's aim of pursuing war in order to fulfil a long-term ambition of creating a 'Greater Serbia' (Maass 1996: 28). Effectively, the international community ignored the complex political questions which underscored conflict, and by so doing failed to transform 'incompatible goals into acceptable compromises and provided security guarantees for individuals and nations instead of for states' (Woodward 1995: 332). In turn, Western attempts to minimize involvement served to help rather than prevent conflict (ibid: 376).

An example of the international community's passivity towards mass slaughter took place in Srebrenica in 1995, where in a designated UN 'safe area' thousands of Muslims were executed and buried in mass graves in what survivors called the 'Marathon of Death' (Rohde 1997). At Srebrenica, Bosnian Serbs 'carried out the most serious genocidal massacre that accompanied the ethnic cleansing of Bosnia and Herzegovina' (Naimark 2001: 165). As the worst war crime in Europe since the Second World War, Srebrenica demonstrated the ultimate failure of Western plans to address the conflict (Honig and Both 1996). The case of Srebrenica provided a clear indication that ethnic cleansing was driven by attempts to gain control of territory as much as it was about trying to eradicate a particular group because of their ethnicity (Naimark 2001: 174), but also overwhemlingly provided irrefutable

evidence of Western indifference. In his account of Bosnia, David Rieff
is clear in his criticism of the West's role:

> Two hundred thousand Bosnian Muslims died, in full view of the
> world's television cameras and more than two million other people
> were forcibly displaced. A state formally recognized by the European
> Community and the United States on April 7, 1992, was allowed to
> be destroyed. While it was being destroyed, United Nations military
> forces and officals looked on, offering 'humanitarian' assistance and
> protesting that there was no will in the international community to
> do anything more.
>
> (1995: 23)

The 'humanitarianization' of the war as Simms describes it, was part of
a broader policy to resist intervention and used in particular by the
British to deflect attention from the 'existence of a major strategic and
political crisis in the middle of Europe', whilst at the same time working
'towards "ameliorating" the consequences of the problem, rather than
addressing the problem itself' (2001: 339). Simms provides a highly critical account of British involvement in the Bosnian conflict, and details
a series of policy approaches devised to defuse pressure for engagement
based on a misappropriation of the reasons for conflict, which served
to promote a view where, 'The risks of action were systematically exaggerated; those of inaction minimized' (ibid: 341). Britain's refusal under
the leadership of John Major to support the Bosnian government, was
a failure to recognize how a foreign policy situation could impact on
domestic opinion, and helped to open splits in the transatlantic relationship, whilst contributing to disorganization and disagreement
within the Nato alliance (ibid: 343). Standing in the way of all international initiatives to help the Bosnian government, British involvement amounted effectively to a stage-management of Yugoslavia's
collapse in an attempt to stay out of the conflict.

Resistance to intervention was also sustained by the mistaken assertion that the war in Bosnia was the resurgence of 'ancient hatreds', and
that Serbian agression was 'driven by irrational blood-lust' (Glenny
1992: 183). However, as Glenny points out, this characterization dis-
guises the territorial ambitions which motivate such aggression and how
important it is that 'In order to comprehend the atrocities, we must
understand the politics and not the other way round' (ibid: 184). Supporting this point, Woodward also highlights how the depiction of

Bosnia was constructed largely through representations of ethnic difference, when 'The problem was not ethnic conflict but the collapse and rejection of an overarching legal authority and of a capacity to tolerate and manage difference. The particular means chosen for accommodating differences in socialist Yugoslavia' she continues, 'had been rejected, and outsiders had helped to disable and diminish the natural constituencies within the country for the values they claimed' (1995: 380). The central reason for war in Bosnia relates to the territorial claims of Serbia and Croatia, both of who were opposed to a unified Bosnia, and it was the betrayal of the Bosnian Muslims by the West which most evidently surfaces in accounts of the war and explanations about the atrocities committed during its course (Vulliamy 1994; Rieff 1995; Neuffer 2001).

By not intervening early enough to stop the genocide, the West allowed Bosnia to be destroyed (Power 2003). However, Western involvement under the auspices of American leadership did occur – instigated by recurring media images of the destruction of Sarajevo and atrocities like the massacre of civilians shopping at Sarajevo's Central Market in February 1994, which triggered a Nato bombing campaign against Bosnian Serbs (Rieff 1995: 217; Glenny 1999: 646, 651) – and a complex series of negotiations which relied on a combination of diplomacy and force produced the Dayton Agreement on 21 November 1995 (Holbrooke 1998; Bildt 1998). The agreement, though the product of a substantive negotiative process, brought an end to fighting, but failed to present an effective resolution of conflict and became problematic as a blueprint for reconciliation (Glenny 1999: 651). This point in the Bosnian conflict, for purposes of this chapter, represents a suitable moment to consider the role of the media in political developments, how it was used for propaganda purposes (particularly by the West), and how it became part of the political policy towards war.

The media and Bosnia

In his account of the Bosnian War, journalist David Rieff hints at the rather contrasting effects which news coverage produced and in so doing invites further consideration of the inconsistent political consequences which reporting came to provide.

First, he asserts that although any possible 'CNN effect' is somewhat exaggerated with regard to news coverage of the conflict (1995: 14), there neverthless existed 'a "CNN effect" in the broad sense that without

CNN, the BBC, and the others showing it all the time, the Bosnian tragedy would have faded from people's minds after the first few months of fighting' (ibid: 216).

Second, Rieff highlights the intention of journalists to incite public pressure because 'The hope of the Western press was that an informed citizenry back home would demand that their governments not allow the Bosnian Muslims to go on being massacred, raped, or forced from their homes' (ibid: 216), before going on to argue that in spite of this intention, 'the sound bites and "visual bites" culled from the fighting bred casuistry and indifference far more regularly than it succeeded in mobilizing people to act or even to be indignant' (ibid.).

Third, Rieff directs us to the power of television news as a political lever by arguing that 'it really was the television cameras and not NATO, let alone the United Nations, that saved Sarajevo after the massacre in the Central Market in early February 1994' (ibid: 217). This massacre had brought to realization, he suggests, the aim of journalists 'to change the sentiments of their readers and viewers about the slaughter' by providing evidence of the Bosnians plight, and demonstrating that 'throughout most of the siege, the reporters and television crews were perhaps the only dependable allies the Bosnians had' (ibid.). Rieff is clear that the moral responsibility of journalists was to 'sympathize with the Bosnian cause, in exactly the way one hopes that if representatives of the foreign press had been stationed in the Warsaw ghetto in 1943, they would have sympathized with the Jews' (ibid: 218).

There are two key points which Rieff raises here which require closer scrunity if we are to more fully comprehend the media's role in Bosnia: (1) how news coverage moved and acted as a form of political pressure; and (2) how journalists came to view the conflict in terms of victims and perpetrators. Rieff's contention that 'to be fair and to be impartial are not the same thing' (ibid: 223), infers a potentially interesting discussion (which I intend to elaborate further in this chapter) about how journalists oriented themselves towards those caught up in the conflict which has been further developed by former BBC reporter Martin Bell, who drew from his experiences of covering Bosnia to make the distinction between what he refers to as 'bystander journalism', and 'journalism of attachment' (Bell 1998). The possibilities of linking news pressures to a clear moral identification by reporters with those who suffer during conflict indicates two interrelated influences which news can have during war, both of which also come strongly into play when considering reflections which debate news coverage of Bosnia. But, before we address the issue of how journalists report conflicts like

Bosnia, it is important to acknowledge some of the key issues about the war which news helped to define and which, for general purposes here, can be categorized as internal and external coverage. To put it another way, we need to have some comprehension of how the media inside Yugoslavia and outside of it, tended to constuct the war and represent its developments.

In her study on how the television news media was used to support nationalist tendencies in Yugoslavia, Basic-Hrvatin identifies three central levels of influence. These influences, which indicate the media's key role in shaping national and public memory, are:

1 television acts to define a specific 'understanding' of nation;
2 its centralized system of information production works to create a 'nationalisation of the public sphere';
3 reports become a factor of conflict because they routinely and systematically create 'the exclusion of the Other' (1996: 64).

In terms of both Serbian and Croation television, Basic-Hrvatin observed how conceptions of nation were drawn from 'a "closed" symbolic way of presentation, comprehensible only to members of the community who share a common national "background knowledge", which relied on expressions of "the canonical nation" (the use of national culture), "the ritual nation" (using a particular style and presentation of politics), and "the popular nation" (created by emphasising the canonical nation as part of popular culture and discourse)' (ibid: 67). The effect of such representations, Basic-Hrvatin notes, is that they induce 'processes of unification and homogenisation of personal memories and collective and national memories' (ibid: 69) and that by isolating images of national mythology and using historical narratives in order to highlight what is threatened (and by association what must be preserved), public memory becomes conditioned to the themes of national memory and alert to the dangers and threats presented by the Other. By emphasizing differences through the presentation of and amplification of national memory, Serb and Croat television effectively not only reinforced the separation of each community, but through exaggerating apparently incompatible concepts of self and nation, stoked fears and anxieties which would ensure conflict.

As Thompson observes, Serbia was more advanced in this process, and focused on the development of a public consensus which would underpin a social preoccupation with 'the national question' (1999: 107). Tight controls over the media and journalists by the Serbian authorities were deemed necessary in order to 'obtain public approval of extreme nationalist policies', and were central for public consent for Serbia's 'extreme nationalist politics' (ibid: 109). In contrast though, Croatia's government was less effective in its attempts to mobilize popular support by trying 'to inspire the people to resist' (ibid: 187). The war expanded hostility to independent media outlets and the government used conflict in order to legitimize its repression of news output which challenged the promotion of state propaganda, disinformation and lies (ibid.). Overall, however, Croatia's efforts to create a unified and clear national consensus were not as successful as Serbia's, whose national interests were promoted more consistently and forcefully through the media.

Thompson makes it clear in his study of the media's role in Bosnia that 'systematic manipulation of the media' was 'instrinsic to the strategies of various leaders', and highlights how the 'most influential media were used to obtain public support or mere tolerance for policies which at best were bound to threaten the peace, security and prosperity of all peoples in the region and at worst were sheerly belligerent' (ibid: 291). The media, he concludes, were essential for cultivating public acceptance of the 'excessive price for the pursuit of nationalist objectives, invariably presented as the defence of national kin and culture', and became 'indispensable in building and maintaining conditions in which war was possible' (ibid: 292). Detailing how the media was used to reinforce nationalist attitudes and therefore intensify the uncertainties which would make war and aggression more likely, Thompson summarizes the process thus: 'The appeal of television seems to draw a good deal upon fear, including the thrill and pang of public fears funnelled ethereally into private homes. Fear engenders hatred and also fosters dependence on authority-figures, the cult of whose personalities is celebrated and policed by the same media which disseminate the fear' (ibid: 297). Paradoxically, though the media may have played a central role in the creation of war, nonetheless its potency was somewhat ignored in the Dayton Peace Agreement of 1995 (Thompson and De Luce 2002) and continues to unsettle efforts to create a sustainable peace (Kurspahic 2003).

In comparison to the certainties of nationalistic coverage which dominated the internal news output of Yugoslvia during this period, Western reporting tended to follow a 'postemotional' course of interpretation. The concept of post-emotionalism is used by Mestrovic to cover 'the confusion, hypocrisies, hysteria, nostalgia, ironies, paradoxes and other emotional excesses that surround Western politics toward the post-communist Balkans' (Mestrovic 1996: 25), and reflects a problem of incoherent and inconsistent policy which was made evident through poor media management strategy by the Western powers (Shaw 1996: 162).

Although American news tended to be generally more sympathetic to intervention than the UK and the EC, it was evident that journalistic calls for involvement were 'appealing to a general sense of the responsibility which went with power rather than a specific sense connected to prior Western actions' (ibid.). The pressure for engagement was also weakened by reports which misrepresented the causes of conflict and those responsible. Sadkovich, for example, in the case of American reporting, observed how 'the coverage itself has often seemed to be misinformed and superficial, when not biased and racist', and continued to 'focus on the sensational rather than the substantive; it has concentrated on personalities rather than issues; and it has tended to recast what is essentially a Balkan affair in terms of American policy or the role of such international organizations as the EC, the UN, and NATO' (1996: 123). Importantly, insists Sadkovich, the American media ignored important distinctions between the parties involved and routinely portrayed the war as resulting from mutually reinforced hatreds, which were driven by clashing nationalistic ambitions and territorial claims. For Sadkovich 'this sort of inaccurate and often apologetic history not only rationalized Serbian actions, it implicated the Croats and Muslims as equally gulity by blaming one group's past actions for the other's current atrocities', and as a result provided analysis which viewed 'the victims as carrying the same bad seed as their torturers' (ibid: 129). Overall, contends Sadkovich, 'the media have displayed a condescending attitude toward the Croats, Slovenes, and Muslims, just as they have dismissed such complex phenomena as neo-nationalism in favour of stereotypical, traditional, and often racist views of the Balkans' (ibid: 133).

Sadkovich seems to be making the point that by misrepresenting and even distorting the reasons for the war in Bosnia, news coverage helped more than hindered the progression of conflict, and argues that 'By focusing on humanitarian aid and peacekeeping forces, the media has given the impression that there is no international security mechanism to deal with the crisis' (ibid: 132). By simplifying the complexities of the conflict (Burns 1996), and concentrating on the theme of ethnic cleansing as an interpretive framework by which to make sense of developments (Banks and Wolfe Murray 1999), reporting routinely played to the preferred responses of Western governments, which were centred on offering humanitarian support rather than intervening militarily.

The media's obsession with ethnic differences confused the demarcations between perpetrators and victims, and in the absence of apparent discernible differences, helped legitimize resistance to intervention. Simplistic 'stereotypes based on the notion of identity, ethnic differentiation, ethnic hatred' did little to help provoke international action which would directly seek to halt the conflict (ibid: 159). Indeed, reports in the United States perpetuated the view that there was no real national interest in the Balkans, and therefore minimal domestic support for involvement which had 'no reasonable chance of sucess' even if it occurred.

The general effect of this emphasis was that 'by recasting the crisis in American terms, commentators and journalists could avoid grappling with complex Balkan politics and Serbian atrocities by arguing that moral outrage was helpless against the stubborn realities of ancient hatreds' (Sadkovich 1996: 133). Such interpretations tended to reflect a rather more widespread selectivity in reporting, which ignored or underplayed occurrences that deviated from preconceived notions of how the Balkans conflict should be represented and understood (Burns 1996: 94). But a propensity to take a homogenized approach to coverage by much of the media, according to Burns, also indicated a 'pack mentality that quite deliberately ignores swathes of evidence which would otherwise balance the picture in a conflict scenario' (ibid: 96). For Burns, 'journalists cannot expect to be received as impartial observers of conflicts' if they form a collective mentality about what they observe, and it is this mentality which he sees as contributing to unbalanced reporting and skewed pressures for political intervention. The danger of such pressure, he continues, is not only that it is unbalanced and not representative of objective reporting, but that it creates a personal responsibility for journalists where 'they may have eventually to account to the peoples about whom they report' (ibid: 98). It is clear that Burns does not think a responsibility for those who are reported on is a particularly good idea and that such a responsibility contradicts the notion of the objective reporter, who should be an observer rather than a protagonist. But, leaving aside the illusory nature of journalistic objectivity, and that the journalist can be a protagonist for non-action just as much as action, Burns surely produces an analysis which is inward looking rather than outward looking and concerned more with preserving the image of the journalist than questioning the consequences of what he or she does. To argue against pressure for intervention when large numbers of people are being murdered, may on the one hand be viewed as an abdication of journalistic responsibility, but it is not an abdication of moral responsibility. It is precisely this problem of distinction which concerned former BBC journalist Martin Bell when he returned home from war in the Balkans.

For Bell, the conventional belief that 'distance and detachment' represent the basic tenets of objective and impartial reporting, has also served to sustain what he calls *bystanders journalism*, which has 'concerned itself more with the circumstances of wars – military formations, tactics, strategies and weapons systems – than with the people who provoke them, the people who fight them and the people who suffer from them' (1998: 15–16). In contrast to this approach, Bell calls for a *journalism of attachment* which 'cares as well as knows; that is aware of its responsibilities; that will not stand neutrally between good and evil, right and wrong, the victim and the oppressor' (ibid: 16). He is, in other words, stressing a need for the closing down of distance between reporter and subject, and a stronger commitment to those who suffer through conflict, rather than arguing for a continutation of dispassionate reporting in such circumstances. Bell refers to examples of media involvement with acts of war which illustrate the protagonist role played by reporters, and also highlights the role which the media can play in peace by citing the presence of news cameras at a prisoner handover in Bosnia, which was requested and used by the parties 'as a means of holding each other to honour agreements already reached' (ibid: 19). Bell is clear that the traditional stance of the bystander journalist breeds indifference to suffering, and that it is this indifference which allows such misery to develop (ibid: 22). Bell's contention that journalism should have a clear moral responsibility towards victims, is distinctly at odds with the conventional image of journalism which prioritises the goals of objectivity, neutrality and impartiality over the misery of others. It is, in other words, an attempt to drag the responsibilities of journalism closer towards those who are the object of its interest and, indeed, unlike the position espoused by Burns, is about holding journalism to account in relation to victims.

The question of moral responsibility towards victims is also raised by Ed Vulliamy, a journalist for British newspaper The *Guardian*, who provided evidence at the War Crimes Tribunal at The Hague about war atrocities. Like Bell, Vulliamy is critical of a journalism which seeks to avoid identification with victims, and is convinced 'that there are moments in history when neutrality is not neutral, but complicit in the crime' (1999: 604). Vulliamy goes on to assert that in the case of Bosnia, 'the neutrality adopted by diplomats and the media is both dangerous and morally reprehensible', and is critical of reporters who abdicated the responsibilty of helping to restore peace and bring those responsible for the genocide to justice. Vulliamy believes that the media's role should be to assist 'the cathartic process' of 'reckoning', which 'means an adjustment of the balance to restore lasting peace' and working to bring about reconciliation. In order to help facilitate this process, Vulliamy argues that 'the press and individual reporters have a duty to abandon their so-called 'neutrality', and 'to reckon with what we witness and urge others to do the same' (ibid: 612). He notes how neutrality towards the genocide in Bosnia became 'nowhere more evident than in the media', and concludes from this 'that after all the huffing and puffing, the spilled blood and broken promises, the graves and families torn asunder, the whimsy and the caprice, the lying and betrayal, the most urgent thing for the West to reckon with is the fact that almost nothing has been learned' (ibid: 620). Vulliamy's desire for a journalism which engages more deliberately and purposefully with the conditions and suffering of victims is clearly an objection to the media's indifference to such victims, and a critique of the concept of neutrality in relation to the circumstances of suffering. It highlights how neutrality can be used to detach journalists from moral responsibility and finds parallels with Bell's analysis, which demonstrates that in the context of the Bosnian genocide, neutrality had political implications which served the interests of those who objected to intervention, rather than those who demanded it.

In response to Bell's argument, Stephen J. Ward tries to disentangle the concept of objectivity from detachment, and advocate a middle way between the two by unconvincingly combining both. Neutrality, he contends, 'demands not the absence of judgement or feeling but the subjection of judgement and feeling to objective, public scrutiny'. Neutrality, he goes on, demands that 'the reporters subject their reports to objective controls, such as the careful presentation of facts, reliable and varied sources, expert opinion, supporting documentation, accurate quotations, and a fair representation of major viewpoints'. And 'a report on any topic is objective if it meets the standards and tests of objectivity to a tolerable degree' (1998: 122). What is needed, according to Ward, is 'both the passion of attachment and the restraint of objectivity to work together to produce solid, yet engaging reporting. Objectivity controls our penchant to speculate and promote. Attachment lifts journalism above a superficial coverage of events that relies on quoting officials and citing obvious facts' (ibid: 123). Ward summarizes his position with the view that 'a narrow standard of objectivity that allows "only facts" in reports is useless for much of journalism. But a journalism of attachment that stresses feelings, value judgements, and interpretations is reckless without objectivity. What is needed is a flexible standard of objectivity that allows us to test both our facts and out interpretations and therefore can be applied to a wide range of stories' (ibid: 124).

Ward's attempt to adopt a centrist position between what appear to be oppositional poles may on the face of it be useful, but raises more questions than it answers and is uncertain, for example, about where one ends and the other begins. The notion that 'flexibility' should occur between objectivity and attachment is not elaborated and so remains ultimately unclear. Ward may have created a theoretical debate about two different journalistic conceptions, but once more there is little room in his argument for applying both conceptualizations in relation to victims. No doubt, there are occasions, as Tumber observes, where a journalism of attachment is faced with the problem of 'how to respond when events force a choice between professional commitment and participatory loyalties' (1997: 7), but this is not a discussion that can be satisfactorily resolved if it remains concerned with conceptualizations of professionalism alone. What Bell and Vulliamy highlight all too well with Bosnia, is the shortcomings of a journalism which is concerned more with its own internal and professional priorities than the victims who suffer in its gaze. Media reports of suffering and political reaction to that suffering in Bosnia combined to present an impression of confusion and indifference, which supported rather than challenged the reluctance to intervene. However, as the conflict continued and threatened to engulf the wider region, it became increasingly difficult to resist intervention, but it would be in Kosovo rather than Bosnia where this action would most take place.

Kosovo and the media

The expansionist policies of the Serbian leadership continued throughout the 1990s and sought to accelerate territorial claims in response to inconsistent articulations of deterrence and containment by the West. Serbian nationalism which concentrated in particular on exaggerating the dangers of Islam, identified Kosovor Albanians as fundamentalist in orientation and as (falsely) planning a 'holy war' against Orthodox Slavs (Malcolm 1998: 351). The Dayton settlement of 1995, may have brought an end to conflict in Bosnia, but did nothing to alleviate the suffering in Kosovo. Indeed, Dayton had served to stengthen Milosevic's hold over Serbia, with Western diplomats thanking him 'for his "peace-making" efforts', and attempts to act 'as a constructive force in the region, whose removal might lead to "instability"' (ibid: 353). The international dissensus about intervention was also taken by the Serb leadership as a clear sign that aggression was unlikely to be halted. Western 'neutrality' (used to help legitimize non-intervention) effectively contributed to a collapse of internal security in Kosovo, and continued to support the 'framework of fragmentation' which had come to symbolize Western involvement (Chandler 2000: 30).

In pursuit of an ethnic cleansing programme, Serbian repression in Kosovo led to the explusion of hundreds of thousands of Kosovar Albanians and a humanitarian catastophe which the West, led by America, dealt with through NATO and 78 days of bombing Serb forces from June 1999 (Naimark 2001: 175). The result of this bombardment was a reversal of ethnic cleansing, where the Serb minority in Kosovo were expelled by returning Albanians. Counter to Milosevic's intentions to cleanse Kosovo of Albanians, his actions had 'ended up condemning the small Serb population of the region to ghettoization and isolation' (ibid.). Though Milosevic had tried to block Kosovo's autonomy and claims for independence some ten years previously (ibid: 176–7), and had stoked tensions between Serbs and Albanians in order to exploit wider tensions in the region which would lead to wars in Slovenia, Croatia and Bosnia (Judah 2000: 59), these actions had gone largely ignored by the West. Indeed, Western inability to comprehend the potential dangers of Kosovo was evident at the Dayton Accords, where Kosovo was seen as an inconvenient complication to the need for a rushed settlement. Dayton therefore offered little in the way of hope to Kosovar Albanians and failed to prevent the disintegation which followed (Naimark 2001: 178). Kosovo was seen within US policy-formulation terms as a problem internal to Serbian affairs, and so tended to elicit indifference in administrative circles (Woodward 1995: 399). The overriding aim of containment by the US failed to halt the fragmentation of Yugoslavia and, indeed, was used by various actors within its borders to help endorse political strategies of resistance and aggression (ibid: 397). Even attempts by Nato to stop the ethnic cleansing by bombardment corresponded with an intensification of expulsions and atrocities by the Serbs, who sought 'to accelerate the Albanians' departure' and gain territorial advantage in advance of further Western intervention (Naimark 2001: 181).

Nato assertions that bombardment was motivated by humanitarian concern was a line reinforced and supported by news outlets like CNN. Routinely, CNN reiterated Nato figures for casualties without critical examination and referred to developments through an 'internalised acceptance of Nato's aims, language, and frames of reference' (Herman and Peterson 2000: 120). The impact of this relationship was coverage which was 'overwhelmingly a version of "press release journalism", based on 'live' news conferences, leaks from government sources, and interviews with US and Nato officials in Washington and Brussels passed along with minimal processing or presentation of relevant context' (ibid: 112–13). Serbian claims were regularly contested through oppositional viewpoints whereas, in contrast, oppositional positions in relation to Nato were lacking. By supporting the Nato agenda and ignoring inconsistencies in the humanitarian argument being forwarded, CNN became instrumental in Nato's promotion and representation of the bombing (ibid: 116).

Even prior to the bombing, Nato's representation of peace talks which took place during February and March 1999 at Rambouillet in France, and which sought to minimize the 'peace process' as an ultimatum for Serbs to accept a Nato military presence in Kosovo, the loss of sovereign rights, or the consequences of military action, was reported supportively by CNN, who portrayed the story as one of Nato justice versus Serbian evil (ibid: 116–17). Here, coverage was seen to have largely ignored the nuances and the implications of the negotiating positions which were conveyed, and provided a platform for Nato, which assisted the case for bombing in the event of Serbian resistance to the conditions set out by Nato in the talks (ibid.). Notably, CNN reporting effectively acted as an extension of Nato propaganda (uncritically reiterating death claims and casualty figures when bombing commenced), and failed to analyse or examine the assertions made both before, during and after the bombing of Serb positions.

Though the British media were seen to adopt a more critical stance in relation to Nato and military intervention (McLaughlin 2002: 122–3), it became evident that there was also a tendency for reporting to become 'part of the moral consensus' that Tony Blair was trying to initiate as part of a broader political project to unite popular sentiment around themes and concerns of moral interest (Hammond 2000: 130). Blair articulated a view of Kosovo based on a model of good versus evil, and attempted to manage a news perception which 'celebrated the bombing as a just war for victims of oppression', whilst 'simplifying and distorting the reality of the conflict' in the process (ibid.). Nevertheless, unlike CNN, the British media also questioned this approach and found themselves being criticized by the government for showing the destructive impact of Nato bombing and that the campaign, as it progressed, was not producing the anticipated outcome (Tait 1999: 41). Government criticisms of the media were founded on accusations about 'too little coverage of evidence of Serb ethnic cleansing and of Nato military successes', along with contentions that reporting had created 'refugee fatigue' and downplayed the suffering of refugees. This perspective, which was stressed by the government in order to try and reinforce the moral credibility of military action, was challenged by sections of the media who continued to report the consequences of the Nato bombing and the plight of refugees against considerable political pressure (ibid.).

But even here, there has been criticism by journalists themselves about the limitations and shortcomings of how news reported Kosovo. Jake Lynch, for example, contends that news coverage 'institutionalised a framework of understanding alien to the principles which kept Yugoslavia if not genuinely at peace, then in some semblance of equilibrium. Gone, in this, is any allowance that violence arises out of keenly felt structural inequities, which must therefore be contained, balanced and ultimately corrected. Instead, there is a model of the conflict as consisting of two parties, one, 'The Serbs,' demonized and requiring punishment; the second a series of other nationalities, straining to express their nationhood and taking turns as the victim' (1999: 51). The effect of this framework, Lynch argues, is that reporting fails 'to connect with any ideas for a diplomatic resolution of the crisis', but becomes intent instead on 'how to "hold the public interest"'. This process of working, Lynch continues, 'enters into a feedback loop, with a measurable impact on subsequent and consequent developments', and routinely categorizes situations 'as a zero-sum game of two parties, one oppressor and one victim' (ibid: 54–5). What Lynch believes needs to be done in order to change this restrictive interpretation is that reporters and editors should 'insist on an equal esteem for suffering, whoever sustains it', and that they should 'seek out peace initiatives, whoever suggests them – severing the umbilical link with official information sources seeking to hold the public interest on their own terms'. If adopted, 'these would be elements of a form of news which would model the conflict as a complex interlocking pattern of fears and resentments, and make it seem to make sense to pursue complex interlocking solutions which do not require a clear winner and a clear loser' (ibid: 55).

Conclusion

Although the cases of Bosnia and Kosovo indicate attempts by some journalists to incite political intervention in order to halt genocide and ethnic cleansing, the general emphasis of reporting was towards a sensationalization of the fighting, which served to reinforce the irrationality of conflict and so underscore the hesitancy of the West, who worked to resist being drawn into action. Significantly, much reporting ignored the historical and political factors which had motivated the conflict, and so could draw no intelligible conclusions about how the war could be stopped. The uncertainties and fears which had been elicited by the collapse of Yugoslavia were largely ignored, as reporting adopted a series of contradictory narratives dependent on changing distance and proximity in relation to war and performing to 'the journalist's role as advocator or as documentarist' (Preston 1996: 113). For some journalists, the ethos of objectivity and neutrality which is used as a measure of journalistic competence and professionalism was also responsible for blurring differences between victims and perpetrators, and it was this blurring which helped legitimize Western hesitancy whilst helping to prolong conflict.

What journalists such as Bell and Vulliamy highlight in their assessment of how the media covered Bosnia is the illusion of neutrality in connection to mass human suffering, and how by not trying to pressure governments to act, journalists are complicit in that suffering. Neutrality therefore has no useful meaning here since to try to create or not create debates about intervention are equally political acts. Although there exist important questions about the morality of journalism and misinformed notions of sentimentalism in relation to suffering (Boltanski 1999; Tester 1997), one should not allow such questions to obscure the point that – by constructing and representing that suffering – journalists become protagonists in how it is perceived and acted upon (doing nothing may also be seen as taking action). Although the media in Yugoslavia (and particularly the Serbian media) were essential for raising nationalist sentiment and in the process, (and, as Ignatieff reminds us about nationalism, key for the denial 'that multiple belonging is possible' (1999: 46)), the international media tended to concern itself with the responses of the West and interpret the war through the policy initiatives of the US, EU, UN and Nato, all of which contributed to contentions about the developing humanitarian catastrophe. As argued, presentation of the war in Bosnia as a humanitarian disaster was used by the West, and especially the UK, to avoid intervention and a commitment to stop the genocide.

The war in Kosovo, which 'occupied such a central place in the Serbian imagination' and 'remained the heartland of Serbian national life', even though Serbs had become a minority group (ibid: 42), became the symbol of Serbian struggle and crystallized the mythology of ancient conflicts were Serbs had fought and lost against Turks. Kosovan moves towards independence reignited fears and anxieties, which Milosevic used in order to 'tap into deep reservoirs of Serb self-pity', and manipulated to promote 'the nationalist dream of reuniting Serbs within one state' (ibid: 42–3). Military bombardment of Serbian positions in Kosovo under the auspices of Nato command produced a largely uncritical response by much of the international media, with networks like CNN tending to reiterate Nato claims of success and accepting official interpretations of action. Although a broader critical stance could be witnessed in British media coverage, it was nevertheless also the case that much reporting complemented Tony Blair's goal of shaping a moral consensus which was based on notions of an 'ethical foreign policy'. Both inaction towards Bosnia and action taken in Kosovo was driven by the West rather than the media. There is no doubt that pressures were made apparent by reporting, and images of suffering caused difficulties for Western governments trying to avoid engagement in the Balkans. However, even here, as the conflict in Bosnia indicates, political attempts to interpret the genocide as a humanitarian issue were part of a resistance strategy designed to avert any military commitment, which the media did little to challenge. Overall, the media provided minimal analysis of the background to conflict, just as it overwhelmingly failed to examine views and perspectives about peace and the de-escalation of war. Nato action in Kosovo was part of a containment policy by the West to halt the refugee crisis, created by the many Albanians who were ethnically cleansed by Serb forces and who threatened to create a humanitarian disaster which could further destabilize the region and augment war.

7
The Middle East

Oslo, secrecy and publicity

The Oslo peace process which sought to address the conflict between Palestinians and Israelis and which came to symbolize the possibilities for peace when Rabin and Arafat shook hands on the White House lawn in September 1993, having committed to the Declaration of Principles, provides an interesting case study by which to think about the media's relationship with peace. Importantly, the Oslo process sought to develop a substantive negotiations dynamic between Israeli and Palestinian delegates in order to bring the conflict to an end. As Corbin points out, this was no small task since the participants were dealing with:

> nearly fifty years of bloodshed and retribution since the founding of Israel, and before that many decades of strife between between Jew and Arab in the region. There had been four wars and countless skirmishes, laced with sustained campaigns of terror that had indelibly marked the psyche of both peoples. The history of Israel and the Palestinian diaspora since 1948 is dominated by a roll-call of tragedy, the stuff of headlines and shocking television broadcasts.
>
> (1994: 14)

Corbin outlines the Palestinian uprising (*Intifada*) against Israeli occupation of the West Bank and Gaza and describes a cycle of violence where 'Palestinians killed Jewish settlers and soldiers and each other, and the Israeli army killed and imprisoned youths and children in the war of stones' (ibid: 15). It is the presentation of such images, she continues, which 'would-be peacemakers had for years fought unsuccessfully to erase from the collective memory of Israelis and Palestinians' (ibid.) and

105

it was these kind of images which the participants carried with them to the peace talks with Norwegian mediators. The main purpose of the 'Oslo Channel', as it became known, was to provide a context in which confidence and trust could develop which would then subsequently feed into more public negotiations carried out with Washington. The Oslo process was designed to 'suggest some solutions that could be implemented through the public channel' (ibid: 40) and was therefore central to the transition from secret contacts to public life. It also relied on maintaining confidentiality in order for this process to take shape.

Significantly, negotiations between Israeli and Palestinian delegations were conducted largely in confidence and it was this secrecy which the negotiators deemed essential if talks were to have any chance of success. Indeed, although secrecy about negotiations was maintained for eight months, the aim had been to reveal the talks 'to the world only with the opening of the archives, long after peace had become a fact' (Beilin 1999: 134), so sensitive had been the contacts. The problem of public knowledge about the secret talks which took place through *back channels* and which were conducted ostensibly through Norwegian intermediaries, was inextricably linked to the media, its potential to interpret events negatively and 'limit the autonomy and flexibility of negotiators' in the process (Aggestam 1996: 5). A further difficulty caused by the media revealing the contacts arises when one considers that 'the news media works to expose and scrutinize activities of diplomats and politicians, thereby strengthening the public consciousness that secrecy runs counter to democratic diplomacy' (ibid: 6). There is an evident disparity between secrecy and the public's right to know which the media stands between. For those involved in the contacts, there was an obvious realization that the media would make the talks public at some point, but in order to try and bind some element of trust between the negotiators, it was seen as crucial that the media should know nothing and that attempts to gain public support would come later. It was a commitment to secrecy which made the negotiators keep moving to different locations so media attention could be avoided (ibid.). Indeed, a fear of leaks, which was shared by all those involved in the contacts, was viewed as one of the main obstructions to progress and the development of trust (Abbas 1995: 107).

The issue of secrecy is a significant feature of sensitive political negotiations for two key reasons. As Bok describes it:

1 those who participate may desire confidentiality about their tentative positions, their drafts and explorations with others. Their claim

to confidentiality draws on the individual's need for leeway in unfinished projects and for freedom from uninterrupted surveillance.

2 a group is less likely to reach a coherent internal position unless it has a chance to explore tentative, even unlikely alternatives; it cannot easily maintain a united position in delicate matters without pressure from special-interest groups and sabotage from opponents unless it has such a chance; and . . . it cannot easily negotiate with other groups without a process of trial and error, of proposal and counterproposal, of persuasion and bargaining and sometimes threat.

In contrast to confidentiality, Bok observes how publicity 'tempts participants to rigidity and to posturing, increasing the chances of either a stalemate in which no compromise is possible, or alternatively, of a short-circuited and hasty agreement' (1982: 183–4). But the reality of the negotiations process is that at some stage both confidentiality and publicity are used for exerting influence on negotiations. The disadvantages of relying on one instead of both are nicely summarized by Bok who contends that although 'true, full openness would doom many fragile talks', negotiators must recognize that 'without accountability and public control, secret negotiations like all practices of secrecy in government go against democratic principles' (ibid: 187) and it is these two situations which need to be reconciled if negotiations are to succeed. Successful negotiations therefore depend upon both working with and within private and public worlds, and using each as part of the negotiative process. But of the two, it is publicity which poses the greater problem for negotiators. As Bok explains: 'negotiators have more to gain from being approved by their own sides than by making a reasoned agreement with competitors or adversaries . . . with the result that short-circuiting or stalemate is more likely' (ibid: 184). In relation: 'if the public exposure is selectively magnified by the media, all the difficulties multiply. Often the media, and especially television, will select a brief, a dramatic moment from the debates, which can skew the public's understanding of the ongoing negotiations. The chances of biased public responses are thereby increased, and this in turn can damage the negotiations, most of all in intense and highly publicized debates' (ibid.).

Reporting negotiations

When made public, a negotiating process operates on two levels. First, through direct negotiation with international actors, and second, indirectly 'with domestic interest groups and public opinion' (Aggestam

1996: 7). Once diplomacy is working at both these levels so 'political leaders conduct two dialogues simultaneously – influencing, as they negotiate, both domestic opinion and their interlocutors' – and this interaction then 'determines the opportunties, constraints, and autonomy of the negotiators' (ibid.). However, provided there is some serious political commitment to negotiate, it is media attention which tends to provide the greater limiting influence on progress. This influence can create two potential consequences where, on the one hand, over-exposure by the media can 'lead to a freeze in the parties' positions and reduce their flexibility', whilst on the other, 'the parties exhibit polarized positions and a low political willingness to negotiate' (ibid.). The news media, to put it another way, can both create pressure on the negotiators and be used by negotiators to create pressure. And, as Aggestam reminds us, the relationship between publicity and secrecy is a relationship of 'two opposing principles that originate from two completely different frames of reference involving the nature of information and who possesses it' (ibid: 8).

The intricacies, complications and contestations within the Middle East negotiations process, which is discussed systematically and critically elsewhere (Ashrawi 1999; Beilin 1999; Said 2000; Rabinovich 2004), indicate a range of unclear political objectives and strategies which contributed to the collapse of the peace process. Even the main broker of the peace deal, America, was constructing policies and initiatives which complemented US foreign policy goals rather than engaging with the immediate needs of the protagonists, concentating 'more on procedures and formalities than on substance' (Aggestam 1996: 17). These discrepancies, which reinforced rather than addressed uncertainties, were, of course, crucial factors in the demise of the accords, but media coverage of the negotiations did not help either. Negotiators from both Israeli and Palestinian delegations 'often attributed the failure of the negotiations in Washington to the high degree of publicity and the complete lack of confidentiality between the opposing parties' (ibid: 18). Although this attribution of blame might be seen as an attempt to divert responsibility for failure of the talks from politicians to the media, there nevertheless exists some agreement amongst the participants that 'publicity prevented flexibility', and 'negotiating positions became rigid so that concessions were impossible'. Furthermore, 'each delegation sought to signal through the media to its domestic constituency that its official negotiating position had not changed and no concessions had been made' (ibid.). This signalling was not only confined to domestic audiences, but was directed towards both delegations themselves, as well as Washington and the wider international community (ibid: 19).

Contacts and talks which took place through the *back channel* with Norwegians in advance of formal negotiations concluded in Washington, established secrecy as a prerequisite for possible progress. Only if secrecy was adhered to would the participants be able 'to elaborate new ideas and make tentative concessions' (ibid: 26). During the early and fragile stages of contacts the media was seen in negative and obstructive terms, and only when the talks had reached a point when the negotiations could stand the pressure of media scrunity would reporters be made aware of negotiations, before then becoming part of the wider struggle for diplomatic advantage in the negotiations themselves. Once secret contacts had developed enough to hold the parties in negotiations, so the media could be used to open the negotiations to a wider level of influence and become central to the internal contestations of the talks process. However, some appreciation for secrecy must be maintained if the talks need to recommence away from the media spotlight because public opposition has increased and in the process made negotiating positions too rigid for progress (ibid: 30).

News and peace: a problematic relationship

Wolfsfeld's work on the media's role within the Middle East peace process provides an important analysis of the complex and changing role of news during the transition from conflict to peace. When a peace process moves from secrecy to publicity, so the media produces a range of influences which are subject to, and shaped by, shifting moments and circumstances within the political field. In relation to the initial phases of Oslo, Wolfsfeld notes how the media created problems by ignoring the more positive aspects of negotiations in favour of emphasizing negative aspects (Wolfsfeld 2004: 75). Significantly, the media tended to view problems in the talks as emanating from the Palestinians and became 'primary agents in spreading fear and panic among the public and in focusing the blame on the Palestinian leadership' (ibid.). But this tendency for the media to act negatively in connection to the negotiations cannot, Wolfsfeld suggests, be entirely attributed to the media. It is also a matter of political incompetence and disorganization when dealing with the amplifying impact of news coverage. As Wolfsfeld points out, 'the political environment was characterized by a lack of elite consensus in support of the process and a large number of serious and violent crises. The ongoing controversy provided journalists with two competing frames about Oslo, while the large number of crises provided important opportunities for the opposition to promote its anti-Oslo frames' (ibid.). However, Wolfsfeld also rightly identifies how the media 'are a poor forum for public discourse' because of a preoccupation with violence and 'a professional interest in bringing it out' (ibid: 102). By reducing complex dialogue to a series of simplistic soundbites, the media act to narrow debate and inflate the more sensationalist aspects of communications. Those dramatic aspects are invariably presented as threats, which are emphasized as more newsworthy than messages of reconcilation and peace because, as Wolfsfeld observes: 'Threats are concrete, specific, and immediate while the benefits of peace tend to be abstract, general, and distant' (ibid: 103).

What Wolfsfeld brings to light in his analysis of the media and peace in the Middle East is how news frames of protagonists shifted and developed in concert with changing political circumstances. When the media became engaged with the Madrid talks which took place in 1992 (the Madrid talks produced exploratory dialogue between Israelis and Palestinians, with a Jordanian contingent working alongside the Palestinians, and took place under the observation of an international panel. The talks ended in stalemate and what Corbin called 'a meaningless war of words' (1994: 16)) – they encountered a new articulate face of Palestinian representation which challenged the stereotypical 'threatening image' and what Wolfsfeld calls the 'Security First frame' (2004: 135). Palestinian delegates at the talks were presented, contends Wolfsfeld, within a 'Peace frame' and so became perceived as integral to any potential shift in the political environment, where the possibilities of peace were now being considered alongside the possibilities of conflict. Though the media would be quick to discredit the peace frame if violence intensified (thereby undermining the credibility and viability of peace), there nevertheless existed a momentum to such developments which the media became participants in. The context of a 'peace process' Wolfsfeld notes, 'introduced an alternative template for covering Palestinians', which also corresponded with 'an increasing willingness to treat Palestinians as independent actors' (ibid: 136). This shift clearly suggested a perception of Palestinians which differed from the security-threat image that dominated coverage. By articulating intentions and goals through the arena of peace talks, the Palestinian representatives offered an alternative image of Palestinian politics which would function as a pressure on Israelis and become part of the discourse about possible peace.

In his conclusion to the role played by news in relation to peace Wolfsfeld writes:

> All other things being equal, the news media generally play a negative role in attempts to bring peace. At the same time, the exact part the press will take in a given peace process varies in conjunction with the political and media environments in which journalists operate. The news media are most likely to play a constructive role when there is a high level of support in favor of a peace process, when the number and intensity of crises are low, when there is a relatively high level of shared news organs and when journalists feel less need or desire to construct sensationalist news stories.

Furthermore, 'Any changes in the political environment lead to changes in media performance that can lead to further changes in the political environment' (ibid: 220). What is evident from this summary is that media influence is shaped ostensibly by what is going on in the political environment at any moment in time, the kind of antagonists involved and the media climate itself (Wolfsfeld 2003: 140). Moreover, the impact of media coverage is more dependent on the political environment than the environment is on media coverage. Within the political environment, the media is concerned primarily with the stronger players and it is the more powerful parties which dominate stories and control the agenda. In turn, 'the weaker the antagonists, the more likely the news media will have an influence on their behaviour and their chances of political success' (ibid: 142). But when coverage starts to become receptive to weaker participants and provides a platform for alternative ways of dealing with conflict which differ from those of the stronger antagonists, then so the media starts to have a greater impact on how conflict and peace might be played out (ibid: 143).

A further obstacle to political control over coverage is a lack of consensus in parties over how to proceed, where the media magnify differences and ruptures, so creating difficulties for promotion of a coherent and consistent approach (ibid: 146). The news media's search for a sensationalist and dramatic interpretation of developments and events does not sit easily with peace politics either, since in the search for peace, messages which inflame reaction and incite dramatic responses tend to obstruct the rather complex and laborious deliberations of the peace-making process. Highlighting the problem of the media's interest in sensationalism, Wolfsfeld continues:

Negotiations about peace are usually difficult and there are always setbacks along the way. When these setbacks occur, leaders will often turn to the press in order to attribute blame. The more heated the media environment the more likely the press is to turn each setback into a major crisis. Journalists will intentionally search for extreme statements from all sides and this will provide the basis for large glaring headlines. The conflict between the two sides will escalate and negotiators will find themselves spending valuable time attempting to defuse the situation.

(ibid: 151)

This propensity to impact on political interaction and influence the atmosphere within which talks take place, indicates the media's involvement as a third party. Operating to exaggerate the drama and entertainment of political interaction by concentrating on conflict, the media are no longer incidental to that conflict, but part of the 'social drama' which takes precedent over political strategy (Arno 1984: 231). As a third party, the media function in conflict 'by participating in discussions between the parties, summarizing arguments, making suggestions, and asking questions' (ibid: 232). Furthermore, the media operate as a third party because they benefit from the conflicts which exist between parties and so depend on conflict to survive (ibid: 234). The political power of the media as a third party exists therefore, not in a conventional political party sense which works to a specific party political agenda, but because of its role as a carrier of conflict between parties. The value of media power for political parties lies in this independence, which enables third-party participation and the development of argument to help legitimize policies and agendas. As Arno points out: 'The value of media support, however, would evaporate if one party were to gain actual control of it. The third-party position would be gone, and with it its power' (ibid: 235).

Clearly, the power of media influence relates to its audience reach and its ability to broaden the field of conflict by inciting other players outside of the immediate geopolitical space within which conflict occurs. Modern technologies demonstrate that as 'the means of communication across national boundaries improve, the opportunities for the development of cross-cutting interest groups and dispersed communities linked by agreement or contention over special symbolic issues increase, and nation-states cease to be the only players' (ibid: 231). It is this third-party role, its potential to complicate conflicts by drawing more participants into disputes and the tendency to read developments through a conflict perspective, which makes the media's influence especially problematic with regard to peace. Secret contacts to initiate peace dialogue do not face the complications and hazards posed by media exposure when dialogue becomes subject to a range of variable and potentially destabilizing effects. The pressures which reporting create do, of course, become absorbed into negotiating processes and are used by the parties to advance/obstruct momentum or stake out potential for progress, but a key problem for negotiators involved in peace talks is weighing the value of confidentiality against the publicity which is inevitably needed to gain support (an evident and recurring headache for those engaged with the Oslo talks) (Abbas 1995: 185).

However, the role of the media as a third party does not mean that it performs mediation in a conventional sense, since the concept of mediation in conflict is built upon the purpose of 'contributing to its abatement or resolution through negotiation' (Zartmen and Touval 1985: 31). As the media has no aspiration to constructively bring conflict to an end (indeed, it seeks to exaggerate and amplify conflict) and becomes part of the dynamic where one party seeks to win over another (unlike mediation which strives for conciliation), so its propensity to act as a mediator is disputable. But even here, within traditional definitions of mediation there is still scope to consider whether the media does actually possess limited mediation possibilities. For example, mediation 'emphasizes changing the parties' images of and attitudes toward one another' (ibid: 32) which the media can also do. Furthermore, although, unlike mediation, the media does not 'negotiate and bargain directly with adversaries' (ibid.) it can and does create the context in which mediation can take place. And like those who perform mediation, the media has to display an independence from the parties in conflict. It is obvious enough that if the media did not have this independence and it was affiliated to a specfic party's interests, then there would be no real point in anatagonists trying to use it to influence positions.

The role of conflict in news is an involvement which is needed by political parties as much as by newsmakers, however. Conflict allows parties to position themselves in antagonistic terms to their opponents and therefore allows for the expression of difference which is necessary to present a party as distinct and seperate from others. Although it is difficult to see how media images of conflict and antagonism encourage audiences to appreciate and consider the possibilities of peace, it is also evident that the conflictive relations between parties is also able to create a dialectical exchange out of which peaceful conditions may develop, even if there is also a tendency within news to miss the substance of conflict by concentrating on the visual drama of conflict itself. Conflict over political issues at least reveals a similiar recognition and commitment to those issues and it is the commonality of conflict which demonstrates a mutual respect for the significance of what conflict might produce. Conflict, then, is about keeping people together as well as keeping people apart and perhaps it is here, even in the highly sensitive and contested nature of peace talks, where news becomes especially important. Even if news tends to overlook how the relationship between commonality and difference works as part of a broader communications dynamic (because of a fixation with the immediate and short-term impact of developments), it is also clear that by providing the space where contestations take place it becomes the environment which shapes the design and flow of communications themselves.

What remains important to consider, given this influence, is whether news might play a more constructive and puposeful role towards generating peace by moving towards an *integrative* emphasis, which can be achieved if intepretations are shifted beyond the limitations of party political discourse to include actors and commentators working outside of those limitations. A more integrative role for news with regard to peace therefore depends upon the expansion of verbal conflict and contestation to allow for a broader range of discourses about peace to emerge (something considered in more detail in Chapter 10). What this suggests is that it is not conflict itself in news which is the problem here, but rather a lack of conflict. By limiting conflicts to a zero-sum game of competition between dominant parties, news fails to allow space for alternative discourses to emerge which could further contest and open up issues and positions in relation to peace communications. Such alternatives would not be in agreement, indeed, they would increase the potential for disagreement, but that is not the point. By opening up the field of contestation, the news media could help shift public and political consciousness towards respecting diversity and difference, which become the basis for rethinking how practical moves towards peace and tolerance might take place. Ironically, it is the restriction of conflict in news which hinders this possibility.

To indicate how such an emphasis might take shape with regards to the Middle East, one needs to look away from the contested nature of politics to the more reflective analyses of writers and peace activists such as Amos Oz (2004) and David Grossman (2003). A challenge to the predictable conflicts which are recycled with unending regularity through news reports can be found in Oz's proposition that instead of relying on the 'right versus wrong' scenario which news perpetuates, another

interpretive framework should come into play which is based on a
'between right and right' model of analysis (2004). Such a framework
seeks to go beyond a simplistic representation of good against bad, or
perpetrators against victims, by arguing that both Israelis and
Palestinians are right in their respective claims for a disputed home-
land. As Oz points out: 'Palestinians want the land they call Palestine.
They have very strong reasons to want it. The Israeli Jews want exactly
the same land for exactly the same reasons, which provides for a perfect
understanding between the parties and for a terrible tragedy' (ibid: 8).
What is required to deal with this dilemma, Oz contends, is 'compromise, not capitulation' (ibid: 9) which derives from both sides' inextri-
cable linkage to the same conflict and a mutual recognition that both
want the same outcome. In that respect there is a common sense of
value here, but what is lacking is a common imagination, and 'a deep
ability to imagine the other' (ibid: 16). The Israel–Palestine conflict, Oz
notes, 'is essentially a conflict between two victims', where each 'sees
in the other the image of their past oppressors' (ibid: 18), which differs
from news representations that oscillate in terms of good and bad,
victim and perpetrator. The territorial claims of Israelis and Palestinians
both have validity and are mutually reinforcing in terms of locking both
sides into conflict. But a key factor which sustains such conflict is the
absence of dialogue and impressions of the 'Other' that strengthen differences rather than indicate similiarities. To achieve a peaceful environment in which constructive exchanges can take place, it seems
logical and vital, as Grossman notes, that both sides will not only 'have
to give up concrete and important assets', but that each 'will also have
to give up the delusions and illusions that have accounted for their
strength and hope and national consciousness' (2003: 97). Issues which
have contributed to separation and prevented engagement with questions of common interest and concern must therefore, Grossman suggests, be reinterpreted in the light of moves which facilitate the opposite
and challenging representations which feed into extremist attitudes and
the polarization of thought.

What this calls for, of course, is the need to further critically engage
with information outlets which concentrate on dominant and predictable divisions, and which appear to legitimize the psychology of sep-
aratism that supports violence. To confront this problem it is important
for news to move away from an obsession with simplistic approaches
to situations and to consider a more complex range of reasons and
explanations for conflict. Instead of viewing events from a simplistic
and dualistic black and white perspective, news needs to become more

receptive both to 'grey' perspectives and to the conflict of dialogue more than the conflict of violence. This means unlocking historical and other contextual influences in order to view the basis of problems and correspondingly, the basis of solutions. Recent analysis carried out by Glasgow University Media Group has identified the omission of contextual perspectives as a key reason for audience (mis)understanding of the Israel–Palestinian conflict, and the authors conclude that 'Television news has largely denied its audiences an account of these relationships and their origins, and in doing so has both confused viewers and reduced understanding of the actions of those involved' (Philo and Berry 2004: 258). Importantly, the GUMG also observe that 'the attitudes of those in our audience groups could change sharply when they did learn more about the origins of the conflict' (ibid.). Although the authors use audiences which are not from the region of conflict and so their responses are not shaped by the historical, social, economic and political conditions which determine reactions and responses to the ongoing war, the research at least raises the point that perspectives can move in the light of different explanatory frameworks and, indeed, point us towards the realization that a shift in contextual information and communications can impact significantly on audience interpretations. The parties engaged in the Israeli–Palestinian conflict have surely drawn from and reacted to the news representations of terrorism and victimhood which news has consistently perpetuated and used to both legitimate response and counter-response against opponents.

In a sense, what I am proposing here is that the news media play a more integral role in peace by providing space for the weaker opponents to articulate ideas and proposals which emerge as part of a peace process (an influence identified by Wolfsfeld earlier). Central questions about territorial claims and security measures, as well as the political issues which sustain division with regard to Israel and Palestine (and thus which must be addressed if division is to be managed rather than used to sustain war) have been, and are being addressed effectively by those outside of the political domain (Lerner 2003; Carey and Shainin 2004), but such 'grey' discourses are ignored by the news media who prefer to reiterate simplistic oppositions in order to infer that conflict and its potential solution is the responsibility of two sides. The news media's preference for the controversial, created problems for the Israeli government in its efforts to gain widespread public support for Oslo and undermined the legitimacy of the accords in the process (Naveh 2001). Moreover, the contentious nature of the Oslo peace process was amplified by the media as voices of dissent were given access to discuss Israeli policy and broad coverage was given to an 'anti-Oslo attitude' (ibid: 221).

Attempting to embrace the conflictive aspects of reaction, the Israeli media concentrated on 'mood-setting', which was 'oriented much more to the public than to the government, and it was very difficult for the Rabin government to transmit opposing messages in these situations' (ibid.). But, even here we should recognize that problems for the Rabin government were made easier by the government's failure to build on majority support for Oslo and a tendency to accede to the more hostile elements of the media. An inability to counter critical coverage by the Israeli government effectively contributed to the demise of policy after Oslo and in the process further obstructed the search for peace (ibid.). Ironically, the media's role in presenting oppositional views with regard to peace is not met with a corresponding discourse which is oppositional to conflict, however. Voices which seek to articulate the case for a de-escalation of conflict (unless promoted intensively by governments) receive negligible publicity in comparison to voices which seek to magnify or exaggerate the difficulties. It is this preoccupation with 'conflicts about conflict' rather than 'conflicts about peace' which perhaps most apparently demonstrates the media's lack of reception and engagement to articulations which seek to develop conflict transformation or conflict resolution discourse.

The influence of the political process on news coverage is greater than any influence which news coverage might bring to bear on the political process and it is for this reason that in general, 'the news media are much more likely to react to political events than to initiate them' (Wolfsfeld 1997: 46). However, it is also apparent that if the news media take a more independent position in relation to dominant political parties, they start to 'play a significant role in defining the political environment' (ibid.). Because of this potential change, it becomes apparent that the interdependence of the media and politics might be better thought of as 'a cycle of influence' (ibid.). Wolfsfeld refers to problems that the Israeli government had in legitimizing the Oslo negotiations, along with a lack of political consensus, media receptiveness to opposition to the negotiations process, and ongoing terrorist attacks as an example of political forces which augmented pressures and difficulties for the government and shifted the cycle of influence away from government to the media (2003: 93). By capitalizing on the problems which the government was experiencing at this time, the news media magnified the issues and concerns which were contributing to such problems and by so doing helped to destabilize political peace objectives.

The substance of negotiations and the nuances of peace dialogue are developments which the news media remain generally unreceptive towards and a collapse in trust after Oslo can be traced to the negative role which the Israeli and Palestinian media played after the accords became public (Wolfsfeld 2001: 116). Highlighting how the media helped to contibute to undermine efforts to facilitate peace, Wolfsfeld identifies news values as a central factor which hinder the possibilties of public tolerance and wider debate:

> It is ironic that most news about a peace process focuses on the ongoing conflict between the two sides. One of the most important reasons for this has to do with the media's unvarying need for drama. A peace process is, for the most part a boring affair. Ongoing negotiations rarely make for riveting news stories. When progress is being made, both sides have an interest in keeping such details secret. When talks break down, on the other hand, antagonists are all too eager to turn to the news media to blame the other side. This is just one of the many media routines that ensure that the public is almost always more likely to hear bad news about a peace process
>
> (ibid: 116–17)

Acknowledging that the news media in providing widespread coverage of signing ceremonies signified the possibility that violence may be ending, Wolfsfeld nevertheless presents a depressing picture of the news and reports about peace, with stories tending to intensify conflict and ignoring efforts to reduce that conflict (ibid: 117). The media's overwhelming concern with those opposed to the Oslo accords far outweighed coverage that sought to examine and broaden perceptions of common interest and demonstrated how reports about resistance to peace took precedence over reports about resistance to conflict. Unsurprisingly, those who need to access the media most if peace dialogue is to be facilitated and more constructively contested seem unable to gain that access (Avraham, Wolfsfeld and Aburaiya 2000). What is also clear is that if media representations of peace are to play a purposeful role in a peace process, then, as Shinar notes, there needs to be a considerable 'updating of media norms and strategies' which move away from conventions of 'trivialization and ritualization' that 'serve to compensate for the absence of a media peace discourse', and moves made towards articulating and 'increasing the news value of peace coverage rather than conducting moralistic attempts to change war-oriented media structures and professional codes' (2000: 94–5).

One further problem with news coverage in the Middle East (and, indeed, the media's relationship with peace politics generally) is that simplistic and sensationalized representations of conflict also serve to intensify and help exaggerate the 'emotional stakes of public discourse', thereby making it more difficult to discuss and reason the shape of peace and the concessions needed to bring conflict to an end (Amin 2004: 9). The media's tendency to exacerbate 'information warfare' means that media dialogue is competitive and functions to hinder much needed trust, as efforts to gain definitional advantage over issues take priority over discussing points of common interest. On the other hand, argues Amin, transnational broadcasting offers the possibility of a more constructive role in Middle East conflict by acting as 'a social engineer' and providing a series of influences:

> including facilitating domestic understanding of regional conflict; providing new neutral perspectives to the general and target audiences; linking the region together and also with the rest of the world; increasing government awareness of other governments' performance in the region and shaping government effectiveness; promoting human rights; advancing formal and informal education; broadcasting news and information about the region and the people and finally familiarizing the region with other cultures, values, traditions and religions, all aspects that work to enhance the culture for peace.
>
> (ibid: 11)

For Amin, the influence of transnational rather than indigenous broadcasting has helped to check Israeli dominance of the 'media war' (ibid: 4), and contributed to 'the creation of a strong pan-Arab public opinion' (ibid: 5) which, by helping to develop a collective consciousness, also assisted the political organization of Arabs and worked to level the discursive field of media communications.

But perhaps here Amin tends to overplay the positive influence of broadcasting and in the process overstates the possibilities for media diplomacy. It is unlikely that transnational media will be seen by indigenous audiences as offering a clearer or more compelling picture of internal affairs than domestic media, or indeed that a greater homogenization of Arabs through coverage would translate into support for peace any more than it would support moves which resisted peace. Indeed, one might argue that for many, fixed and more traditional images and representations of separation are believed more than images which signify change, since such images challenge what is traditionally known. It may well be that transnational broadcasting is a significant factor in representations of the Middle East which feed into public awareness of political conditions, but we should also remember that transnational broadcasting also has its own representational restrictions which undermine public understanding and effect the potential for how audiences engage with conflict (Philo and Berry 2004). The concern of transnational broadcasting with transnational audiences rather than any one national audience may free it, to some extent, from the cultural and political preferences of that national audience, but we should not think that this global reach also frees it from simplification. Indeed, one might argue that in trying to make sense to transnational audiences, broadcasting must simplify even further in order to stimulate the universal desires, emotions and concerns of global audiences. One can see that transnational broadcasting (and I am thinking primarily of CNN and BBC) also relies on the 'emotion of opposites' and the 'discourse of extremes' to tell stories and that the world is constructed to a large extent in black and white terms because of this tendency.

Nor should we confuse the development of collective consciousness, which Amin mentions, with a greater role for the public sphere in political life. This consciousness is ultimately a consciousness of difference and a limitation for recognizing the position of the Other. As such, the construction of collective identity reinforces a barrier to tolerance and accommodation with the Other, and tends to be acknowledged by news as interesting because of its potential to translate into an opposing force within the zero-sum game of media politics. We should not assume, then, that transnational broadcasting (given news values and the imperative of conflict) is any more likely to shift national audiences away from the competitive nature of dominant politics and the dominant political figures which represent those parties than national broadcasting. The overriding concern with the power of politics rather than the power of political ideas is endemic to news and a central reason why it fails to move away from the black and white images of power and control.

This propensity to construct politics in such antagonistic terms has negative repercussions for the development of peace, which can only be transformed if news becomes receptive to the greyness of discourse (discourses which have a tangible and positive role to play in relation to public debates about peace beyond the confines of mainstream party politics) and ideas which lay in between the extremes. By allowing grey discourses to emerge and gain public attention, awareness becomes more attuned to possible ways of dealing with political problems which do not feature in the articulations of dominant parties who have party interests to protect. Moreover, it is the grey discourses which allow the black and white discourses to be bridged and which bring the possibilities for a peaceful resolution of differences into view. The cultural and political homogenization, which television news in particular promotes, inevitably works against the expression of difference, and so inhibits appreciation of similarities and common interests between communities. Only by shifting its focus from division to diversity will the news media then come to play a truly productive and facilitative role in the development of peace, and to do this, a transformation in the relationship between news and the public sphere is required.

Conclusion

The Oslo peace process demonstrates a problematic relationship between peace politics and the media. Balancing secrecy with publicity presents a dilemma for politicians engaged in sensitive and fragile negotiations, and indicates how the development of trust and commitment must precede trying to use the media for political advantage once talks become public knowledge. What is evident from the Oslo talks is that publicity tends to hinder flexibility and adaptive dialogue, whilst secrecy lacks public support and social validity. Both are necessary and yet both impose significant restrictions on how far and in what direction politicians can manoeuvre. The influences which news have on a peace process are widely examined in Wolfsfeld's work on the Middle East, which concludes that reporting exerts a largely negative impact on peace because of an obsession with conflict, drama and simplicity (all of which do not sit well with peace-making). Although the news media's influence on peace varies in connection with changing circumstances and conditions in the political environment, and although by allowing weaker antagonists to access reports the news media can find greater media independence from the mainstream parties, this independence is also shaped by how organized and consistent the mainstream parties are in their pronouncements about peace. Notably, then, the media's independence is shaped more by the level of consensus and credibilty displayed by the dominant parties than any journalistic intention to increase the amount of pressure on those parties.

What is underlined in this chapter is that the news media's influence on peace politics can only take a full and purposeful role if it seeks out the messages and arguments of parties, individuals and agencies outside of the dominant mainstream political sphere. Released from the confines of party political interests, these parties, individuals and agencies could expand the possibilities of dialogue beyond the zero-sum and largely counter-productive exchanges of dominant parties. Such voices could also add flexibility and bring a creative dimension to dialogue which is lacking in the narrow contestations of elite party positions, whilst influencing the possibilities of political movement by drawing more imaginatively from the diversity of the public sphere. The notion of 'greyness' is useful here to think about how alternative discourses might pull the extremes closer together and facilitate dialogue which moves towards inclusivity and away from the exclusivity of restrictive political debate.

8
The Northern Ireland Peace Process

Political background

The Northern Ireland peace process grew out of a series of dialogues and exchanges between SDLP leader John Hume and Sinn Fein president Gerry Adams in the late 1980s. These dialogues sowed the seeds for a departure in Republican thinking about British involvement in Northern Ireland and encouraged a move away from paramilitary violence which activated the involvement of British, Irish and American governments, and produced an expansive peace process designed to entrench attitudes of conflict resolution and draw paramilitary groups into the arena of democratic politics. The interactions between Hume and Adams captured wider political interest from the early 1990s, when the British and Irish governments recognized the possibility for transforming the political environment in Northern Ireland, and a series of communications and contacts followed which culminated in The Good Friday Agreement of 1998. The agreement provided a constitutional settlement based on themes of equality, human rights and consociational change (O'Leary 2001), and was based on years of bilateral and multilateral negotiations which concentrated on developing three interlocking strands. The first strand focuses on the formation of a new assembly which fully represents the different communities and parties. The second seeks to facilitate stronger liaison and co-operation between Northern Ireland and Dublin. And the third is concerned with tightening relations between all parts of Britain and Ireland. The significance of this triangulation lay in its potential to formally attach the interests of parties to each other and to draw political representatives of paramilitary groups further into the political arena. A central feature of the peace process has therefore been to address the underlying causes of conflict and division by working to build a 'totality of relationships'

(Bew, Patterson and Teague 1997: 203–15) which respected the concept of inclusiveness, and which sought to integrate into the institutions and structures of democratic politics those whose exclusion had been sustained during the course of political violence.

The role of governments within the peace process has been key to its momentum and consolidation, and in relation to republican engagement with the peace process, the Irish, and to a lesser extent, US governments, (especially under Bill Clinton's presidency) have been particularly important. Together, Ireland and America have been instrumental in promoting a broad-based Nationalist front able to exert considerable pressure on the British, who, during the formative years of the process, tended to reflect Unionist concerns. Recognizing the significance of Irish involvement, Sinn Fein president Gerry Adams has made clear that 'Sinn Fein's recognition of the central role of the Dublin government in the creation of the peace process was a major shift in the traditional Republican and Northern Nationalist attitude to Dublin' (Adams 1995: 206). For the Sinn Fein leadership, Irish engagement was crucial to help advance a national consensus on the issue of constitutional change and for promoting Irish unity by using positive relations with Britain, Europe and America (ibid: 206, 208). Moreover, Ireland's role within the peace process has been very much slanted towards reinforcing the case for a political settlement favourable to nationalists, along with the expectation that Dublin would take the initiative whenever possible to develop broad international support for such an outcome (ibid: 237).

Under the leadership of Albert Reynolds, who 'wanted to subsume Sinn Fein into the democratic process as swiftly as possible' (O'Brien 1995: 300), the overriding emphasis was on producing a political dynamic which would bring gains that political violence had failed to achieve. The British government, who had long held 'back-channel' contacts with Provisional IRA representatives, were also aware that changes were under way in Republican thinking, but were less receptive to the momentum being encouraged by the Irish because of fears about a nationalist-led agenda and its influence on the marginalization of mainstream unionism (the Conservative government under John Major relied on the Unionist vote across a range of domestic and international political issues). Resistance by Unionists towards talks, which they saw as an attempt to renegotiate Northern Ireland's relationship with the UK in ways favourable to Nationalism, resulting in the eventual disengagement of Northern Ireland from the UK, exacerbated tensions with the British and undermined the support which Unionists had traditionally provided. A tendency for the Irish to sympathize with Nationalists, while the British responded to Unionist anxieties, created a process of contrasting pressures and imperatives which both governments sought to influence through the media as well as at the negotiating table. And, although both governments reached agreements on key issues and documents during the course of the peace process, it was the twin-track approach which enabled exclusive concerns to be embraced and which provided the middle ground where the divided communities of Nationalism and Unionism could meet.

Reynolds provided both private and public clarification to Sinn Fein about negotiations and worked closely with SDLP leader John Hume 'in trying to pressurise the British into becoming persuaders for a united Ireland' (Hennessey 2000: 76). He also dedicated himself to the task of developing constitutional Nationalism and convincing the Republican movement 'that more progress towards a united Ireland could be made through the political process and the abandonment of armed struggle' (ibid: 77). Reynolds commitment to 'momentum and reconciliation' (Coogan 1995: 379) helped to produce, along with the British government, the Joint Declaration document in December 1993. Although the document outlined a common set of principles for British and Irish handling of Northern Ireland, and established 'the principle of consent', which effectively meant Irish unity could only occur with majority consent in Northern Ireland and enshrined a Unionist veto, it was also apparent that the declaration was 'weighed heavily in favour of Nationalists' (ibid: 374). Also evident was the 'skilful and abundant use of coded language' which allowed for 'constructive ambiguity' and signified 'a political statement of attitude and intent directed primarily at the IRA' (Arthur 2000: 243).

The importance of the Joint Declaration lay in its ability to couch the prospect of change, which appealed to Nationalists, within a context of majority consent, which appealed to many Unionists. Furthermore, the document 'marked an end to Republican hopes that the principle of consent would be on their terms', indicating 'the point at which constitutional Nationalism in Ireland finally embraced the principle of consent on Unionist terms and abandoned previous hopes of manoeuvering the British into being persuaders for a united Ireland' (Hennessey 2000: 81). Clarifications and negotiations which followed the document helped create conditions which led to cease-fires by the IRA in August 1994 (Bew and Gillespie 1999: 293–5) and in October 1994 by the Combined Loyalist Military Command (ibid: 297–9), and reflected wider anticipations about the possibility for peace in Northern Ireland.

When John Bruton succeeded Albert Reynolds as Irish prime minister in December 1994, his commitment to the peace process was seen as less intense than Reynolds's (Coogan 1995: 387–8), however Bruton did play a key role in producing the Frameworks Document which was announced by the British and Irish on 22 February 1995. Consisting of two sections, the first part contained 'The British Government's understanding of where agreement might be found among the parties on new institutions for Northern Ireland', while in the second part 'the British and Irish Governments present their best assessment of where agreement could be found concerning new political arrangements between Northern Ireland and the Republic and between the two governments' (Dixon 2001: 251). The Frameworks Document, building from the Joint Declaration, thus drew out the parameters for how a settlement might be achieved and focused on the three interlocking strands designed to facilitate 'shared understanding' and provide a framework for further negotiation (O'Brien 1995: 340–2). However, the general thrust of the document was oriented towards Nationalists and its emphasis on 'harmonization' gave it an all-Ireland leaning which alarmed Unionists (Dixon 2001: 252). Constructed with the aim of keeping Sinn Fein inside the peace process, the Irish government continued to hold together the pan-Nationalist consensus, much to British consternation (ibid: 258).

A lack of progress in negotiations led to the IRA ending its cease-fire with the bombing of Canary Wharf in London in February 1996. The Sinn Fein leadership related the act to Unionist and British intransigence, whilst Gerry Adams maintained contacts with key players and worked to 'retain his image as a peacemaker' (Bew and Gillespie 1999: 323) against a background of growing fear and unease. A reinstatement of the IRA cease-fire in July 1997 coincided with a change of British government and a Labour Party less restricted by Unionist opinion. Along with the newly elected Irish prime minister Bertie Ahern, British prime minister Tony Blair brought a new impetus to the peace process, which was also supported by America and the mediator Senator George Mitchell, who worked with the parties through to the Good Friday Agreement which was signed the following April.

News and the peace process

The role of the news media in the Northern Ireland conflict has demonstrated a tendency to view developments by way of a 'terrorism-as-cause' paradigm (Butler 1995), with Republican violence seen as a threat to

British state control and the disruption of social order. Noticeable in much of the literature which analyses reporting and Northern Ireland is the media's preoccupation with the criminal consequences of terrorism and British state propaganda which sought to demonize and pathologize those who perpetrated and supported acts of violence (Curtis 1984; Schlesinger 1987; Miller 1994; Rolston and Miller 1996). Throughout the modern period, and up until the development of the peace process, the submissiveness of the news media to elite interpretation of Northern Ireland gave credance and apparent validity to articulations and viewpoints that worked to delegitimize the motivations of Republican paramilitarism, whilst functioning to provide a framework of condemnation which obscured the implications of British state policy. A political consensus developed based on criminalization of the Republican position which also served to help legitimize the British government's containment and management of the conflict.

This policy of division which dominated the period more commonly referrred to as the 'Troubles' (from the late 1960s until the 1990s) was transformed with the development of the peace process, where attitudes began to shift from the politics of exclusion to a growing awareness of the need for inclusion, and it was this realization which helped to influence a departure in the British government's traditional relationship with the Northern Ireland problem. Representatives who were previously excluded from news reports because of affiliations with paramilitary groups were now, through changes in the political environment, able to articulate their positions quite openly and, as a result, the political arena became subject to a broader range of discourses trying to contest various positions and interests which were emerging in debates and negotiatons about peace. Significantly, the peace process (re)politicized the political sphere in Northern Ireland and the media's role became central in this (re)politicization. By promoting contestations between parties, carrying dialogue and communications, and publicizing the dynamic and direction of talks, the news media became political participants in the peace process and produced expectations and pressures which were absorbed into negotiations. The importance of television news within this environment proved central in shaping public perceptions about the possibilities of peace, and became especially potent as a force of influence because of its ability to reach all audiences simultaneously (unlike the print media which attracts specific audiences and reflects the segregations of the Northern Ireland polity). Notably, then, by exerting a range of influences and consequences on peace politics, the news media provided a space for dialogue and interaction to occur which impacted on negotiations and public opinion (Spencer 2001; 2003; 2004a).

Contestations between parties and governments produced varying degrees of success in the battle for public relations initiatives, but the efforts of Irish and British governments perhaps more succintly indicate attempts to try and shape news agendas during the formative stages of peace. A particularly useful study which highlights this contestation in relation to television news is provided by Feeney (1997), who looks at three case studies of how the British government used the media to try and gain advantage over the Irish in 1994. Feeney explains how the British centralized communications at Whitehall (away from the Northern Ireland Office), where it could more effectively maintain a unified government position when dealing with the media (ibid: 45). Also interesting is Feeney's account of the British government's attempts to create a primary definition of two political summits in 1995 and a document called 'The Mitchell Report of 1996', which tried to map out a way forward for dealing with the impasse over decommissioning of paramilitary weapons. Rapid and comprehensive responses to news interest surrounding these events significantly influenced the course of news emphasis and facilitated subsequent political responses in ways which favoured the British position. Feeney also points out how a slow response by the Irish government and a lack of unified statements assisted the British in gaining public relations advantage. However, efforts to try and secure control of news agendas in this way also suggest difficulties for developing structures of trust and accommodation. Feeney, notes, for example, that British government efforts to promote an image of control over the peace process were directed at the British electorate rather than designed to incite constructive dialogue. He also observes how attempts by the British to exert control over the Irish created suspicions in Nationalist constituencies, where 'because there are two communities watching the same news which transmits a message designed for Britain, the result is to increase division in the North' (ibid: 48). Indicating how British activity might be interpreted more critically by Nationalists, Feeney suggests that 'if the British were trying so hard there must be another story' and that because of this other story, political opposition would read events differently (ibid.).

This centralization of communications and preoccupation with using news both to maintain credibility amongst the British electorate and control the news agenda also underpinned the British government's efforts to provide a primary definition of peace process developments.

An example of such primary definition can be found in Miller and McLaughlin (1996), which looks at how the British government dealt with press revelations about secret contacts with Sinn Fein when such contacts were leaked to the press in 1993. The authors point out how the leak about the government's 'clarification' to Sinn Fein of details relating to the Joint Declaration (also called the 'Downing Street Declaration', itself a good indication of British efforts to claim responsibility for negotiating the document) was dealt with both as a damage limitation exercise and as an attempt to regain the public relations initiative from Sinn Fein, who tried to use coverage in order to try and exploit potential weaknesses and inconsistencies in the British government's account of events. Though Sinn Fein provided some problems for the government by releasing detailed evidence of the contacts which had stretched back for some time (Sinn Fein 1994), it is clear that British attempts to try and manage reporting at this time were generally successful and that 'TV journalists refrained from asking the hard questions about British government strategy and about contradictions with previous policy' (ibid: 431). Comparisons wth the example of primary definition presented by Miller and McLaughlin can also be found in how television news treated the IRA cease-fire announcement of 1994 (Spencer 2000: 141–57). Caught somewhat unawares by the cease-fire annoucement, the British proceeded to stress how the word 'permanent' had been omitted from the cease-fire statement in order to place deliberate doubt on its reliability and assert control over the news agenda, even though this emphasis differed strongly from that of Dublin and America.

The IRA announcement and Sinn Fein's manipulation of news attention to maximize the impact of the announcement also brings into view the propaganda opportunities which can be seized by groups other then governments during a moment of political change. Indicating how the news media can be used with varying degrees of success by different parties, Sinn Fein has used the support of Irish and American governments to put pressure on the British government and exploit propaganda opportunities much more effectively than Unionists (Coogan 1995: 371–8), who have demonstrated a less sophisticated understanding of how to use the news to further their position. As Parkinson concludes in his study of Unionism and the media, it is because of Unionism's 'failure to project its cause and elicit sympathy either at political level or in the national media' that 'their own propaganda and political pressure have had little effect on influencing the policy of the main British parties' (1998: 161).

Lago's (1998) analysis of how Sinn Fein was dealt with in news reports once the peace process gained credibility as a substantive political process provides us with a highly relevant case study about how representations can change alongside shifts in the political landscape. According to Lago, not only was there a notable increase in the number of interviews conducted with Sinn Fein after the peace process started, but the nature of the interviews and the questions changed (ibid: 678–9). Unlike before, when the questioning of Sinn Fein was hostile and concerned with the actions of Republican 'terrorists', 'journalists seemed to be searching for greater involvement and "clarification" by Sinn Fein representatives, in turn suggesting that journalists regarded the party's stance as increasingly important' within the dynamic of the peace process (ibid: 680). Furthermore, contends Lago, this change in approach to Sinn Fein by the media tended to coincide with a more critical stance towards those seen as opposed to, or obstructive towards, the peace process. The media's positive attitude towards the early stages of peace, which as Darby and MacGinty (2000: 93) observe was almost universal, was also a key factor influencing the growing critical coverage afforded to Unionists. The more positive approach used in the interviewing of Sinn Fein therefore had consequences for Unionism, with its representatives questioned more than before, sometimes to the extent where broadcasters appeared 'to favour Republicans in ridiculing Unionism' (Lago 1998: 684).

It is clear that television news plays a significant role in the dissemination and distribution of political information and that it takes on particular importance in the shaping of public perceptions about politics and political life. It is the ability of television news to broadcast to a variety of audiences simultaneously which demonstrates its communicative power and which highlights its potential to become an active agent in the process of megaphone diplomacy (Miller 1994: 283–4). However, this propensity to develop broader political and public awareness needs to be considered in the context of the conflict and antagonism which symbolizes media politics. This competitiveness may be attractive to journalists, but it also serves to inhibit conciliatory gestures and can create obstructions for delicate negotiations, which in turn tends to slow down the dynamic of interaction and halt progress. This problem brought about some frustration for the negotiations Chairman, Senator George Mitchell, who in his account of events which led to The Good Friday Agreement, described how:

All of the participants sought to advance their negotiating positions by manipulating the press outside. Whatever the result from the standpoint of the parties, it made the process of negotiation much more difficult. Countless hours were to be consumed by attacks and counterattacks, accusations and recriminations, over what had appeared in the morning newspapers. It didn't just take up a lot of time, it poisoned the atmosphere, creating and exacerbating hostility among the participants.

(1999: 62)

Mitchell's point about the media's negative impact on peace talks occurs not only between parties, but also within them. McDonald, for example, highlights how splits within the Ulster Unionist Party over The Good Friday Agreement were exacerbated by television pictures of early released IRA prisoners at a Sinn Fein annual conference. The reports created considerable problems for those within the Ulster Unionist Party who were trying to sell positive aspects of the agreement to their constituencies in the build up to a referendum, and assisted the case being made by anti-agreement factions within the party (2000: 210).

Developing conciliatory positions and negotiations through television news is, therefore, clearly problematic given the emphasis which reporting gives to the more negative or conflictive aspects of a situation or event (Bantz 1997: 134) and where positions are routinely constructed within the 'presentation of conflicting possibilities', frame or perspective (Tuchman 1999: 299). Yet it is also apparent that even though news prioritizes negativity, there is the potential for pressures to be applied which can underpin momentum and facilitate exchanges through this negativity, and that this dynamic can help reinforce expectations of change.

The ability of television news to act as a lever of influence on talks indicates its potential to exert pressure on the political process. A number of editors and journalists who I interviewed about the role which reporting played in the final stages leading up to The Good Friday Agreement, supported this view (Spencer 2004a). The presence of the media outside the talks in Castle Buildings, Belfast, was seen to create a 'pressure-cooker' atmosphere, which reinforced expectations of a peace deal and pressured the participants to be seen working to bring that deal about (ibid: 611). Furthermore, the participants were routinely going outside the building in order to brief the media about developments, and trying to use the real-time communications of broadcasts to move the direction of the negotiations in ways which favoured the party position being communicated (ibid.). Significantly, the television media were useful in relation to interaction and dialogue on key issues within the peace process such as the release of political prisoners as part of a final settlement. Government ministers would routinely comment on the prisoner issue to journalists, who would then seek responses from Sinn Fein. Comments from Sinn Fein would be returned to ministers through interview thus producing a momentum of dialogue, where each would attempt to exert negotiating pressure on the other. Not only did the media therefore play an important part in providing the space for such debate, but it also, at the same time, functioned to prepare the viewing public and other parties for the politically contentious possibility of prisoner releases (ibid: 612).

Television news also helped to create the climate for public recognition of cross-party communications and dialogue between those who had previously refused to meet or engage with each other. A good example of this development took place during a BBC2 *Newsnight* broadcast (12.8.97) when Ulster Unionist Party representative Ken Maginnis took part in a studio debate with Martin McGuiness of Sinn Fein. As the first time on British television when a Unionist had been seen talking to a Republican, the meeting was expectedly hostile, but in terms of its symbolic power and as evidence of the two sides meeting, it was seen by many as a sign of considerable movement and a commitment to the contestations of peace politics (ibid: 612). The meeting was indicative of the media's role in the choreography of the peace process and but one example of many where diplomacy was pursued through the channel of news. This was particularly the case during the early and more tentative phases of the peace process. At this time former Northern Ireland Secretary Peter Brooke used journalists to send messages to the Republican Movement about the unlikeliness of British forces defeating the IRA, signalling a reappraisal of the stalemate between the two (Taylor 1997: 316). Picked up by republicans, a counter-response was also carried through the media, with Sinn Fein representatives Gerry Adams, Martin McGuiness and Mitchel McLaughlin admitting that Brooke's comments had created some 'partial debate' within the Republican Movement (Mallie and McKittrick 1996: 101).

One year later Brooke went further and made a keynote speech were he announced that 'The British Government has no selfish or strategic or economic interest in Northern Ireland . . . Partition is an acknowledgement of reality, not an assertion of national self-interest' (Taylor 1997: 318). The fact that most of the media missed this comment and that the government was angry that the message had not been covered as the ground-breaking communication it was intended to be, once more demonstrates the importance of the news in a changing politicial climate (Spencer 2004a: 612). The comment, however, stimulated a sequence of secret contacts between Sinn Fein and the British, until those contacts were made public in November 1993. Then the publicity of talks had damaging consequences for the British who had previously denied talking with republicans, once more highlighting the problem of both using and trying to prevent news from covering sensitive political communications. The impact of news coverage on political contacts and the varying effects of that impact, both negatively and positively, bring to light the complex relationship which exists between news and politics when the political enviroment is undergoing significant transformation (ibid: 610).

At governmental level discourse tended to revolve around specific and repetitive themes. For the Irish, this meant playing up the positives of the process, which as former Foreign Affairs official Eamon Delaney put it, depended on creating an enviroment where:

> the same language was constantly regurgitated and turned around. This created a problematic paradox; each speech had to sound fresh and different, while essentially saying exactly the same as previous speeches. The language on Northern Ireland was tightly controlled ... The language went something like this; the situation was a tragedy, and needed a new beginning, an agreement in which all sides could be accommodated and in which one tradition does not dominate over the other. The two Governments must ensure that negotiations lead to a settlement which honours the rights and aspirations of both communities equally. Unionists must be assured that Northern Ireland will remain a part of the United Kingdom for the forseeable future, while Nationalists must be assured their cultural identity will be secure in Northern Ireland, as well as in an all-Ireland context. We need to open doors, not close them.
>
> (Delaney 2001: 325–6)

In his memoir, Delaney also highlights the meanings of specific terms which were constantly articulated so as to become absorbed into the ideological parameters of peace discourse (ibid: 335–6), and points out how this formulation was drafted into key documents which became the foundation for future talks and negotiations (ibid: 347). What emerges from Delaney's account of planning and co-ordinating speeches for political and public consumption is the importance of holding a line through the media and using reiteration in order to establish positions which would influence talks in ways favourable to governmental aims. Those aims, as far as the Irish were concerned, were designed to help accelarate the process and to pressure the British who wanted to slow the process down and work to designated time frames (Spencer 2003: 66–7). This attempt by the Irish to promote a 'peace first' initiative, created major difficulties for the British Government and sometimes contibuted to a break-down in the co-ordination of messages and statements made to the media, which was taken by journalists to be evidence of dissensus rather than consensus over the way the peace process should proceed (ibid: 67).

One means used by the Irish to intensify pressure on the British was to make statements which would appeal to Nationalist audiences. By making comments favourable to Nationalist opinion, the Irish worked on the assumption that Unionist unease and dissent would in turn put further pressure on the British Government who, given the need for Unionist support over other aspects of government policy, would then need to act (ibid: 68). The risk here however, is that pressures can lead to further intransigence because of the potentially negative impact on relationships. Morever, the tendency of television news to increase tensions and antagonisms between parties, along with a propensity to concentrate on a short-term advantage of political strategy, created problems for long-term political objectives and the complex issues which sustained the peace process.

It is the media's ability to exacerbate tensions and amplify potentially destabilizing communications, which explains why some participants view the media so critically. Indeed, because the media tend to narrow the possibilities for flexibility, it is argued that its most effective use for politicians is to state and reinforce known positions (ibid: 70). During periods of intense political activity and movement, it is seen as preferable to remain reticent in the wake of journalistic inquiry, where an emphasis on the zero-sum game of winners and losers can set back trust and confidence. Restricting the flow of information is thus as integral to political control as promoting information (Manning 2001: 19) and suggests that although news coverage is necessary for the legitimacy of political action, it is also necessary to keep political activity away from the media until positions are developed enough to survive any negative repercussions created by the emotive atmosphere of news broadcasts. Effectively, when politicians talk to the news media, they do so for two primary reasons. First, to reassure their constituents and second, to try and strengthen their negotiating position. Because of a fear amongst the parties that they will be seen as weaker than their opponents, or conceding to the pressure of their opponents demands, there is a tendency for politicians to take a hard-line stance towards issues which can hinder constructive interaction and impede progress. This has negative consequences for positive relations and does little to encourage engagement with the core themes and concerns of peace. It is for this reason that confidentiality is so important in the early stages of a peace process. One former Irish prime minister made it clear to me in interview that the IRA would have broken contacts if leaks were made to the media during the formative stages of talks (Spencer 2003: 72), and that the competitive atmosphere of news would have ended the trust and confidence which were slowly being built.

For the Irish, the main imperative of communications was to keep both sides within a talks process. This inevitably required a sequence of messages, where a positive gesture given to one side would have to be reciprocated with a similiarly positive gesture to the other. The symbolic and public content of such gestures also helped to entrench confidence in the commitment of the Irish government and proved vital for pulling the paramilitaries further into the democratic process (ibid: 74). The symbolism and communicative implications of television messages was able to convey messages and signs in ways which were unachievable within the confines of private talks.

It is also important to recognize that in the case of Northern Ireland, Loyalists and Republicans watch the news closely in order to try and assess the thinking and intentions of each other (Spencer 2001: 69). Loyalists talk about how television news was used by Sinn Fein to put pressure on opponents during the talks in the build-up to The Good Friday Agreement, and refer to the example of Sinn Fein representatives walking around the car-park space outside of Castle Buildings, smiling and looking relaxed with each other. This was then broadcast to Unionist (as well as all other) constituencies who would interpret the body language and non-verbal communication as a sign of the talks going well for Sinn Fein, and by association going badly for Unionists (Spencer 2004b: 48). As a consequence, Unionist audiences would contact their representatives and demand that they take greater control of the negotiations, such was the ability of non-verbal communication to evoke fears and anxieties within Unionist/Loyalist communities. Although, an indication of how unsophisticated Loyalists and Unionists are in dealing with the power of the media compared to Sinn Fein, this example nevertheless reveals how crucial performance is when interacting with the news cameras and how non-verbal communication can be a persuasive device for applying pressure. But even taking this into account, it remains evident that for Loyalists at least, the media has tended to be somewhat unreceptive to the smaller parties and what they might offer to the peace process. Loyalists are critical of the media's inability to engage with the dialogue they have been trying to promote and the constructive gestures which they have made in order to try and develop peace (ibid: 44–7).

This problem is also experienced by parties such as the Northern Ireland Women's Coalition, who provided an important contribution to the negotiations by working to promote political inclusivity and inclusive discourse (Spencer 2004c). For the NIWC, the media are largely uninterested in the role of the smaller parties and any potentially constructive role which they may play in the development of peace. In a series of interviews carried out with representatives of the NIWC, it was perceived that female politics was not taken as seriously as male politics by journalists and that one reason for this was because the competitiveness of male politics has much greater appeal as news drama. Furthermore, argued the respondents, the competitiveness of male-dominated politics which is commonly used to make sense of political debate, is emphasized so much in news that this representation becomes a legitimizing presence in a process which suggests that politics should be practised in that way. The representation of dominant political agendas from male perspectives makes it very difficult, for parties like the NIWC, to access mainstream political debates and, indeed, the media's tendency to view the smaller parties as peripheral and insignificant in relation to what is happening increases the unlikeliness of those parties being seen as having any noticeable impact in the political arena. Another important reason for the media's lack of interest in women's politics, insists the NIWC, derives from a negative conceptualization of women's activism compared to that of men, with female politics invariably seen as subordinate to male politics and therefore passive in orientation. Ironically, although the work of the NIWC might be seen as offering a credible and legitimate alternative to the rather obstructive and antagonistic practice of male politics, and so constructive within the development of peace discourse, a perception was nevertheless perpetuated which saw women's politics as weak precisely because it does not engage in the restrictive and conflictive interactions of conventional male communications.

The NIWC's efforts to strengthen cross-community relations through articulations which prioritized non-confrontational discourse and a mutual respect for all sections of the community, were seen as a weakness by many. It was because the party refused to take a clearly partisan position on the constitutional question of Northern Ireland's status with the UK and Ireland that they were accused of lacking political credibility. And it was because the NIWC's politics were not complementary to journalistic interest that the media reinforced rather than challenged this accusation. The experience of loyalists and the NIWC thus tends to confirm that the news media regard the smaller parties as less consequential in the Northern Ireland peace process, and that the ideas and articulations which they might bring to peace therefore deserve marginal interest, regardless of their political relevance. The NIWC's emphasis on inclusivity and their role as mediators between the participants highlight a positive and helpful contribution to the progression of peace, but the importance of their input was minimized by the media's obsession with the dominant parties and the predictable scenario of confrontational politics. Although the dominant parties themselves are seen by the media as 'cruch actors' because they can 'move things one way or the other' (Spencer 2004a: 615), we need to bear in mind that by reinforcing this perception, the news media help to invest those parties with the ability to operate as cruch actors. When thinking about the importance of news within a peace process therefore, it is vital to recognize the media's connection with the dominant parties since it is they, rather than the smaller parties, who benefit most from the media's communicative potential.

A comparison of how Sinn Fein and the Ulster Unionists operate in relation to the media provides us with an interesting insight into how two of the dominant Northern Ireland parties deal with and respond to journalistic attention. From the perspectives of key editors and journalists working in Northern Ireland (Spencer 2004a), it is apparent that Sinn Fein's superiority in managing the media derives from the centralized way in which the party is run. Unlike the Ulster Unionists, which operate as a bottom–up organization, and which allow representatives to freely say what they want to the media, Sinn Fein is extemely careful about how it conducts debates within the party, and is careful to advocate a single line of analysis to the media about whatever issue is of interest at that point in time. Editors note that it is nothing short of catastrophic for a political party to send out a number of messages (often contradictory) to constituencies and that a fragmented approach to issues increases fear and uncertainty amongst audiences (ibid: 616). The Ulster Unionists have routinely used the media to try and influence internal dissent and disagreement in the party about the direction and demands of the peace process, rather than take a unified approach to situations and the moves of opponents, and this has contributed to a decline in their influence (demonstated by losses at the elections in 2003, which resulted in the Democratic Unionist Party gaining the most votes for a Unionist party and superseding the UUP's dominance which had prevailed throughout the peace process until that time). In contrast, the image which Sinn Fein have cultivated for themselves suggests a largely reliable, well-organized, coherent and unified party which has translated into ongoing electoral gains and the position of becoming Northern Ireland's dominant Nationalist party. Although there are obvious important structural and organizational differences between the two parties and how they work with communities at a local level, it is clear that the rise of Sinn Fein and the fall of Ulster Unionism is also connected to image management and how the media is used to publicy promote positions and objectives. The impression which audiences have in their heads about political parties is one which is largely shaped by how those parties present themselves. If the representation is carefully maintained and developed then the party begins to appeal as more reliable, and it this reliability which tends to ease the fears and insecurities of audiences. Image management is therefore inextricably linked with public support, whereas poor management invariably contributes to dwindling support.

The media's shift of attention after the 2003 elections from contestations between Sinn Fein and the Ulster Unionist Party to Sinn Fein and the Democratic Unionist Party further highlights the obsession with political power and party dominance. It also indicates that discourse and discussion about the peace process (and the political issues which underpin it) is conveyed by the media primarily from the vantage point of extreme positions, at the same time ignoring or giving minimal attention to those parties who operate outside those positions. Moreover, one might argue that the attention given to the extremes encourages those parties to maintain extreme positions in order to continue using and exploiting coverage. Even when moves towards peace occur, it is evident that certainly in the case of Northern Ireland (from 2004 on), such moves take place because of a political interest by the extremes, and not because of the media's ability to bring debates and perspectives to the fore which offer constructive alternatives to the obstructive and resistant moves of the dominant parties. Loyalist parties and the Northern Ireland Women's Coalition received minimal coverage by the media after The Good Friday Agreement of 1998, when the search for peace became portrayed as essentially a straight contest between Republicans and dominant Unionism. Indeed, Loyalist political representatives could be forgiven for thinking they have no role to play in the development of peace, so absent have they been from coverage. Furthermore, this exclusion creates disruption and concern within constituencies which impacts on the public mood and social attitudes about peace. In disappearing from reports, Loyalist representatives are perceived as having no influence over the course of events by their supporters and therefore find it difficult to persuade those supporters that they are being heard and actively involved in developments. This point returns us once more to the issue of inclusion and reaffirms the importance of diversity in peace politics. By reducing the complexities and political nuances of the peace process to a contestation between two opposing voices, news effectively denies the existence of viewpoints and contributions which may widen the possibilities for progression and operate beyond the narrow limitations of the zero-sum game which the dominant extremes occupy.

Although it appears obvious, given this involvement, that the media are players as well as observers in relation to this process, it is the preoccupation with the entertainment of division that seems to demand we bring into question the responsibility of this engagement. The television images which personalize the peace process and depict it as a confrontation between individuals, by so doing, reduce the complexities and details of political change to a battle of wills (at the time of writing this can be seen between Rev. Dr Ian Paisley of the DUP and Gerry Adams of Sinn Fein) which has consequences for how peace is handled. Importantly, this also has repercussions for other parties and how their constituencies view the process. As mentioned, the marginalization of Loyalism from reports has brought about considerable pressures on Loyalist leaders who are inclined to adopt a defensive (and so reductive) position in order to try and convince constituencies why support is still needed for the role they have to play in peace politics. Moreover, the clear gains being made by Sinn Fein (which is reinforced by their continuing presence in news) compound the difficulties for Loyalists who find themselves having to work harder and harder to maintain any kind of credibility as players with influence over events.

The absence of political participants from news who represent the smaller parties has produced problems for the development of peace. Loyalist paramilitary violence has considerable potential to destabilize the peace process, and is not best dealt with by Loyalists being marginalized from events. Frustrations about the absence of a Loyalist contribution to debates about the peace process, which are being controlled and shaped through the contestations of dominant Unionism and Republicanism, are more obviously a result of news selectivity than political incompetence (for example, the involvement of Loyalism was vital for The Good Friday Agreement and bringing about a paramilitary cease-fire). This selectivity extends to other parties (notably the Alliance Party and the NIWC) and reflects an inability to seek out, question and communicate other discourses that challenge the rigidity of dominant positions. It is, in a sense, a continuation of the divisiveness which the media emphasized throughout the years of violence, but is now constructed through words and expression rather than the effects of physical violence. The coverage given to a range of parties in the build up to The Good Friday Agreement demonstrates that the media's receptiveness to alternative discourses does happen, and that when it happens it does so at a very specific political moment when the dynamic of political interaction dramatically changes. But once that dynamic is seen to develop into core themes and issues of contestation, then the media tend to revert attention back on the dominant parties, whilst the smaller parties start to disappear along with the alternative discourses which they articulate.

Conclusion

There is little doubt that the news media plays a central role in the development of a peace process, most notably in terms of ability to both include and exclude political representations. During the intense negotiations in the build-up to The Good Friday Agreement, the parties and governments sought to use the media to promote negotiating positions and key aspects of policy were discussed effectively through news channels. The dramatic and simplistic emphasis of coverage was used to apply pressure on opponents and press for responses and commitments on key issues and concerns, as well as used to communicate expectations of change to a broad range of constituencies simultaneously. For the momentum of the peace process, news proved especially important during the early stages of contacts and was instrumental in the development of a communications dynamic. However, this potential must also be seen in the wider context of a commitment amongst the parties to engage with talks. As Wolfsfeld noted in relation to the Middle East peace process, it is politics which is the determinant of political activity; the media's influence is secondary. But what is also apparent is that the media can influence the level of pressure exerted on parties by allowing alternative discourses to hightlight shortcomings, obstruction and lack of imagination amongst the dominant extremes. It can, in other words, help audiences and opponents think more broadly about the parameters of political discussion and bring to question the unhelpful and narrow choices which tend to befall those who rely on intransigence, confrontation and hostility as devices to engage with the uncertainties of peace. It could also be argued that a wider range of voices in peace dialogue might increase the possibility of risk-taking and encourage a greater flexibility and adapatability towards peace politics that is lacking in the conventional struggles between two opposing forces.

What news reporting of the Northern Ireland peace process highlights is that the media have played both a positive role and a negative role in relation to the development of peace, but that this role is mainly negative. It is fair to say that there has been a general tendency for the journalistic community to support the prospect of peace in Northern Ireland and, unlike the Middle East, there has been some consistency in the level of support shown by successive governments (both British and Irish). However, the news media has inevitably interpreted the peace process through the prism of news values and continued to emphasize events through a conventional narrative format which relies on simplicity, conflict and drama, and this creates problems for informing audiences about the details and complexities of peace politics. Obsession with antagonisms of the dominant parties prioritizes confrontational discourse and undermines rather than constructively engages debates about peace and alternative conceptualizations of peace politics. Notably, it remains in the interest of dominant parties to manage and reinforce their dominance in order to maintain media attention and political influence. Unfortunately, since the media emphasize divisiveness over difference, and assess ideas about peace within the narrow parameters defined by the more powerful parties, they effectively reinforce the power and influence those parties have and thereby help to amplify the fixed positions they tend to occupy.

9

The Gulf War, the 'War on Terror' and Iraq

News coverage of the Persian Gulf War in 1990 offers some useful portents for Western reporting of the Iraq War of 2003 and more broadly the 'War on Terror' which developed after 11 September 2001. Significantly, the American invasion of the Gulf to reverse the Iraqi invasion of Kuwait highlights a drive towards war which was barely questioned or critically examined by news. The media's tendency to represent the American-led incursion as a battle between Western respect for freedom and decency, against the devious and over-zealous Arab community (whose point of focus was the Iraqi dictator Saddam Hussein) (Schiller 1992: 23), was an impression sustained through a carefully controlled and choreographed news environment. Throughout the campaign, US national interests and the relationship of foreign policy to those interests was largely ignored by the news media (Lang and Lang 1994: 59), who reported developments as disjointed episodes without explanation or context (ibid: 58). Instead, the emphasis provided a distortion of the conflict by way of exaggerating 'a diabolical enemy-image; a virile self-image; a moral self-image; and selective inattention' (Dorman and Livingston 1994: 75).

The rush to war was contributed to by coverage which 'failed to examine U.S. policy claims, moral or otherwise, within the context of alternative historical settings', and because the media framed public communication through themes and concerns articulated by the Bush administration (ibid: 76). It was this submissiveness to dominant opinion that led to a situation where 'journalists tended to perform as passive "chroniclers" rather than active "examiners"'; neglecting to inform the public of other debates which countered elite articulations (ibid.). Those elements of the news media which sought to present counter positions and arguments adopted a critical stance which 'was procedural rather than substantive', and contained within 'definitive boundaries' in relation to the position taken by the Bush administration (Entman and Page 1994: 96). The impression of criticial distance from the government line was therefore seriously limited as well as somewhat indicative of a 'failure to recognize that slight alterations in news practices could have promoted more informed public participation' in debates about the legitimacy of war (ibid: 97).

On the point of the media showing any real interest in war being averted, Chomsky notes that 'The silence in the United States was deafening and instructive. Throughout Iraqi democrats were in essential agreement with the mainstream of the U.S. peace movement and indeed most of the world. But all these sectors were opposed to the stance of the U.S. government and were therefore not fit subjects for the media, which had quite different responsibilities' (1992: 56). 'In short', continues Chomsky, 'had minimal standards of journalism been observed, it is doubtful that the administration would have been able to pursue its wavering commitment to undermining the pursuit of peaceful means and establishing the preferred rule of force' (ibid: 59). By constructing Iraqi leader Saddam Hussein as an equivalent of Adolf Hitler, the war took on a moral imperative which ignored the importance of oil supplies and domestic interest, and converted the problem into a simplistic consensus/conflict paradigm of right over wrong. The propensity of journalists to question this argument was limited not only by a clear inabilty to challenge and expose weaknesses in the pro-war case, but, once again, because the war complemented news rituals and values. As Hallin and Gitlin note on this point: 'The war had a narrative logic full of suspense, crescendoes, and collective emotion. It was the stuff of high drama – valuable not only for high ratings but for high excitement in the community and the newsroom alike' (1994: 161). Journalists who were allocated into 'pools' connected to military units and who had reports veted by military personnel inevitably produced coverage which was 'restricted to military questions', along with issues of tactics and strategy (Schiller 1992: 23). But, the saturation coverage given to the military campaign also served to support the inevitability of conflict which was the key goal of the US government. Discussion which centred on themes of military activity rather than peaceful alternatives to the war therefore had a two-pronged impact. First, it complemented US foreign policy aims, and second, it complemented the conventions of dramatic news construction. By reinforcing the military emphasis, supporting political aims and amplifying the dramatic appeal of the conflict, the media produced a war, as Hallin and Gitlin observe, 'that fits very closely that old romantic image – clean successful, largely painless, exciting, and suffused with good feelings of potency and solidarity alike' (1994: 162).

During the war, the role of CNN proved vital in the communication of events and exerted considerable 'ability to control the agenda for many other press outlets in print and broadcast journalism' as well (Corcoran 1994: 108). But CNN's presentation of the conflict, as with most television coverage, held a 'fascination with the minutiae of war, which creates a depthless, ahistorical presence' that itself became 'a powerful form of censorship', and helped to 'turn journalism into moral persuasion of the public that the war is fought by decent people for honorable objectives' (ibid.). CNN therefore helped to promote a version of the war which was consistent with American government aims and did little to interrogate the legitimacy of the invasion or the concerns of those opposed to the conflict. Though CNN created the immediacy of experience for viewers and thus perpetuated a feeling amongst audiences of being 'participants in events' (Vincent 1994: 199), its function was crucial for promotion of the view that the war was a justified action; a position further reinforced by the apparent excitement which direct coverage provided. This tendency was reflected by the television media generally, which drew from similiar sources and so adopted a shared approach to reporting the war, as well as official propaganda (Taylor 1998: 268). This war, Taylor argues, could not have taken place without co-ordinated and extensive propaganda. It was this propaganda which fomented the view that military action taken by a US led coalition, would be a 'just war', and so a 'justified offensive against the Iraqi enemy by largely democratic governments which enjoyed popular support for their actions' (ibid: 271). The demonization of Saddam Hussein helped to personalize the reasons for war and keep the emotive level of debate away from those who challenged this narrow frame of reference. Indeed, in relation to voices of dissent reaching audiences, it was clear that 'This was not a war in which the "vocal minority" were to be given a magnified voice' (ibid: 272).

For Taylor, the Gulf War provides an example where the distance between governments and public is narrowed (ibid.). Live television coverage allowed elites to communicate instantaneously thereby minimizing the interpretive role of journalists and producing uncertainty about the media's public role (ibid.). If television not only reinforces distance but magnifies it (ibid: 276), then what becomes evident from real-time news in war zones is that speed of communication also renders the journalist increasingly powerless. Instead of instantaneous coverage making life more difficult for politicians, perhaps we should also consider the possibility that such speed might make life more difficult for journalists by eroding their ability to make critical interventions between the flow of political messages and the public. It seems reasonably clear that in the case of the Gulf War, the television news media overlooked its public responsibility and became an extension of the propaganda flow from governments. In the case of Britain, the television media's part in this flow was instrumental in moving public opinion from initial resistance to being convinced about the need for war in a very short time (Philo and McLaughlin 1995: 146). The linkage of Saddam Hussein to Hitler helped to eradicate resistance to war and presented armed intervention as the only effective policy (ibid: 147). By focusing on Saddam in this way, contentions about the moral basis for war became increasingly incidental to a growing emphasis on character and individualization (ibid.). Moreover, this focus helped to divert the media's attention from civilian casulties and dislocate the war from its social consequences (ibid: 149). Such had been the onslaught of propaganda (carried by CNN and the American networks) that even in the build up to the war, reporters rarely ventured outside Washington to seek alternative interpretations about the recommendations for military action. Unable (or unwilling) to counter the growing consensus about the inevitability of conflict, even Democrats grew reticent about war and therefore added to the credibility of a military campaign (Merin 1999: 99).

This tendency to largely ignore oppositional opinion illustrates how the public's right to be informed about a range of perspectives was notably absent from coverage (Taylor 1998: 274). As with war reporting itself, which reduced the experience of military conflict to a video game of graphics supposed to demonstrate the accuracy of 'smart' bombs, or adventure film sequences where fighter planes would set off from and return to aircraft-carriers against dramatic skylines, the media's commitment to public information was illusory (ibid: 278). The impression that the war was clean and that civilians were not killed, but merely turned into 'collatoral damage' was a premise reiterated by journalists, many of whom reported the war through the CNN perspective and had become caught up with the 'logic of simulation' (Baudrillard 1995). As Patton writes about the propensity of news to construct the war through a film narrative consistent with American ideals and myth in the introduction to Baudrillard's provocative text *The Gulf War Did Not Take Place*: 'The Gulf War movie was instant history in the sense that the selected images which were broadcast worldwide provoked immediate responses and then became frozen into the accepted story of the war' (1995: 3). By using visual technology which was incorporated into military operations, the media contributed to the sensation that war was being fought efficiently, and in so doing became vital to the political deception that war lacked serious consequences. In conveying the war as a 'hyperreality', the news media constructed the spectacle of war as low in critical interrogation, but high in drama and emotion. It is not suprising given this general apathy to analysis and questioning, as Kellner notes, that 'the Bush administration and the Pentagon carried out one of the most successful public relations campaigns in the history of modern politics in its use of the media to mobilize public support for war' (2004: 136).

When troops and reporters had been deployed to the region, it was noticeable that 'no significant television debate took place over the dangerous conseqences of the massive US military response to the Iraqi invasion, or over the interests and policies that the military intervention served' (ibid: 137). Yet once the deployment had taken place, it was the media's obsession with military procedures and the drama of visual technologies which helped to ensure that the war effort was maintained. Through carefully choreographed political statements and the global coverage of CNN, which promoted an orientalist and American perspective, it was evident that the US administration had created a 'total media' environment which served to build and sustain popular support for the policy of war (ibid: 148). The net impact of this approach, as Kellner reminds us, 'was a militarization of consciousness and an environment dominated by military images and discourses' (ibid.). Although prolonged coverage of war has political implications which might destabilize policy objectives and produce long-term negative perceptions amongst voters, and although coverage of the Gulf War also raised questions indirectly about broader American policy intentions in the Middle East, it nevertheless emerged, as Kellner concludes, that 'the woefully one-sided coverage of the Gulf crisis and war by the mainstream media calls attention once again to the need for alternative media to provide essential information on complex events like the Gulf War' (ibid: 151). What the Gulf War revealed is that politics is increasingly acted out on screen and that the relationship between politics and the media is prioritized over the media's relationship with the public, which is neglected. Because of this, there exists a real need for the 'reconstruction of television and the mass media' which engages with public concern (ibid.) and which gives space and opportunity for discourses of peace as well as discourses of war. The media's enthusiasm for the war to take place and its supine reaction to opposing discourses which sought to articulate the effectiveness of sanctions against Iraq, or other alternatives to the killing, not only negate any idea of objectivity and balance in coverage, but, more seriously, have moral consequences for dealing with foreign policy crises and public understanding about how such crises might be dealt with. By removing the inconvenience of misery, violence and death from coverage, the media effectively reduced the war to Hollywood entertainment, where killing is without consequence and where the 'good guys' win. In so doing, coverage was able to supplement the myth of American righteousness and thus give further credance to the orientalist perspective of American interventionism against an uncivilized enemy.

The 'war on terror'

Although the Gulf War demonstrated a general passivity in reporting and a tendency to uncritically support US and coalition aims, it did at least offer some semblance of reasoning for Western invasion of the Gulf, which was to expel the actions of a dictatorial regime and restore some semblance of order to the region. The Iraq War of 2003 offered a different scenario, however, in that it was a war without any credible reason and no real attempt to provide a justification which would stand a modicum of critical assessment. It was a war that had been pursued as part of the Bush administration's 'war on terror' policy which had been hastily constructed after September 11 (9/11). That Iraq was seen to have no role in the attacks of September 11 was a point barely worth considering in the wave of American media coverage which carried the momentum of demands for war by the Bush administration, and in the process contributed to expectations about its inevitability.

In the immediate aftermath of the attacks on the Twin Towers in Manhatten that slaughtered thousands of people, the conclusion in political circles was that the action had been carried out by Islamic fundamentalists, and that retaliatory measures would take place against the supporters of Islamic militancy. On September 11 George Bush made it clear that those responsible were terrorists and that they would be hunted until found. As part of what became known as the Bush Doctrine, Bush was emphatic that he 'would make no distinction between the terrorists who committed those acts and those who harbor them' (Singer 2004: 144). Bush had been (and continues to be) deliberate in his many references to define those responsible as evil, but rather than using a discourse about evil which acknowledged political and social factors, Bush was intent on depicting evil as an internal condition of the individual (Collins and Glover 2002: 65–77), thereby personalizing the concept and promoting retaliatory measures through a process of individualization (Bird 2002).

In relation, the construction of the 'Islamic peril' (which became associated with the spectacle of 9/11) requires recycling the use of certain characteristics in order to help focus the demonization (Karim 2002). A tendency to refer to the threat of Muslim fundamentalism through a paradigm of 'Muslim terrorism' has enabled journalistic representations to provide dominant articulations which sustain the perception that 'Islamic violence' arises because of an attachment to Islam rather than because of efforts to provide an extremist reading of the Islamic code (ibid: 102). Without making clear distinctions between extreme and moderate elements of the Muslim experience, the news media effectively homogenized Islamic traditions and, more importantly, helped to present the Muslim tradition as a dangerous threat to Western capitalism and the 'free world'. In the immediate aftermath of September 11, media reports drew heavily from the frame of interpretation perpetrated by the Bush administration which concentrated on the search for 'Islamic terrorists' and supressed the development of 'a nuanced and contextual understanding of Islam, Muslims, or the nature of the Islamic peril' (ibid: 105). As the news media reproduced this emphasis it became increasingly evident that journalists were interested primarily in views which confirmed 'their perceptions about endemically violent Islam' (ibid.). In relation to this concern, as Karim observes 'the dominant discourse's sheer ubiquity and manoeuverability overshadow the presence of alternative perspectives' (ibid.).

Though the failure to generate a coherent and responsible articulation of the Muslim world also relates to some extent, to the failure of Muslim voices to resist and counter dominant discourse, it is noticeable, Karim argues, that the scale of simplifications in journalistic narratives has substantially overwhelmed this possibility. Islamic religious belief is routinely referred to as a form of fanaticism and the 'generalization and polarization of all Muslims as "fundamentalists" and "moderates," "traditionalists" and "modernists," "fanatics" and "secularists" serve to distort communication' (ibid: 107). Furthermore, there exists a regular attempt by reporters 'to make the Muslims who are interested in constructive dialogue with non-Muslims apologetic about their beliefs or, contrarily, disdainful about any interaction' (ibid.). This propensity to neglect appreciation for the diversity of Muslim societies supports dominant discourses which systematically relate Muslims to Islam and thereby to violent extremism which has become familiarized by its linkage with Islamic belief (ibid: 108). The humanist expressions of Muslim life hold little interest for the bulk of Western journalists who ignore the symbolic and mythical narratives which sustain spiritual aspirations and non-materialist approaches to existence (ibid: 113). At odds with the emphasis of journalistic exposition which considers the world through a rationalistic logic, it is unsurprising that reporters have been unreceptive to a world view which does not conform to such rationalistic interpretation (ibid.). However, any understanding of the apparent distance between Northern and Muslim societies, as Karim puts it, depends on 'an appreciation of the continual assault by the dominant technological discourses on the spiritual as well as the rational sensibilities of people in these societies' (ibid: 114). This inability of journalists to properly conceptualize the Muslim Other, contributes to misunderstandings which derive, first, from a bias towards dominant discourses, and second, from a tendency to deal with conflict scenarios by pursuing a course of action which appears 'to react first, using cliches and stereotypes in almost unrestrained manners, and then to reflect upon the matter' (ibid.). Initial media reactions thereby both frame subsequent enquiry and influence public understanding of the Other. The problem with this approach is that by imposing limitations on interpretations of the Other which are invariably negative, the media construct the Other as a perceived threat, thereby hindering tolerance and sustaining antagonistic relations.

Of course, this relationship which is built on the consensus/conflict foundations of 'us' and 'them', has been exploited by the Bush administration and the UK government to help exacerbate military action as a response to the 'war on terror' and the proposed elimination of the 'axis of evil', which motivates the permanently elusive terrorist threat. The epitomy of that evil took form through Osama bin Laden and Al-Qaeda who, as purveyors of radical Islam, were deemed by the US and UK (in particular) to be the 'cornerstone of terrorism', and so the hub of the 'axis of evil'. Retaliations against Islamic groups and those who came under the umbrella of 'terrorism' were constructed through the language of freedom and the dangers posed to that freedom by anti-Western factions. The apparently illogical notion of a 'war on terror', which was espoused by the Bush administration, proved useful for political action in the sense that it allowed anyone opposed to American activities against terror to be deemed sympathetic to terrorist causes and allowed a simplistic yet emotionally effective 'them' and 'us' categorization to prevail. Bush continued to emphasize the values of freedom

and democracy under threat by terrorism and succeeded in marginalizing America from much of world opinion in doing so. This helped to
excerbate feelings of fear and isolation among much of the American
public and minimized critical resistance against Bush's drive to pursue
aggressive foreign policy interventions as part of a 'first strike' strategy
(Singer 2004: 143–53). Bush's language, which concentrated on themes
of evil, freedom, justice, fundamentalism, and civilization verus barbarism (amongst others), was promoted with little critical scuntiny by
the news media, which became part of the crucial propaganda campaign
in the drive towards wars carried out in Afghanistan and Iraq (Collins
and Glover 2002).

The general picture of Al-Qaeda conveyed by the media after September 11 was one of a complex and well-organized network which
possessed considerable ability to destabilize American domestic life and
its vital interests abroad. But, as Burke points out, the idea that Al-Qaeda
is a well-organized and expansive network is somewhat misleading. He
argues that 'it is important to avoid seeing "Al-Qaeda" as a coherent and
structured terrorist organization with cells everywhere, or to imagine it
had subsumed all other groups within its networks. This would be to
profoundly misconceive its nature and the nature of modern Islamic
militancy' (2004: 6). In order to conceive its nature properly, Burke
observes, one must be aware that Al-Qaeda 'is not about being part of a
group. It is a way of thinking about the world, a way of understanding
events, of interpreting and behaving. It is the composite of the common
elements of all the various strands of modern Islamic radical thought
and currently it is the most widespread, and the fastest growing, of what
makes up the phenomenon currently, and largely erroneously, labelled
"Al-Qaeda"' (ibid: 14). Burke also contends that the personalization of
the Al-Qaeda threat though the figureheard bin Laden 'is convenient
and reassuring. It is enormously difficult to conceive of the nature of
modern radical Islamic militancy without simple ideas that make sense
of hugely varied and shifting phenomena. Blaming bin Laden implies
that his elimination will end the problem. A "gang of evildoers", to use
President George W. Bush's term, can be hunted down. Creating "Al-
Qaeda" as a traditional terrorist group constructs something that can be
defeated using traditional counter-terrorist tactics' (ibid: 15).

This simplification of Al-Qaeda therefore relates to political articulations and utterances which perpetuate simplifications in order to avoid
engaging with the complexities of radical Islam, and which have been
well served by news representations also eager to avoid grappling with
the details of Islamic militancy as Burke has done. As he concludes:

'Contemporary Islamic militancy is a diverse and complex phenomenon. To blame it all, or even a substantial portion of it, on one man is gross over-simplification. Building bin Laden up to be a global mastermind directing a well-organized and effective network of terror is counter-productive'. Since, as Burke contends, we have entered 'a "post-bin Laden" phase of Islamic militancy', perhaps we should be more sceptical of dangerous ideas circulated by politicians and large swathes of the American media that 'the 11 September attacks were a product of some kind of inevitable "clash of civilizations" between the Islamic and Judaeo-Christian worlds' (ibid: 21). In relation to this, if Islamic militancy is more about thinking and behaving, then perhaps an obvious question would be how can a counter-terrorist war be used to eliminate this thought and behaviour? Such questions have been notably absent from media analysis and representations of the war on terror. Instead, the terminology of 'Al-Qaeda' and 'Islamic terrorism', have, insists Burke, been used as 'catch-all' phrases 'in helping us to comprehend the phenomenon, and address the threat confronting us' (ibid: 22).

As a symbolic representation of the 'axis of evil', images of bin Laden have usefully served propaganda purposes of the Bush administration. However, it is also important to acknowledge that the US has used a range of interlocking communication strategies in its campaign against terrorism. Those strategies have been concerned with 'military concepts of information warfare, foreign policy concepts of public diplomacy, and approaches to media management drawn from domestic politics' (Brown 2003: 90). The first of these three 'can be seen as a systematic attempt to make sense of warfare as an exercise in information processing' (ibid.). The second 'draws together international broadcasting, cultural diplomacy, educational exchanges and overseas information activities' (ibid: 91). And the third relates to news 'spin' carried out by 'press offices that focus narrowly on short-term media coverage and a strategic communications function that develops proactive communications strategies, for instance by using the activities of leaders to communicate key messages' (ibid.). Central to the push for war has been the depiction of the enemy as criminals and it is this frame of emphasis which emerged as a paradigm by which to make sense of progress and development (ibid: 95). Representatives of Al-Qaeda contributed to this perception by sending video messages which sought to mobilize popular support for a broad uprising against America and those areas of the world which supported American interests. This response served to sharpen the apparent inevitability of conflict and also helped carry the message that the US was engaged in a war against Islam which must be resisted and met with retaliatory or instigative actions (ibid.). For Brown, the apparent intransigence displayed in media communications between the US and Al-Qaeda functioned, on the one hand, to draw the actors into a dynamic relationship with each other, whilst on the other, it helped to determine reponses and counter-response (although we should bear in mind that Al-Qaeda media communications were far outweighed by American communications) (ibid: 97). Ostensibly, news reporting served to support rather than resist the momentum of this conflict and in the process, marginalized voices of dissent about a global war against terrorism. Discourses of peace have been notably absent from reporting the war on terrorism and, indeed, the association between terrorism and war has been established as a normative framework to interpret events, with images of war being the key determinant for constructing narratives about conflict.

It is important to recognize here that although the public relations machinery of the Bush administration is both vast and instrumental in shaping the frames of reference used by news in relation to global terrorism, the representatives of this terrorism have successfully manipulated news images to promote their own viewpoints. In the absence of clearly demarcated territories and spaces where terrorists exist (meaning that global terrorism is both potentially everywhere and nowhere at the same time), it is evident that media space has become the key ground where the conflict takes place. Islamic militants have realized the importance of using the media to both affirm their role in a terrorist war and to create footage which communicates a narrative of control and continuing presence. This presence acts as a counter to American assertions that militants are being defeated and seeks to incite further Islamic support. To demonstrate this influence one need only think about video footage made by militants in Iraq of (largely) Western hostages released to Al-Jazeera television news and placed on the internet. Such videos, asserts Burke, 'are rooted in the essence of the militants' project, which is the project of all terrorists – dramatic spectacle'. Burke continues 'videos have become the most potent weapon of modern Islamic militants. They realised long ago that Al-Qaeda and its offshoots could not take on the military might of the US and its allies. But when it comes to propaganda – the key battlefield in the "war on terror" – the advantage clearly lies with the militants' ('Theatre of Terror', the *Observer* 21 November 2004). It is no longer merely images favoured by Western governments that appear on the television screen, but images crafted and controlled by Islamic militants. The message of such militancy is now able to enter the domestic setting and contribute to the communication of fear which has come to symbolize the political environment in a post-9 11 world.

The communication of threats, assurances and intentions between America and Islamic militants through the news media therefore indicates that television is the prime territory where the 'war on terror' is being waged. The expression 'war on terror' may be confused as a concept because it lacks specificity or theoretical concision, but it is precisely this absence of specificity and concision which is used by the West (meaning principally the US) to support ongoing global military actions against those who appear every now and then on our television screens. If terrorism is terrorism because of its power as a media event, then in essence the war on terror is a war of television images. It is a conflict of mediated space and a constant reworking of the threats and fears which derive from the dramatic narratives which are constructed within that space. And, significantly, the increase of communication outlets has helped to generate a greater exchange of images and messages which serve to intensify and concentrate the apparent seriousness of the situation, thus reinforcing the credibility of retaliatory response and counter-response in the process.

Al-Jazeera and propaganda

What is of particular interest in this battle of images is the role played by television networks which do not conform to conventional expressions of dominant Western political interpretation. The role of all-Arab television news network Al-Jazeera, which is based in Qatar, illustrates an important influence here. Since 2001, Al-Jazeera has regularly broadcast video recordings made by Islamic militants and Osama bin Laden which have been screened globally by other networks and absorbed into debates about the 'war on terror'. The channel has come to challenge traditional notions of impartiality (as defined by journalistic communities who represent the world by way of American or Eurocentric perspectives) by screening voices and representatives from Arab worlds which remain largely invisible to media audiences on Western networks. Because of efforts to communicate a plurality of voices and opinions, Al-Jazeera has experienced hostility from both Western and Arab governments (Maladi 2003: 150), but it is American criticism which has been most prominent against the network. The tendency to emphasize Arabic perspectives has wrought particular criticism from the United States which views Al-Jazeera as a threat to its policies and attempts to win over the Arab mind (ibid.). Amongst Western politicians, Al-Jazeera is seen as 'regularly airing bin Laden's version of the "war on terrorism"' (ibid: 158) and it is seen as a direct result of Al-Jazeera's ability to present oppositional considerations of US foreign policy that its news stations have been bombed by American forces, killing a number of its news personnel (ibid: 159).

In the wake of September 11, when the US implemented an aggressive foreign policy agenda, it became quickly obvious that for the idealism of American Republicanism to prevail, the news networks would be necessary to promote and so help legitimize The Bush Doctrine of pre-emptive action. This change, which signalled 'a fundamentally new era in international relations' (Singer 2004: 179), also required the removal of any distinction between terrorism and those who might be seen to be sympathetic to terrorism (as encapsulated in speeches by Bush which espoused a 'with us or against us' ethos). The tendency of Al-Jazeera to challenge the simplistic premise articulated by the Bush administration (and other supportive allies like the UK) raised questions about underlying reasons for Arab hostility that notably connected with the Israeli–Palestinian conflict and the Afghanistan war (ibid.). In its coverage of the Afghanistan war, for example, Al-Jazeera 'presented live coverage of the aftermath of American air strikes and emphasized civilian casualties and reactions to the war' which resonated with Arab audiences and raised serious concerns about American interventionism (Seib 2004: 107). On a regular basis, Al-Jazerra has been viewed by US diplomats as promoting an 'anti-American bias' and deliberately inciting Arab hostility because of this approach (ibid: 108). In contrast to the Gulf War of 1991, which was covered by the heavily pro-American bias of networks such as CNN, the Iraq War of 2003, saw 'the establishment of Arab media as a viable alternative to Western news organizations and its role in attracting global recognition of Arab media voices' (ibid: 110). Not surprisingly, because of this difference, 'CNN and Al-Jazeera often presented conflicting reports, particularly about the success of the coalition forces and the impact of fighting on Iraqi civilians' (ibid: 119), which impacted on the apparent homogeneity of much Western television news coverage and exposed the absence of objectivity in reports. It is because of this impact that coverage produced by Al-Jazeera is seen by some to 'have helped create an urgent necessity for a meaningful analysis and re-evalution of war coverage to include an assessment of contextual objectivity as a barometer for fairness and balance in reporting around the world' (Iskandar and el-Nawawy 2004: 332).

Al-Jazeera's identification with the plight of Palestinians has raised questions about its ability to mobilise Arab opinion against Israel and the US (el-Nawawy and Iskandar 2003) and has proved to be a point of concern regarding bias and balance. However, such criticisms tend to ignore how the language and emphasis of Al-Jazeera's reporting is deeply constitutive of Arab consciousness and the Arab condition (ibid: 53–4), as well as overlooking how this association plays as an antagonism to the conventional emphasis of Western news coverage. Not surprisingly, Al-Jazeera's connection with Arab perspectives and its use as an outlet for videos released by Islamic militants, means that the channel is sometimes viewed as part of the West/anti-West duality which has come to symbolize discourses based along civilization versus barbarism lines. In the struggle to win a war of ethics and values (Singer 2004), perhaps it is somewhat expected that Al-Jazeera's receptiveness to critical Arab opinion and Islamic militancy has led it to be mistakingly interpreted, in the eyes of the US, as 'the enemy itself or at least a conspirator' (ibid: 189). However, regardless of this perception, it is now apparent that Al-Jazeera plays a prominent role in informing Arab opinion and has become a key channel for American diplomats to appear on when trying to impact on that opinion (ibid: 199). Moreover, the Bush administration inspects reports from the channel for signs or clues of secret messages from bin Laden (Miles 2005: 181).

Al-Jazeera's reporting in the Iraq War of 2003, accused by many of anti-American bias, showed images of civilian casualties and atrocities which were notable by their absence on CNN and its internet service was the most accessed for the duration of the war (ibid: 203). Whilst recognizing the importance of the network to reach Arab audiences, the Bush administration has also been subject to critical reporting which has made it more difficult to justify policies and actions to Arab audiences. In turn, this makes it harder to achieve 'the strategic objective of US communication', which 'was to neutralise international and especially Arab Muslim public opinion' in pursuit of its 'war on terror' campaign (O'Shaughnessy 2004: 195).

The use of video footage made by Osama bin Laden and Islamic militants and screened by Al-Jazeera (before being used globally by other networks) has been a potent force of communication in the war of images. The communications, which are placed to affect 'two targets of persuasion, the international court of Islam and specfically Arab opinion and the United States and its allies' (ibid: 2001), outline the features of an American enemy which is dehumanized (much like American messages dehumanize Islamic militants), and position that enemy as a major threat to sacred values. This dynamic of good and bad, the pure and the contaminated (ibid.), is, of course, systematically connected to opponents who promote similar viewpoints and use the polarity of differences to demarcate values of right and wrong. But, the images also symbolically communicate the personality of leadership and help to construct war as an 'asymmetic' process 'fought on an imaginary as well as military plane' (ibid: 9). Moreover, as is the case in war propaganda generally, the exchange of images which take place between the West and Arab/Muslim communities is concerned with impacting on the psychology of audiences in ways which, for both parties, might help induce a winning end to conflict. As O'Shaughnessy writes on this matter: 'War is communication. The aim is seldom the complete physical extermination of the enemy but to persuade them to surrender: the object of war is therefore the enemy's morale' (ibid: 35). Response and counter-response are therefore confined to the confrontational limits imposed by the intransigence of personalities fearful of offering any sign which may be read as moving away from a desire to defeat opponents. Though these communications strive to create fear and tensions in order to unify public support, they are simplistically repetitive and it is this repetition which erodes the possibility for thinking outside the narrow limits needed to keep debate under control. The power of such communications to work effectvely on an imaginary level depends on restricting the imaginations of audiences by reinforcing myths through the repetition and non-deviation of messages. At its most effective this process can convince audiences to believe in things that do not exist, as in the American invasion of Iraq in 2003 when the public were encouraged (along with other politicians) to believe in a threat without any supportive evidence to justify this threat.

With regard to the propaganda campaign carried out by the Bush administration, the news media were crucial in the development of what O'Shaughnessy calls 'emotional proof' as a means for legitimizing invasion. Much of the American media coverage in the build up to the Iraq War, proved vital for allowing emotional proof to be established as a credible position in relation to invasion. The concentrated campaign carried out by the Bush administration provides us with a good example of how idealism was used and reinforced by the news media to generate emotional proof, which as O'Shaughnessy defines it: 'is where we feel intuitively that there is a causal connection which is highly significant to the creation of some event and yet which cannot easily be pinned down, but where we believe this thing to be true because we have a deep emotional need for it to be true' (ibid: 224). It was this emotional proof which enabled the Bush administration to insist that Saddam Hussein was linked to Al-Qaeda and that Iraq possessed weapons of mass destruction. Although both these claims were false, they provided the grounds for debate and momentum which led to war and were reinforced by media coverage which absorbed the emotional proof approach and accepted it as a basis for military action.

The Iraq War, 2003

The advocation of war by the US – in the absence of any evidence which might provide a justifiable case for military intervention – required what Weber has called 'the circulation of non-knowledge' (2003) in order to acquire public support. Analysis of non-knowldege in this context is concerned with what the American public were not told about the 'war on terrorism' and Weber's interpretation of how non-knowledge became circulated is drawn from examination of 'the incessant, conscious exchange of some narratives, images, and ideas so that others remain unconscious' (ibid: 190). This process, she notes, is attained 'not by ignoring news stories but representing them in such a way that their exclusive focus on one aspect of the story makes it possible to neglect other, potentially more important aspects of the same story' (ibid.). For Weber, CNN played a particularly important function in this process and contributed to public ignorance about the Bush administration's obsessions over war through identifying with Hollywood narratives which drew from previous attacks on America from Pearl Harbor on. In response to such attacks, the interpretive framework for understanding American action would invariably centre on 'heroizing the global mission of America as the benevolent leader of the "free world", loved and admired within and beyond its shores' (ibid: 192). Furthermore, continues Weber, this narrative 'taps into America's pre-Vietnam belief that its history is the history of progress' (ibid.) and informs subsequent responses to future acts. It is the historical memory of events such as Pearl Harbor and how that event has been constructed through the cinematic tradition of action films which also produces a reference point by which to make sense of expected responses to other attacks on America. In relation to this, the articulation of myths and projected notions of the 'American way' (impressed continuously through government speeches about values) are used as determinants for marking out parameters of debate and courses of action. What Weber's argument points towards here is not therefore the news media's detachment from political power in the event of disaster, but rather its attachment and identification with historical and cultural values which surface in defence to the threat which has occurred. Morever, if the

Hollywood tradition becomes the context for introducing those values, then it is plainly evident that force rather than peaceful dialogue is emphasized not only as the *preferable* course of action, but the *only* course of action.

Once September 11 had happened, the question was not whether there would be retaliation, but the scale of it. It was this expectation which significantly influenced news coverage to drive the retaliatory debate forward and create what came to be the inevitability of conflict. The absence of much of the US media from the conflict in Afghanistan was significantly reversed with Iraq. Here the networks would provide saturation coverage of the incursion and journalists were embedded into military units so that journalistic access and output could be carefully monitored and audiences would be provided with the military per- spective. Importantly, real-time coverage within this context obstructed the possibility of objective analysis and provided military leaders with the means to observe and control military moves as the war progressed. Once this process was underway, voices advocating peace were reduced to sloganizing protests and became increasingly absent from reports as time went on. Instead, the focus was necessarily oriented towards Saddam Hussein and his demonization. The formation of rhetoric and symbolism were crucial with regard to this representation, but we should also remember that the American propaganda effort depended on a number of interrelated processes. Those processes included, 'the continuing part played by the rhetoric of enmity, the role of fantasy and willed belief in propaganda, the significance and completeness of the coherent organising/integrating perspective, the on-going role of myth (not least how much can be fabricated on a conspiracy of false beliefs), the concept of emotional proof, the problem of imagistic control, and propaganda as the search for retrospective justification' (O'Shaughnessy 2004: 210).

In Qatar, a stage-set headquarters was set up – under the design of a Hollywood art director who had also worked with illusionist David Blaine – which would accommodate journalists and provide them with representations of conflict through the wizardry of advanced techno- logical communications (ibid: 214–15). This carefully controlled and choreographed environment produced round-the-clock information which effectively minimized any oppositional reports emerging and was used to restrict the scope for journalistic interpretations which departed from military lines. By filling airtime with propaganda, the Bush admin- istration and the military succeeded in keeping Iraqi reports from infiltrating coverage and thus helped to maintain the illusion that the war was progressing in much the same way as a Hollywood cinematic experience, with America fulfilling its mythic role as a civilizing force bringing freedom to those subject to barbarism.

Effectively the bulk of news coverage failed in its responsibility to inform the public about the issues which underpinned the drive to war. Although in comparison to the American media (which ostensibly promoted right-wing agendas), British news coverage was more critical about the march towards war, even here the broad thrust of coverage was sympathetic to the Blair government's pro-war position (Lewis and Brookes 2004). Notably, this sympathy was created by 'the focus on the progress of war to the exclusion of other issues, the tendency to portray the Iraqi people as liberated rather than invaded, the failure to question the claim that Iraq possessed WMD [weapons of mass destruction], and the focus on the brutality or decadence of the regime without putting this evidence in a broader historical and geopolitical context' (ibid: 298). The decision to embed reporters with military units and provide them with expansive access to the fighting was part of a strategy to fill airtime with coverage about the progress of US and British forces (America and Britain forming the majority of the 'coalition of the willing') in order to avoid the possibility of reporters filing reports from other, potentially more critical sources. Moreover, as Lewis and Brookes observe, 'by giving broadcasters access to highly newsworthy action footage from the frontline, they were encouraging a focus on the actions of US and British troops, who would be seen fighting a short and successful war. The story was thus all about winning and losing, rather than a consideration of the context in which the war was fought' (ibid: 299). This militarization of journalism signalled a transformation from the kind of reporting which took place during the Vietnam War. Then the relationship between journalists and the military was considered to be adversarial (Reese 2004: 250). With Iraq, the 'national solidarity' that had been forged by September 11 was carried into the war, used to help silence voices of resistance, and supported efforts to frame news 'within military logic' (ibid: 259). The strategy of embedding journalists therefore 'created a strong dependency relationship between journalists and their units' (ibid: 261), which meant that the production and distribution of information reinforced rather than challenged the military policies of the Bush administration. This emphasis was further assisted by the lack of any embedded reporters providing reports from the Iraqi perspective (Alex Thomson, 'To get the whole picture we need embeds on both sides', the *Guardian*, November 22 2004) and so benefited from the absence of alternative positions which deviated from the broad thrust of US military policy.

If the demands of speed in reporting 'keeps coverage shallow' and allows 'quasi-political negativity' to produce interpretive frames (Seib 2004: 64), then clearly it becomes problematic to ascertain what the real outcomes of conflict are or what they mean. By producing reports which sanitize the Iraq conflict, the news media effectively provide a narrative of combat which avoids rather than confronts the true hostilities of war, and in so doing also help to marginalize discourses which object to a war which appears to be progressing 'cleanly' and without horrific con-sequences. In a sense, the Iraq War has been covered more as an adven-ture story than an invasion of doubtful legality for reasons which seem to lack substance (particularly by the US media), and indicates standards of reporting which adhere to the notion of 'balance' (which has been shaped through reference to the right-wing consensus) in order to avoid exposure of the false claims which were used to perpetuate the momen-tum of conflict and which have become the foundation on which the 'war on terror' has been built (David Edwards and David Cromwell, 'Balance in the service of falsehood', the *Guardian*, December 15 2004).

The media's inability to critically evaluate the substance of claims made by the Bush administration about Iraq's supposed role within the 'war on terror', reflects a growing inability to distinguish between reality and fiction. This obviously has highly useful implications for the Bush Doctine of pre-emptive action where those deemed to be enemies can appear and disappear with convenient regularity, and where enemies are no longer identifiable by their geographical position, but by an ephemeral presence which shapes media interest. But, within this new environment, as Jonathan Raban observes (2005), the demarcations between war and peace become confused, with one vanishing into the other and at the same time blurring responsibilities for how to deal with potential threats and crises. This predicament of being unsure whether the climate is one of peace or war derives from thinking about oppo-nents who emerge and disappear, in Dick Cheney's analogy, from the 'arena of shadows' (ibid.). The absence of an enemy in this climate is therefore as worrying as the emergence of an enemy and reflects the need to maintain constant fear as a device for helping to legitimate response and action. But, as Raban contends, this attitude 'has been thickened by the political and journalistic habit of using speculative – often wildy speculative – conjunctions' to connect people to organiza-tions which are seen to be bent on the destruction ot America and its civilians (ibid: 23). Raban is astute to note that the list of demands made by militants such as bin Laden relate not to the destruction of America, but changes in its foreign policy (ibid: 22), and that somehow this important point has escaped the attention of the dominant right-wing media who prefer to perpetuate the destruction myth, and by association the simplistic (as well as inaccurate) civilization versus barbarism thesis.

New media

Although it appears that the news media is generally unwilling to examine the consequences of this development, and indeed tends to reiterate the idealism which has come to reflect dominant political thinking on the global terror debate, it is also important to acknowledge the emergent power and influence of the Internet as a communicative source within this climate. Significantly, the Internet, unlike television, refutes passivity and demands engagement by the user. In so doing it releases possibilities for active citizenship which are routinely denied by much of the mainstream media. Moreover, the Internet in relation to Iraq allowed users to criticize and evaluate events and occurrences which were shown on television, bringing into question the immediate (rather than co-ordinated) experience of reported acts (Allan 2004: 349). The development and use of weblogs, or blogs, which as Allan notes 'may be characterized as diaries or journals written by individuals with net access who are in possession of the necessary software publishing tools to establish an online presence' (ibid: 357), have functioned as 'unofficial' news sources and allowed interpretations and articulations to emerge which have transgressed 'the border between "professional" and "amateur" reporting' (ibid.). As Allan also observes, the production and distribution of what he calls 'personal journalism' provided outlets for observations and accounts of the conflict in Iraq which countered emphasis of mainstream reporting and offered a space in which alternative perspectives could be formed, pursued and elaborated. As a resistance to the obvious pro-war bias of the right-wing media and its acquiescence to the policies of the Bush administration, internet bloggers were able to communicate viewpoints and arguments which 'were able to show, with little difficulty, how voices of dissent were being routinely marginalized, when they were even acknowledged at all' (ibid: 358). Serving to create a space for alternative discourse to circulate and challenge the interpretations of the mainstream media, the internet posed a significant resistance to the narrow dimensions of coverage, and was released from broader institutional constraints and the interests of dominant political power (ibid.). This tendency for new media to allow users to 'connect with distant voices otherwise being marginalized, if not silenced altogether' (ibid: 361) exposes the news media's tendency to exclude those arguments which do not complement the dramatic thrust of events as they exist on the ground. A tendency, which, because of the news media's absorption into the process of conflict and the politics which shape it, appears unable to assess alternatives which operate outside of those parameters. Voices of peace and resistance to the real-time 'noise' communicated by much mainstream reporting indicate only too well an abdication of journalistic responsibility in the wake of war, and raise serious questions about news and the public sphere.

One of the more significant advantages of new media therefore relates to its potential for 'the collective interrogation of mainstream media', and the ability to facilitate and 'develop a collective and social perspective on events of the day' (Williams 2003: 187). As a means for expansive communication, it is evident that forums and chatrooms also present a resistance to the conventions and dominant frames of mainstream media reporting (ibid: 188). And, while it cannot be claimed that new media is as influential on public opinion as television, it is evident that television also draws from the Internet and that it is a growing source of influence in the media environment. In the absence of diverse information within the mainstream media, new media provides a space that 'opens up the possibilities for critical discourse', which in the process challenges the narrow interests of elite political discourse that the news media draw from and perpetuate (ibid: 188). Used as a means of communication in the Balkan wars, the Internet has steadily grown as a news medium and became an important source of information in the wake of September 11 (Seib 2004: 89). Its role as an alternative communication source indicates its capability to weaken government propaganda and to incite involvement in political debate (ibid: 95). Islamic militants have clearly recognized the propaganda value of using the Internet to influence news agendas whilst retaining their invisibility in the physical world, and communicative exchanges in the 'war of terror' occur with increasing frequency in the 'cyber territories' of new media. The possibilites of new media thus present challenges to the conventions of mainstream news reporting, and although we should be careful not to overstate the influence and significance of such technology, perhaps we should at least recognize that it signals a real challenge to the news media's close relationship with political power (rather than the public) and, as such, indicates potential for a reinvigoration of the public sphere. New media, in other words, offers users the possibility of accessing alternative discourses which are ignored by much mainstream coverage, and can give attention to ideas and responses about peace that are notably absent in comparison to news reports obsessed with the drama and politics of war.

Conclusion

The Gulf War of 1990 and the Iraq War of 2003 both indicate the media's role as a participant in, rather than observer of, conflict. However, reporting of the Iraq War of 2003 demonstrates an intensification of this role and must be considered in relation to debates which concentrated on the 'war on terror' and viewed pre-emptive conflict as a legitimate strategy of response to those deemed to be terrorists (or supporters of terrorism) after September 11. The American media's inability to expose clear falsifications about Iraq's connection to the actions of September 11 highlight not only a lack of interest in viewpoints and arguments which challenged the false claims, but gave credence to elite assertions that Iraq was affiliated to Al-Qaeda and possessed weapons of mass destruction. Media support for these arguments, which was reinforced by negligible interest in counter-arguments, reveals a clear abdication of journalistic responsibility to hold political leaders to account and present alternative discourses in measure to government and official opinion. The news media both in America and the UK (but especially America) has served to support government accusations about an Islamic threat, but given next to no attention to 'voices of reason' with the Islamic communities. Indeed, when representatives for Islam have appeared, the overriding emphasis has been for reports to present them in defensive positions, or apologists for militant Islamic movements.

A personalization of the 'enemy' has been particularly emphasized by news coverage and has contributed to a lack of discussion about political, social and historical reasons for militancy and resistance. Most notably, news coverage has failed to offer the public an informative picture of the 'Other', instead chosing to draw from and, indeed, support distortions provided by the Bush administration (and its supporters) and the actions of an aggressive foreign policy agenda. Simplistic portrayals of those seen to be players within the 'axis of evil' have amplified the emotive expectations of audiences and obstructed rather than generated a broad appreciation for the complex range of factors which underpin the conflict between the West and ' global terrorism'.

News outlets which challenge this representation, such as Al-Jazeera, have been viewed (as well as used) by US officials as an extension of Islamic militant ideology and obstructive to American aims. The militarization of news reporting provided a very one-sided account of the conflict in Iraq and by focusing primarily on the actions of the military campaign, remained blind to questions about its legitimacy. By ignoring the atrocities of war and the suffering of Iraqi civilians, television news helped to create the impression that the war was progressing cleanly and in keeping with the 'civilized values' which provided the basis for intervention. Voices of peace were noticeable by their absence as the momentum of the war provided the narrative for reporting developments.

Significantly, the 'war on terror' is a media war. It is a war of imaginations, images and words. The appearance and disapperance of terrorists and militants takes place within the media space and, indeed, terrorism is foremost a communicative act which takes place through the publicity of news reports; it is a spectacle. But, what is less considered is the problem of how a media war can become a media peace. If the media is the arena of conflict, then isn't it also by association the arena for peace and, indeed, cannot a media war, only be ended through a media peace? Furthermore, if this is a media war, then where is the possibility for a media peace? It is the problem of how the media can play a more constructive role in conflict and how they might adopt a peace-oriented approach to reporting (along with a conflict-oriented approach to reporting) to which we now turn.

10
Peace Journalism

Journalism and peace dialogue

Although there has been much attention given to the media's relationship with conflict, it is noticeable that this attention has not generated a comparable level of concern about the media's relationship with peace. However, consideration of this interaction has taken shape through a small, but significant body of work which looks at how a peace-oriented journalism might develop and what it might bring to public understanding in terms of conflict causes, varying approaches to conflict interpretation, and the articulation of a dialogue which proposes constructive solutions to division. One of the earlier studies which recognizes the shortcomings of journalism in this regard is the UNESCO-funded MacBride Report *Many Voices, One World*, which set out to highlight inequalities in the 'new information and communication order' (1984: 18): The pupose of the study was to advocate recommendations for a communications order which would be adaptive and reflexive in order to meet a need for 'more justice, more equity, more reciprocity in information exchange, less dependence in communication flows, less downward diffusion of messages, more self-reliance and cultural identity, more benefits for all mankind' (ibid.). Acknowledging the legacy of inequalities in communicative exchanges and the changing communications environment, the Report also sought to raise awareness about the media's role in making issues of common concern known and producing public action against governments in order to elicit peace initiatives. The emphasis towards peace is clear in the Report, which argues that although disturbing or unpleasant events and facts must be made known, so should positions which offer the 'reminder that peaceful solutions exist' (ibid: 140). Morever, the thrust is not just towards public knowledge which provides awareness, but knowledge which translates into action against governments who aim to exaggerate dangers in order to try and legitimize war and conflict. The responsibilty of the media, the Report asserts, is to try and mobilize public opinion against those who operate against the interests of peace, which is of universal importance and a condition necessary for positive human expression (ibid: 141). Journalism, it suggests, should not contribute to fears which are 'heightened by intolerance, chauvinism and a failure to understand other points of view. Those with responsibility in the media should remember that, beyond national interests, there is the supreme interest of humanity in peace' (ibid.).

Highlighting the global inequalites which exist and which are reflected by access to dominant communication outlets, *Many Voices, One World* attempts to provide a case for an expansive and inclusive communications policy which allows for a more equitable exchange of viewpoints and discourses, and which takes into account the complexity and range of human experiences in relation to events. In a real sense, the Report strives to articulate a need for democratic participation in the media, where public opinion can be mobilized to impact on political life and where the cultural and social concerns of individuals are recognized alongside the collective concerns of communities and nations (ibid: 192). The development of such a policy depends on extensive consultations between a range of social, economic and cultural groups in order to bring about an integrative process designed to help foster democratic relations both nationally and internationally (ibid: 193). Promoting this initiative globally, the aim is to strengthen democractic participation, produce greater 'independence and self-reliance amongst nations' which will assist the realization of individual expression, the development of democratic organization, and help to reconcile communication inequalities. Central to the goal of greater global communications equality (and by extension political equality) is the need for news to adjust its approach to conflicts by moving away from the exclusive frameworks of interpretation that are routinely used to explain problems far away, and which serve to maintain the communications inequality that obstructs rather than assists the potential for public understanding. As the Report concludes:

> Conventional standards of news selection and reporting, and many accepted news values, need to be reassessed if readers and listeners around the world are to receive a more faithful and comprehensive account of events, movements and trends in both developing and

developed countries. The inescapable need to interpret unfamiliar situations in terms that will be understood by a distant audience should not blind reporters or editors to the hazards of narrow ethnocentric reporting . . . Higher professsional standards are needed for journalists to be able to illuminate the diverse cultures and beliefs of the modern world, without their presuming to judge the ultimate validity of any foreign nation's experience and traditions.

(ibid: 211–12)

The rather ambitious recommendations of The MacBride Report, which appears to be constructed with aims of political equality in mind (albeit expressed through the notion of equality in communications), brings to light important questions about the media's inability to act receptively in relation to a diversity of viewpoints, which is taken and developed more systematically into a framework of proposals by Galtung and Vincent in their proposals for how a peace-oriented media might be developed. The authors contend:

1 '[W]henever there is a conflict, one of the basic tasks, indeed duties, of the media is to give a voice to both or all parties in the conflict' (1995: 126).
2 '[T]he media should try to make explicit some theories, the intellectual frame of reference, and the "discourse" or "paradigm" within which a conflict is to be understood' (ibid: 129).
3 Media ownership should not matter and 'the two foregoing demands should also be directed to media that are owned by big governmental or corporate interests' (ibid.).
4 '[M]edia should be less the victim of the four key tendencies in news reporting; over-emphasis on elite countries, over-emphasis on elite persons, over-emphasis on personalization and over-emphasis on negative events' (ibid: 132).
5 '[T]he media should pay attention to enhancing the retention elements of news reporting, and not talk down to its audience and readers' (ibid: 134).
6 The media should strive to understand the realities of armed conflict and try to offer space which minimizes the 'tendency to seek recourse to armament' when conflicts are unsolved (ibid: 136).
7 '[T]he media should pay more attention to the inner dynamism of the arms race and armed conflicts' (ibid: 137).
8 '[W]hen it comes to disarmament in general, disarmament negotiations and conferences in particular, and summit meetings even

more particularly, media should pay more attention to their own weaknesses when reporting such phenomena' (ibid: 138).

9 The media should 'look at the North–South conflict formations relating peace and war to development and not only to the problems of peace and war amongst industrialized countries' (ibid: 139).

10 The media should seek 'to portray more clearly the benefits of peace' (ibid: 140).

The overarching theme of these proposals, it seems, is to develop collective public conscience and awareness through diversity of opinion and it is this diversity which is emphasized as key for facilitating peace. The prospect of the media being used to shape a 'peace consciousness' rather than a 'war consciousness' is created precisely because the parameters for contestation are expanded beyond the narrow intransigence of two oppositional forces which tend to inform news discourse. As intimated earlier, the potential for peace is heightened not by the eradication of conflict, but its development into a broader arena of contestable positions which make recourse to a single line of conflictive action less likely. By opening discussion to a full and diverse range of communicative participants, it could be argued that war becomes harder to achieve and this is so because a range of opinions act to dilute or confront the premise for war which is so often unchallenged within the frames of conventional media reporting. Here the tendency is for two dominant oppositional voices to determine the likelihood of armed confrontation, which itself is made more likely by the apparent intractability of the two positions. By allowing more viewpoints to enter debate, the potential for looking at conflict by way of constructive counter-argument is augmented and with that augmentation, the legitimacy of claims for conflict is brought into question, exposing possible motives for war as unimaginative and largely driven by specific national interests rather than moral reasons. Currently, the mainstream news media rely on the exaggeration of conflict by focusing on two antagonistic forces and contributing to zero-sum politics. By helping to lock two positions into a simplistic game where each is mindful of conceding to the other and each is working to defeat the other, it is evident that scope for facilitating dialogue which moves away from the fixations of the win–lose scenario is minimal. To address this problem, a marked shift is required from the exclusive paradigm provided by news, to an inclusive paradigm where contestations over a single line of communication give way to collective contestations and a multi-layered dynamic of communication. If the media is to stress peace initiatives, then it must also, as Galtung and Vincent note, recognize its own bias and move to report all sides, which means being receptive to 'non-elite' as well as dominant sources (ibid: 199). In turn, peace groups which may be hostile to the news media and see it as an 'obstacle to the creation of a peace culture' (Bruck and Roach 1993: 88) must work to make their message more readily available, and at a wider social level non-elite sources must seek to develop 'active participation from civil society' in order to enable alternative discourse to flourish and promote public activism (ibid: 94).

The ideas proposed by Galtung and Vincent, in order to suceed, depend on the media recognizing its shortcomings in the way it deals with confrontation, and working more specifically as a third party which seeks to constructively help in the resolution of conflict. To operate in this way, as Bote argues, the news media must also play an educative role, where, by giving voice to all parties, each becomes more informed about the 'other's point of view; stereotypes are challenged; and initial perceptions can be re-evaluated and clarified' (1996: 7). This change requires a 'reframing' of issues and debates which is 'aimed at helping disputants identify the shared problems that are causing the conflict'. The reporter's position of being able to facilitate a series of exchanges that may be unlikely in the real world indicates the potential for reporters to 'spot a problem-solving option or basis for agreement that the parties have not considered' and, in turn, 'to put these ideas into circulation' (ibid: 7). By functioning as a non-partisan third party along with other conflict resolvers, Bote argues that the media's role should be to focus on 'the possibilities of conflict escalation, de-escalation, or settlement' and to monitor 'adherence to or breaches of agreement' (ibid: 8).

Attempting to establish what constitutes a positive media role in this context, Bote asserts that good reporting 'should look beyond stated positions toward the interests and needs of the parties' and that by bringing to light historical and social perceptions about conflict, journalists can help 'call attention to dangers of escalation and to opportunities for settlement that the parties may not have recognized (ibid.). Furthermore, they can become part of an 'early warning system' that identifies the underground tremors of impending conflict, thus permitting earlier responses to it'. It is only 'on the basis of thorough and sensitive analysis' (ibid.) that parties can determine agreement and Bote would like to see the media moving to provide such analysis. Bote's emphasis on an inclusive approach to what he calls 'conflict resolvers' is also shared by Adam, who similarly argues for a more expansive consideration of viewpoints by the media. In the case of war situations, Adam believes that the target audience (which has involvement in the consequences of conflict) itself should become involved in news coverage, allowing issues of social concern to be more widely discussed and enabling public opinion to become absorbed 'in the planning and execution of the media campaign' which promotes a participatory approach (1997: 50).

Robert Manoff's work, which is concerned with the problem of how the media could prevent and moderate conflict, provides a list of recommendations which are systematic in orientation and which relate more specfically to creating a journalistic paradigm which creates what he calls 'social invention'. This paradigm is based on the attempt to produce a communications dynamic 'in which the spontaneous, largely uncoordinated, but not random activities of diverse actors could create new institutions and behaviours', thereby cultivating an approach to conflict which draws from and serves social interests rather than political interests (1997: 27). Manoff draws up a 24-point plan to achieve this process which builds extensively upon similar recommendations made by Galtung and Vincent. Interestingly, for Manoff the news media should not operate as independent observers of conflict, but should actively seek to prevent it. Journalists, in other words, should work to try and stop conflicts (the distinction between war and conflict is not elaborated, but it appears that Manoff is referring ostensibly to developing war situations) rather than help protagonists exacerbate the tensions that make the path to conflict more likely. The media, he argues should give attention to conflict in ways which 'bring pressure on the parties to resolve it or on the international community to intervene' (ibid: 26). To assist prevention, Manoff wants the media to help 'establish the transparency of one conflict party to another', and 'engage in confidence-building measures'. In order to fulfil this aim, it is important not only to disclose the interests of parties to each other, but also, as Manoff recognizes, to 'prevent the circulation of incendiary rumours and counteract them when they surface' (ibid.).

The emphasis on prevention as a core value of the paradigm is essential to the facilitation of conflict resolution and provides the framework within which constructive dialogue and discourse take shape. Working to address and clarify the needs of the parties in conflict is connected to framing 'the issues involved in conflict in such a way that they become more susceptible to management' and developing common ground which pulls parties together. Further recommendations such as trying to 'enable the parties to formulate and articulate proposed solutions by serving as a non-antagonistic interlocutor', or helping to 'participate in the process of healing, reconciliation and social reconstruction following conflicts', infer a strong moral imperative to try and level power between parties rather than simply magnify power struggles by promoting images of success and loss. For Manoff, the media should work to 'encourage a balance of power among unequal parties where appropriate, or, where the claims of parties are not equally just, strengthen the hand of the party with the more compelling moral claim' (ibid: 27). Noticeably, these recommendations are not merely concerned with the news media developing a greater receptiveness to voices that challenge dominant articulations, they are about developing an approach to reporting that prioritizes the value of peace rather than war. As such, Manoff attempts to define an interpretive context framed with a strong moral dimension in mind, which stands in contrast to the zero-sum scenarios that news tends to favour and exacerbate in the coverage of conflict.

On the face of it, the argument posed by Manoff that news attention should be concerned with 'convincing moral claims', rather than the conflicts between the most politically powerful protagonists is problematic. Yet it is evident that the recommendations he provides are deduced from a moral position. This position is based on the thesis that it is better to prevent conflict than to create it (again bearing in mind when Manoff talks about conflict, he is referring primarily to war). The idea that the journalist should actively strive to try and bring about the prevention of conflict also immediately counters the expectation that he or she should not seek to become a political protagonist. Though, as the case studies in this book demonstrate, journalism is actively political and integral to the conduct and development of political life, the criticism that journalism should do what it already does but differently still manages to raise concerns about a slippage of standards and the erosion of objectivity. As a journalist himself, Manoff is quick to dismiss the idea that journalism can report the truth, but concedes that the objectivity debate is useful to determine the parameters of journalistic practice. However, even here, he acknowledges how it is 'an article of faith for those who practice objectivity that they can neither intervene in events they are covering nor take responsibility for the consequences of their decision to abstain from doing so' (1998: 3). To deny the need to try and help peace is, he suggests, an abdication of one's human responsibilities, aside from what it means in journalistic terms. Manoff is clearly right when he points us towards the realization that a journalist cannot extricate him/herself from the social consequences of what is produced, or that journalism is a social practice. To not actively try and bring about peace, or to not try and prevent war, raises important moral questions about journalism which the objectivity debate does not answer. But by preferring not to work to create peace, news is in fact choosing to assist the case for war and in doing so not only undermines the objectivity goal, but does so with moral consequences which are far worse than undermining objectivity by attempting to prevent conflict.

Admittedly, there are a number of issues entwined in this argument which are complex and really need to be examined on a case-by-case basis in relation to specific conflicts. But the idea of striving to prevent or moderate conflict does not contradict my earlier contention that more conflict rather than less is called for in reporting in order to achieve this. Of course, there is another problem here, however, and it is this: if the news media actively seeks to prevent conflict, then presumably they also come into difficulty with the objectivity debate by removing discourse which seeks to create conflict. As a response to this, one might argue that both types of discourse are needed because the more desirable goal of peace will gain greater legitimacy against the evident limitations and shortcomings of confrontational discourse. To put it another way, peace discourse needs conflict discourse in order to expose conflict discourse as unreasonable, unimaginative and ultimately destructive. By developing a greater receptiveness to alternative voices which seek to articulate the possibilities for peace, there is a stronger possibility that voices which promote conflict will be represented as extreme rather than moderate, as they may appear if unchallenged. Furthermore, if the media were to give more attention to the 'grey discourse' which operates in between extreme positions, they would increase the chances of the grey discourse acting as a bridge between extremes, and so offer improved potential to help overcome problems by way of a connectiveness which operates when extreme positions are pulled closer to constructive debate and interaction.

Obviously, such a change demands a reversal in the conventional priorities of news construction and the dominance of key values. If the media are to become receptive to the quest for peace, then they need to emphasize the grey discourse over the black and white. They need to emphasize complexity over simplicity, diversity over division, the undramatic over the dramatic and the political power of ideas over the ideas of political power. They need, to put it another way, to exchange the politics of exclusivity for the politics of inclusivity and, when dealing with war or the confrontations which favour war, look at discourses which talk about forgiveness, empathy and justice as well as those voices which call for revenge, retribution and retaliation. With 24-hour rolling news, there appears to be no real basis to arguments which stress there is not time for news to do this. Indeed, if news cannot possibly have more time than it already does, then time cannot be the issue.

Paradigm shift

What is required is a shift in the practice of journalism which, according to Manoff, operates at two intersecting levels: which he labels *operational and paradigmatic*. At the operational level, Manoff argues that 'we need to consider what can be done to prevent and resolve conflict through activities consistent with existing journalistic practices', whilst at the paradigmatic level, there is a need 'to conceive of media-based preventive actions that are possible under current professional paradigms' and which 'are not fundamentally at odds with the profession as it is currently understood' (ibid: 5). The development of a paradigmatic approach to bring about a change in reporting must be made outside of the journalistic field, and operational change is seen to result from a reorientation to conflict because of debates which shape the paradigm shift. As journalism is protective of the conventions it adopts and a change to conflict prevention interferes with existing ideas of professionalism, so the responsibilities of the profession must be brought outside of the industry into the public domain if change is to occur. As Manoff notes, 'instead of starting with the media's understanding of their own possibilities, as determined by current paradigms', there should be a process of debate about change which is driven by, and based on, the work of conflict resolution theory and 'the work of negotiators, diplomats, "track two" practitioners and protagonists who have participated in the resolution of conflict or who have studied the process'. It is this shift of emphasis, contends Manoff, which then begins to address 'the question of what conflict prevention and management require of the media' (ibid: 6) and which moves discussion of key issues and themes outside the narrow limits of professionalism and the insular discussion of how such change would impact on and interfere with journalistic standards. The transformation which Manoff proposes is therefore premised on the question of what society wants from the media rather than what it is expected to accept. And it is clear that if the news media are to help bring parties to the table, promote active listening, work to move parties off positions towards interests, help to dispel misperceptions and stereotypes, question assumptions, facilitate a joint problem-solving agenda and act to deconstruct divisive language (Baumann and Siebert 1997), such change must be facilitated from without rather than within.

Given the unlikeliness that a shift in reporting emphasis will be initiated from inside the journalistic profession, it is clear that pressure for change must be carried through a 'paradigm of peace' which is shaped, debated and developed from perspectives in the public domain. Recognizing the importance of promoting the need for a paradigm of peace that changes the orientation of reporting in relation to conflict, Reardon appears to offer a reasonable assessment when she argues that:

> We engage in war and violence because we think violently in images and metaphors of war. If we are to experience an authentic, fulsome peace, we must think peace. If we are to think peace, we need a paradigm of peace. We need not only a vision of peace but also the concepts, the language, the images, and the metaphors that will comprise a functioning and equally vigorous paradigm *of* peace, so that from it we can construct paradigms *for* peace, those explicit conceptual and political models around which we can organize a peaceful society in which we can conduct human affairs in a more humane manner.
>
> (1989: 16)

Not only is it vital to articulate peace though language which advances the prospect of non-violent settlements to disputes, but, Reardon insists, it is also necessary to conceptualize peace 'in structural or political terms' which emanate from 'social and economic structures' (ibid: 20) and which in the process engage with the issues of inequality and injustice that tend to underpin tensions and violence. The inception of a peace paradigm which informs the interpretive and explanatory positions taken by journalists, conceived within this context, operates as an 'organic' process which must remain 'an active, dynamic state' (ibid: 21), designed to encourage journalists to recognize that 'integration of diversity in a mutually enhancing relationship is a fundamental process for maintaining life and achieving peace' (ibid: 23). For Reardon, a receptiveness to diversity is the foundation of the peace paradigm, for 'the reluctance to see things holistically also may well contribute to the current alienation of individuals and to the disintegration of society'. The logic of this perspective, Reardon concludes, is to 'manage and control the conditions of separation and alienation' rather than contribute to those conditions (ibid.).

Although it would be unfair to suggest that journalists themselves have not grappled with questions about peace or tried to re-evaluate their responsibilites when reporting conflict (Lynch 2004), it is also evident that this receptiveness has been largely influenced by debates outside the profession, where dialogue between reporters, academics and peace workers has tried to negotiate the operational and paradigmatic gap which Manoff refers to (*The Peace Journalism Option* 1998). But even here, a recurring theme seen as essential for the emergence of peace journalism (as with all the positions outlined in this chapter) is diversity, for it is this which is seen as 'the antidote to the demonization/humanization polarity of war journalism' which contributes to the effect of 'humanizing all sides of the conflict' (ibid: 16). The typical representational emphasis of war journalism contributes to a war psychology whereas, in contrast, peace journalism tries to create a peace psychology. In the absence of a receptiveness to diversity, as Galtung notes, war journalism tends to promote a zero-sum analysis, depicts violence as self-generating and without background causes, focuses on the visible consequences of violence, views conflict from the perspectives of two sides, instigates us/them differences, demonizes the enemy whilst humanizing 'our' side, maps conflict in terms of loss and gain and ignores peace proposals (Galtung 1998: 13–14). Much of this interpretive framework evaporates if journalists move towards a diversity framework since, as Hollingworth acknowledges, by drawing from a range of sources outside the narrow information order generated by elites and officials, dialogue starts to connect rather than divide, thereby producing a situation where 'attention switches from victory to transformation of conflict' (Hollingworth 1998: 23). Enabling dialogue to move beyond a winner and loser scenario, a journalism which brings participants to debate on level terms also helps to 'disaggregate a body of interests or opinions and create a polygon of perspectives' (*The Peace Journalism Option* 1998: 24). This shift clearly requires a relocation of emphasis where the political sphere interacts in dialogue with the public sphere and vice versa, and as such seeks to empower non-elite groups and agencies who have ideas and recommendations that serve the overriding goal of peace and the avoidance of war. The power of narrow political interests can only be effectively diffused when comprehended alongside a wide range of alternative perspectives.

The tendency to not fully distinguish between conflict and war in much of the literature cited above overlooks the distinctiveness as well as interaction between the two conditions. Significantly, conflict is both necessary to help avert war as well as intrinsic to its development. The more important questions here, it seems to me, should be concerned with the specific nature of conflict, about how that conflict is reported, who participates in that conflict and for what reason. Evidently 'conflicts can be positive and constructive, by opening avenues of change' or, they can be destructive and used to close down the possibilities of change (Lynch 2002: 29). But perhaps here we should attempt to separate out conflict which seeks to create war from conflict which seeks to create peace, and perhaps we should think differently about conflict where one side strives to defeat another for a specific end from conflict which seeks to confront this outcome by working to move parties from incompatible positions and unreasonable demands. Clearly, for peace journalism to occur it is the latter definition of conflict which should prevail whereas with war journalism (or, indeed, reporting generally), it is the former. By opening up the scope for dialogue, the news media not only encourage greater social participation in reports but they also have an effect which is central to averting violence and war, namely 'the more alternatives, the less likely the violence' (ibid: 30) This sits in contrast to the competitive approach to conflict where two parties each use conflict to try and overwhelm the other. In this context, the two parties:

> feel they are faced with only two alternatives – victory or defeat. Defeat being unthinkable, each party steps up its efforts for victory. Relations between them deteriorate, and there is an escalation of violence. This may further entrench the 'us and them' mentality, causing gradually growing numbers of people to 'take sides'. They may ask themselves 'who will protect me?' and find the answer is 'my own kind'. Goals become formulated as demands to distinguish and divide each party from the other. Demands harden into a 'platform' or position, which can only be achieved through victory.
>
> (ibid: 31)

By creating awareness of differing types of violence which relate to groups or individuals, myths and narratives which sensationalize violence, structural violence which produces inequality, repression or exploitative systems as well as both the visible and invisible impact of violence, a conflict analysis approach is developed which opens up the space for wider debates and contributions relative to the complexity and dynamic of the emerging (potential) violence. Moreover, identifying the various types of violence and the relationship of each to the other encourages a greater need to expand the number of participants to discuss those types, thereby helping to facilitate a situation which moti-vates a broader range of articulations and interests that collectively assists the development of potential solutions and a transformation of relationships. Comparing the advantages of this collaborative approach to a simple competitive conflict model, it becomes evident that: 'A con-flict presented as two parties contesting the same goal (like territory, control, victory) is so naked there is very little to play on. When the conflict is more complex, constructive deals can be made, like X yield-ing to Y on one goal, Y to Z on a second, Z to X on a third' (ibid: 32).

The shift from a war journalism approach to that of a peace journal-ism approach indicates a shift in values which is almost diametrical in orientation. What underpins this discussion is an emphasis on 'balance' as a key determinant for story construction, within which, for example, debate moves to dialogue, difference to common ground, event-based reporting to process-based reporting, newsroom agendas to public agendas, objectivity to fairness, commentary to communication, watch-dog to enabler, and emotive imagery to public participation in problem-solving (ibid: 36). Collectively this paradigm seeks to become 'part of a strategy to make the conflict transparent, to understand and uncover it by exploring complexity, rather than perpetuating the distortions inher-ent in seeking simplicity' (ibid: 37). Applying the paradigm to initiate dialogue about various forms of violence and the separations as well as interconnectedness of 'the structural, relational and cultural contradic-tions which lie at the root of conflict' (Miall, Ramsbotham and Wood-house 2000: 56), it is plain that the recommendations provided by much of the literature about peace journalism are designed to prevent the esca-lation of conflict by transforming the competitive win–lose model into an ongoing process of management and flexibility to the issues which arise.

When one looks at the typical conditions which help entrench con-flict, one can also see how those conditions are absorbed and, indeed, amplified by much news reporting. As Deutsch argues: 'The tendency to escalate conflict results from the conjunction of three interrelated processes: (1) competitive processes involved in the attempt to win conflict; (2) processes of misperception and biased perception; and (3) processes of commitment arising out of pressures for cognitive and social consistency. These processes give rise to a mutually reinforcing cycle of relations that generate actions and relations that intensify con-flict' (1973: 352). In its coverage of conflict news seems to reinforce these processes, and therefore makes the likelihood of increased conflict and violence more rather than less likely. Moreover, if the news media's tendency to promote a win–lose competitive model of conflict encourages the parties involved 'to see their interests as diametically opposed', the more common outcome to this tension is not compromise, but one where both parties lose (Miall, Ramsbotham and Woodhouse 2000: 5). Admittedly, we must distinguish between influences of third-party intervention which exert 'hard' power (seem as deriving from government and non-government agencies able to force negotiating positions) or 'soft' power (parties and organizations who try to influence and facilitate moves towards an outcome) within this process (ibid: 10–12), but even here it seems likely that representations of weakness and strength, or loss and gain, negatively shape the perceptions of parties engaged in conflict and make agreement more difficult to reach as a result. The change needed to achieve such agreement is dependent on moving the win–lose scenario of conflict to a 'non-zero-sum' model where parties start to see that 'both may gain or both may lose' and then use this reinterpretation 'to assist parties to move in the positive-sum direction' (ibid: 8). This requires an equalization of power and, invariably, in the case of parties with antagonisms about identity and relationship, a need to try and bring the weaker party into a stronger position so it will be able to more effectively confront the power of the stronger party. It is this support for the weaker party which is needed to help transform 'unpeaceful, unbalanced relationships into peaceful and dynamic ones'. Recognizing that unequal power contributes to unbalanced relations, it emerges that balance is best created by working to level power, so transforming the structure of relations to bring about greater stability (ibid: 13).

A conflict resolution dynamic

The idea of lending extra support to the underdog and confronting the power of the stronger party, though essential for levelling out the conflict dynamic and more effectively addressing the attitudes, behaviour and contradictions which constitute the conflict process, pose obvious problems for the media and ideals about journalism refraining from direct or active participation in the political process. However, if the news media is to assist in the development of a conflict resolution dynamic by operating in ways which support peace journalism then it must do precisely that. The idea of moving from the zero-sum emphasis to a non zero-sum emphasis clearly means avoiding the construction of winners and losers and shifting from an interest in confrontational discourse to non-confrontational discourse. But even here, there remains a problem about supporting the underdog since an evident bias may impact negatively on the stronger party and reinforce a siege mentality. Similarly, if the face of conflict requires a levelling of positions to push parties towards conflict resolution positions, there arises a difficulty with the distinction between victim and perpetrator which may confuse responsibilities and once more create negative repercussions. Though it appears a moral imperative to try and help victims, it is evident that in conflict nearly all parties view themselves as victims in some sense, and to try to support 'real' victims may encourage the perpetrators to accelerate moves towards violence as feelings of resentment increase. Notably, it is not possible to try and move a stronger party towards peace without resistance and this resistance may manifest in greater tensions and violence which work against the development of relations and trust. An intensification of support for victims or weaker parties will, in all probability, be read by stronger opponents as a growing danger and lead to an escalation of conflict as the stronger party feels blamed, isolated and increasingly desperate to try to defend its position. Thus the development of support for the underdog in order to try and level the playing field between parties indicates problems if the media were to merely resort to more sympathetic coverage for weaker parties against greater critical coverage for stronger parties.

One way to try and improve the situation for weaker parties is not to provide an obvious sympathy for weaker parties directly, but to diffuse the superior position of stronger parties by drawing from dialogue and viewpoints through other sources who are able to articulate alternative perspectives which move between the two sides. A development of dialogue which works between the two sides and improves the chances of moving towards some degree of co-operation on issues is central to a conflict resolution dynamic which helps both sides to realize that each would be better off if agreement is reached (Deustch1973: 216). Moreover, a wider range of contributions to debate also helps to open up the potential for different resources and considerations to appear, giving the parties more room for manoeuvre and more communicative positions to draw from (ibid.). In contrast, the less alternatives available to draw from, the less likelihood of moving forward and the greater the potential for hostility and competitiveness. Indeed, not only is a competitive environment likely to hinder the chances of constructive progress, but it makes retaliatory gestures inevitable (ibid: 248). A significant benefit of enabling a diversity of voices and positions to enter the process of conflict resolution relates to the probability that the two sides are less susceptible to being seen as losing face to their opponents when suggestions and proposed solutions are offered outside of the destructive and counter-productive exchanges that the competitive model produces.

The fear of losing, which is magnified by competitive interaction, also means that this fear restricts the possibility of positive dialogue and bargaining. Through competitive exchanges: 'Little confidence is placed in information that is obtained directly from the other . . . poor communication enhances the possibility of error and misinformation of the sort that is likely to reinforce the preexisting orientations and expectations toward the other' thereby encouraging the exertion of superior force in order to avoid defeat' (ibid: 353). These issues reveal a noticeable complexity in the news media assisting a conflict resolution process and this becomes even more problematic if we bring to mind the possibility that direction and strategy for change might also be obstructed or lost beneath the cacophony of suggestions that diversity might bring. Though it is not my intention to develop this problem further here (essentially because this problem is so unlikely to arise), it is still worth considering what we mean by diversity and whether it can lead to a situation where, to use a cliche, 'too many cooks spoil the broth'. Perhaps an answer to this is that we need to try it in order to find out. And, perhaps the best conflict resolution is not to try to produce finite ends, but to develop a process of ongoing engagement and change. A dynamic, in other words, of perpetual transformation carried out within a framework of discourse which is perpetually peace oriented.

Conclusion

Studies which seek to address the possibilities for a peace-oriented journalism, immediately expose shortcomings and deficiencies in the way the news media report conflict. They also throw into relief the illusion of objectivity and raise questions about the role of the news media in relation to an informed public sphere. Importantly, peace journalism does not seek to disguise deliberate intentions to affect political outcomes and brings to the fore moral concerns which are about human responsibility as well as journalistic responsibility. By trying to develop a paradigm approach which is shaped by emphasizing the benefits of peace rather than war, peace journalism is about journalists actively working to try and prevent war by focusing on the possibilities of peaceful resolution or management of conflict. As I have tried to argue here, this does not mean the eradication of conflict, but the opposite: broadening the field within which contestation, argument and disagreement can take place. But, along with widening the space for such contestation, peace journalism is also about moving away from obsessions with simplistic and narrow positions that serve to inflame conflict and make war more rather than less likely. The potential for conflict to be exacerbated is intensified when two opponents dominate news and feed a zero-sum political game which creates a win–lose outcome.

The broadening of debate to include a variety of perspectives and propositions about how to try and facilitate a de-escalation of conflict is dependent on complexity rather than simplicity. The tendency to present conflict issues through two oppositional forces not only makes concessions and positive gestures more difficult to achieve, but also conveys the impression that conflict is *only* about those forces and that the outcome is entirely dependent on their actions/reactions to each other. By bringing other agencies and parties into the field of contestation, alternative discourses emerge which are less contained by the simplistic demarcations of the win–lose game. As stated, the zero-sum contest is about black and white positions, whereas the more constuctive contributions that help work towards peaceful resolutions or management are necessarily grey; able to blur and dissolve apparently incompatible positions into areas of common interest. Then, a shift can take place which encourages a problem-solving approach to difficulties that challenges the constant tilting of who has made ground and who has lost ground, towards a more balanced position of ongoing negotiative exchange and interaction. Drawing from groups and agencies that articulate positions outside of the predictable and inward-looking positions of dominant political parties, articulations emerge which are able to expose the obvious and damaging stereotypes that permeate and sustain confrontational dialogue. In the process, there is a greater chance of discussion emerging which humanizes all sides and more informatively elaborates on those underlying tensions and fears which provide the basis for antagonism and increased conflict.

In a very real sense, peace journalism poses a vital debate for journalism in terms of how conflict is currently constructed and represented. It also looks outside of the profession to conflict analysis and uses key ideas from this discipline to highlight evident problems with journalism with which the profession appears unable to deal, and with which it will continue to remain unable to deal all the time it pretends that it works objectively, and so in the best way possible. What the peace journalism debate exposes most of all is that reporting falls far short of a comprehensive approach to problems which increase the probability of war and therefore falls a long way short of human responsibility to try and avert such conflict. Given the increase in national and international conflicts, its relevance as a critique of journalism is central for thinking about how the media might best help to try and prevent or de-escalate such conflicts. It is a critique which brings to light that journalists are human beings first and journalists second rather than the other way around, and that the obsession with conflict between extremes indicates an abdication of human (if not journalistic) responsibility. Though there are evident problems with the coherence of the peace journalism debate which relate to how conflict debate is managed and constructed into definitions and narratives about events and exchanges, it engages with a key question about journalism and war, which is what should journalism try and do to help prevent war and so help avert the deaths of many people?

The evident lack of receptiveness to peace discourse and de-escalation initiatives trying to prevent wars and humanitarian crises not only demonstrates the illusion of objectivity in reporting such situations, but raises serious moral concerns about journalism's role within this process. Although there may be journalists who actively set out to challenge expectations about the inevitability of military and civil conflicts, it appears to be very much the case that the institutional and occupational bias of reporting is concerned more with amplifying the extreme (and so dangerous) aspects of communications than using contestations in dialogue to help resolve or more effectively manage imminent dangers. What the concept of peace journalism brings to this discussion is the fundamental recognition that all the while the news media is preoccupied with centres of power and elite influence, it is unlikely to take account of discourses which operate outside that narrow domain of power. The idea of journalism redefining its take on conflict by applying a conflict analysis model of working signifies a need for reporting to rethink its relationship with power and to introduce changes that radically challenge the established conventions of the profession itself. The news media's lack of interest in peace discourse represents a notable absence of obligation to view peace as a lively and contestable point of debate in public life, and in the process indicates a diminished responsibility towards variety of opinion and discussion which devalues democratic society.

Conclusion

What this study has set out to do is encourage further discussion about how politics and news interact in relation to military and civil conflicts, and humanitarian crises. The conventions of news culture, which determine what Bourdieu calls the journalistic field, indicate a preoccupation with values that tend to sensationalize political life and reduce it to a series of personalized conflicts. The emphasis on drama and emotive 'win–lose' scenarios has contributed to a trivialization of political life, and by focusing on the interests of the few rather than the many, has reduced the public to powerless spectators rather than active citizens. This suggests notable problems for believing that reporting operates in an objective and balanced way and is a starting point for thinking about how alternative discourses might permeate official discourse and help shape discussion about conflicts which have major social implications. Within the bounds of news production, it is apparent that political conflicts are played out, but that those conflicts are confined to the political field and rarely opened up to broader consideration from groups and representatives who are less concerned with protecting narrow political interests. Since news is the central arena where politics is now played out, it is clear that image management and performance are key determinants of political success and that entertainment has become the basis of generating public attention. Politics, in other words, must present itself in the form which the media requires in order to be noticed. The media is the space where politics takes place, and as Castells observes, 'without an active presence in the media, political proposals or candidates do not stand a chance of gathering broad support' (2004: 375). The media, as he puts it 'frame politics' (ibid: 371). Furthermore, although the news media do not create politics, they reinforce the presence of those who represent politics and in so doing, perpetuate the political system within which parties rise and fall. This enclosure signifies a relationship between news and politics which is inherently problematic for those seeking to challenge the dominant parties occupying the media space. With regard to military and civil conflicts and humanitarian crises, the news media has regularly failed to engage with debates which emphasize moving away from the zero-sum political game of negative conflict and this has had serious consequences for the development of peace.

In this book I have attempted to create a distinction about how conflict is handled in news. We might refer to this distinction as *negative conflict* on the one hand, and *positive conflict* on the other. Negative conflict is concerned with the narrow meanings and antagonisms which dominate zero-sum exchanges. It is also about the use of oppositional viewpoints which makes violent conflict more likely and which heightens the possibility of military confrontation. Significantly, negative conflict is also about using zero-sum arguments to avoid acting to prevent humanitarian crises and mass slaughter. It is about constraining arguments within the bounds of dominant elite discourse and amplifying simplistic responses to problems in black and white terms. Positive conflict, on the other hand, is about providing a broad arena where contestable positions and debates come into play which make violent conflict less likely and constructive intervention more likely. As explained earlier, within this space the complexity of 'grey' discourse takes precedence over the simplistic emphasis of 'black and white' discourse. Here points of common interest are explored alongside points of difference and antagonism, and a number of potential solutions are worked towards based on a conflict analysis model. Essentially, this paradigm relies on the use of more conflict rather than less, but conflict in terms of argument, discussion, contention and reason. It also relies on the news media looking away from the dominant political parties to other fields of expertise in order to better contextualize the details and nuances of debate. Dominant political positions therefore, are but one part of this dynamic which seeks to locate politics more firmly in the public sphere. This distinction is all the while encased in a moral imperative which is that violent conflict should be prevented whenever possible. This imperative is clearly jeopardized when contestations about probable violence are controlled and dominated ostensibly by actors who adopt hostile positions and increase tensions towards each other.

Against this recommendation for change, this study also acknowledges that modern political communications operate with some sophistication and that the news media can exert certain influences on the political process during moments of crisis. The speed and magnifying power of real-time news (the CNN effect) produces pressures which operate on a number of levels, and which create demands for: snap decisions, the exclusion of diplomats and experts, a facilitation of diplomatic manipulation, the creation of high expectations, the broadcasting of deficient reports, instant judgement and containment of discussion (Gilboa 2003). The role of the news media within the foreign policy setting may also be viewed in terms of controlling, constraining, intervening and instrumental spheres of activity (depending on context and circumstances) which compel politicians and diplomats to adopt strategies of presentation and planning that address media demands (Gilboa 2002). Diplomatic efforts must now consider when to conduct diplomacy behind closed doors and when to use the media as part of that process. But even bearing these points in mind, it seems apparent that news cannot offer an alternative policy to the one currently on offer. It can highlight problems with that policy and expose inconsistencies which politicians need to respond to in order to sustain credibility and public support, but it cannot offer a replacement and it cannot change political will. It's influence is therefore connected to presentational issues rather than substance.

The media's use in signalling between diplomats and politicians has become a vital part of the diplomatic apparatus in modern politics and the global reach of news is allowing conventional diplomatic interaction to be surpassed by the speed of instantaneous statement and counter-statement. Problems with the media's simplistic take on complex issues create difficulties for the detailed and laborious process of diplomatic interaction and thus indicates how those involved in the diplomatic process must use the media selectively and strategically. Its importance to convey non-verbal communication, presentations of the self, images of leadership, threats and reassurances, the potential of movement or intransigence, commitment and ambiguity as part of the diplomacy dynamic, demonstrate the range of political uses and functions which news can serve and highlight its centrality in political communication. What we need to bear in mind however, is that this complex role depends on using and reinforcing the parameters of elite discourse and power. This is not to deny that those in power are not motivated to find constructive solutions to problems, of course not, but that in relation to a journalism which is oriented to peace and which draws from a conflict analysis paradigm of interpretation, this indicates an obvious disparity. If peace journalism depends on opening up the arena for positions and viewpoints which are outside the realms of elite discourse and interest, then this may hinder diplomatic activity which requires complex knowledege and understanding of the elite discourse within which it is contained and, in turn, the exclusion of contributions which do not operate within the same closed circle of priorities. Contributions from outside diplomatic circles, then, may interfere with and further obstruct the potential for diplomatic resolution and agreement. On this point, though one must add that elite discourse offers only a limited range of options for agreement based on the restraints and imperatives which frame that discourse. Alternative viewpoints may help to inform diplomatic procedures and present constructive and purposeful options which conventional diplomatic practice, because of particular ways of working, is unlikely to access or relate to. Moreover, since diplomacy has social consequences, it is important that society and the public has a stake in what that diplomacy is trying to achieve (one of the criticisms of the Northern Ireland peace process is that the process has failed to gain social roots or broader public support because developments and debates have been too contained within elite circles). This requires building change from the bottom up rather than the top down and maintaining a vibrant dynamic between politicians and the public where each draws from and informs the other.

The conflicts which are analysed in this book demonstrate a lack of interaction between news and the public sphere. They demonstrate a preoccupation with the concerns and articulations of elite power and they tend to confirm the zero-sum approach to political life and debate. Throughout, complex issues and problems are addressed from within a framwork of specific political interests, with little recourse to alternative discourses. Though of considerable social and public importance, the international conflicts examined detail an exclusion of social and public discourse and, as such, show a notable absence of public engagement with vital concerns. From a media perspective (ostensibly American and British) violent conflict and humanitarian crises are routinely seen in black and white terms and as struggles between positions of power and domination. In the case of the Vietnam War, peace protesters were not interrogated for the intellectual or moral merits of their argument, but for their ability to represent an image of threat to social order and political authority. Ironically, the news media succeeded in helping to portray the peace movement as a destabilizing influence and so a potential danger rather than as a necessary resistance to violent conflict calling for an end to slaughter. By concentrating on images and slogans which associated the peace movement with a left-wing political agenda, the peace movement became synonymous with an agenda which stood in contrast with notions of capitalist freedom and democracy. The media's ability to reduce articulations about peace to a potential threat to peace, also fulfilled the news requirement of amplifying anatagonism between two opposing forces and diluting discussion to a simple authority/anti-authority bias.

With regard to reporting Africa the news media tend to adopt a formulaic approach to conflict and humanitarian crisis which relies on predictable images of dependency and suffering. All too often that suffering is without political context, but conforms to a narrative about the savage Other, who is found to exist in desperate circumstances because of affiliations with tribalism and brutality. This frame of interpretation clearly helps to minimize the possibility of embracing debates and arguments that promote a more sophisticated understanding of the situation. Instead, the inclination is to provoke a gesture of help from the viewer who looks at the voiceless object of misery staring back at the camera. A general and understandable response to this dilemma is to demand instant help and to push for humanitarian assistance. In the wake of this recurring nightmare (because such situations seem to appear with some regularity), there is no room for assessment or comprehension of intervention to stop genocide because it has already happened.

As with Rwanda, by focusing on the refugee disaster which the genocide had created, and failing to engage with questions of responsibility or Western inaction, news effectively contributed to the indifferent attitude displayed by the West and in doing so assisted dominant political arguments which sought to confuse the nature of the violence, its underlying motivations and its human consequences. To have comprehensively engaged with viewpoints and discourses which addressed these crucial issues would have intensified pressure markedly and made the management of indifference much harder to maintain. What played into the hands of governments seeking to avoid engagement in Rwanda was, in fact, the images of disaster and misery which provided the face of war. By concentrating on the humanitarian disaster which the genocide had created, the news media effectively helped to legitimize a humanitarian response from governments. By not taking a critically engaged position towards the genocide during its early stages (and before the scale of the slaughter had reached its peak), the news media failed to hold governments to account on intervention, and in the process also made peace dialogue unimportant for the immediate requirements of assistance and support. Clearly, the debate was not about prevention, but response and being seen to be helping to alleviate the desperate circumstances faced by victims.

The images of refugees and suffering demonstrated an inabilty to distinguish between victims and perpetrators and perhaps was reflective of
a broader failure to distinguish differences, inequalities and the struggle for control of Rwanda. When the news cameras arrived at the refugee
camps, it was obvious that the kind of images shown would be consistent with Western coverage of the African plight. Reduced to objects of
misery and silent suffering, both perpetrators and victims were portrayed as victims. No doubt, perpetrators also had an awareness of the
media's inability to discern the guilty from the innocent, for if this
ability had existed, there would have been no chance of perpetrators
finding refuge with victims. In this context of confusion, how can one
talk about guilt and justice in any meaningful way? The failure to separate the guilty from the innocent perhaps most forcefully symbolizes
not only government indifference to the genocide, but media indifference. If the media is unable to identify differences when the genocide
has transmuted into a clearly categorizable refugee crisis, how might
the case for intervention be made outside that frame of reference?
There have obviously been a number of journalists concerned about this
problem (who wrote accounts when they left Rwanda), but this post-
genocide reflection has no significance as a form of pressure. Rather,
such accounts merely confirm the politics of indifference and the lack
of forceful debate about intervention to stop the murder. The indifference to genocide is ultimately a crisis of explanation. On the one hand,
it returns us to the media's lazy and stereotypical interpretation of
African conflict, but on the other it marks serious moral concerns about
Western government inaction with the full knowledge that genocide
was taking place. Media apathy and the political evasion of responsibility to intervene combined to make the case for non-intervention reasonable, and by association the case for intervention questionable.

In relation to news reporting of Bosnia and Kosovo, there was a
notable attempt to identify and separate victims from perpetrators, and
the process of categorization, though reliant on simplistic polarities,
created pressure and debate about the responsibility and necessity for
Western intervention. However, it must also be said that the news media
characterized conflict as being driven by civil intolerance and the resurgence of historical ethnic hatreds, which hindered clear debate about
the nationalist tendencies of leaders seeking to ethnically cleanse territories of now clearly defined enemies. Western reluctance to engage in
the conflict meant that governments (especially British) used the media
to help exaggerate the impression of action, whilst simultaneously
downplaying inaction. This image of action, however, amounted to a

stage-managed collapse of potential policy consensus amongst Western governments, therefore inhibiting intervention.

Much of the Balkans coverage served to intensify the dramatic emphasis of conflict through a personalization of responses and approaches, and it was this personalization which also served to reinforce the idea that in the absence of a clear and agreed approach, intervention would be not only unadvisable, but counter-productive. Recognition that personalized approaches to issues of policy and military engagement served to support a broader policy of non-intervention received negligible analysis by the news media. Varying responses about reaction to suffering and violence created a picture of confusion which buttressed the case for non-intervention, and it was such confusion which also enabled action, in the form of aerial bombardment, to be presented as a constructive response to a growing humanitarian crisis. The television news media's tendency to uncritically reproduce Nato briefings about the bombardment of Kosovo not only meant that political assertions about the bombing being necessary to help victims went unchallenged, but further hindered the possibilty of facilitating any diplomatic outcome. This stance reflected a lack of interest in peace intiatives along with questions about inequality, common fears and geopolitical change in the post-communist world.

However, although it would appear that news reporting of the Balkans made little difference to British and American policy, it is still important to acknowledge that the presence of the television cameras meant that violence in the Balkans was kept in the public consciousness and therefore a significant pressure for politicians to handle. News kept the shock and horror of ethnic cleansing at the forefront of attention, and as Chapter 6 makes evident, a number of journalists sought to bring pressure on Western governments to act decisively against the perpetrators. Just how this pressure impacted on those governments and what difference it made to policy is contentious, but what is less contentious is the general absence of peace discourse and a media receptiveness to non-confrontational dialogue. Once more, the Balkans episode indicates a lack of interest in the political complexities which underpinned conflict and a lack of attention to constructive and purposeful dialogue which offered a counter-argument to the nationalistic tendencies that were promoted through the media and which, in turn, served to exacerbate the violence.

The news media's relationship with the Oslo peace process and the Israeli–Palestinian conflict highlights the problematic tension which exists between confidentiality and publicity and underlines the difficulties that politicians can have when moving from closed-door to open-door diplomacy (Gilboa 2000). The media's ability to expose tentative moves and gestures within negotiations tended to reduce flexibility between parties, as each sought to send the message to respective constituencies that negotiating positions had not changed. News reports which conveyed that concessions or constructive exchanges had been proposed also risked being interpreted by respective constituencies as having arisen through weakness, thus intensifying fears that the parties were threatening to sell their own support base short in any potential deal. This pressure encouraged parties to adopt a more hardline stance when appearing on television, and contributed to a more competitive negotiating environment than would have been the case if talks had been conducted in private. The competitiveness of public diplomacy was augmented by a media emphasis on the negative features of communication and the drama of antagonism. Conducting exchanges through this emphasis invariably intensified the flow of threats and counter-threats, which in turn, made it more difficult to explore points of common interest and develop conciliatory themes.

Although news coverage of negotiations changed in terms of influence, along with rises and falls in political commitment to negotiations and movement, it is clear that the role of stronger parties was given extensive coverage and that weaker parties were seen as peripheral to any prospective agreement. This lack of interest in the weaker parties reflects an exclusive attitude to the talks which hinders the development of integrative discourse and a broader public understanding of political associations with conflict and its possible resolution. As Amos Oz has argued (2004), the media's tendency to promote a right versus wrong scenario is ultimately destructive for public understanding and therefore inimical to the tolerance needed to accept risks for peace. The absence of alternative viewpoints able to expose the lack of flexibility and imagination in the extreme positions also reflects a lack of media imagination to access discourses which have contributions to make towards peace and which are less transfixed by a desire to protect power and influence. As suggested, alternative discourses can act as bridges between extreme positions and help draw those positions closer together. Alternative discourses can expose the similarities of interests and loosen the fear of appearing weak. A wider range of voices about peace can help promote a growing awareness about peace and more clearly outline the advantages. Significantly, voices which approach conflict from a conflict resolution perspective are not restrained by the short-term goals of elite political negotiation, which strives to use negotiation as a means for augmenting political support as much as achieving agreement. The roles of elite and non-elite discourse are both crucial for the successful development of peace. Paying attention to elite discourse only locates discussion in a sphere of competitive win–lose argument which does little to promote tolerance and understanding. It also serves to give control of momentum and debate to elites who foremost seek to achieve results which improve popularity and credibility with audiences and cement electoral success. Important though that is, it is but one means to argue and debate peace.

Although generally speaking, the news media were more supportive of the peace process in Northern Ireland than in the Middle East (Wolfsfeld 2004), there is a similar concern with elites which has, over time, reinforced public mistrust and anxiety about what peace means. During the build up to The Good Friday Agreement, the television media were particularly attentive to a range of parties about the prospect of reaching a settlement and it was apparent that the smaller parties were playing a key role within the negotiations, whether as intermediaries or in providing a flexible response to the demands of the stronger parties. However, since The Good Friday Agreement, this interest in a range of debates has once more shrunk to the apparently intractable positions of dominant Unionism and Republicanism. News coverage has returned to a preoccupation with drama and sensationalism and zero-sum politics. Throughout the peace process, the smaller parties have found it difficult to get news interested in the message they are trying to get across and this is seen by those such as the Northern Ireland's Women Coalition as a key reason why they lost public support and failed to regain seats at the Assembly. We cannot of course, blame this entirely on the media, but even so, it is obvious enough that without public awareness, no party is going to garner the electoral support it requires to take office. For weaker parties trying to gain a foothold in a new political dispensation, this makes growth and success especially hard.

It is necessary to recognize that in Northern Ireland the news media created expectations about peace which acted as a form of pressure on the parties to work towards that end. Even though the issue of commitment and pursuit towards that end is another matter, there are numerous examples of the media operating as a platform for megaphone diplomacy and journalists assisting communications between sides who, early on, refused to meet face to face (Sparre 2001). Issues such as the release of prisoners and the decommissioning of paramilitary weapons have been discussed through news and become important points for conveying to the public that positions must move and concessions will need to be made if the parties are to effectively manage a conflict transformation process. But hopes and expectations which surround this perception have changed considerably since The Good Friday Agreement, however. As I write this, the peace process has returned to another crisis (concerned with Sinn Fein's commmitment to democratic politics and IRA criminality) which has been amplified by the dramatic emphasis of coverage and the competitive response, counter-response scenario of elite discourse. The political conflict over political inclusion has now shifted to political conflict over exclusion. This has reinforced the divisiveness of political identity and badly damaged the public tolerance needed to move forward. Perhaps expectedly, there has been no attempt by the news media to accommodate suggestions and viewpoints from non-elite groups during this period of difficulty. Rather, the tendency has been to further isolate the crisis from public consultation and conduct debate within the competitive elite environment of claim and counter-claim.

The media's relationship with the 'war on terror' raises a number of very serious questions about journalistic responsibility and information. As a media war, the 'war on terror' is about an 'enemy' who is simultaneously everywhere and nowhere. The enemy is especially dangerous when they seem to be nowhere, because this invisibility creates the anxiety and fears which are realizable only when the enemy appear (or the consequences of their actions appear) somewhere. In the 'war on terror' the 'enemy' is for most of us (the exception being those who are victims) a media construct only. Interestingly, much of the media reporting about those who have come to symbolize the 'enemy' is not only speculative but based on non-information. The reporting confirms the existence of threat and potential devastation, but is a process without end. In such an environment the perception is created that peace is impossible without the elimination of the enemy, but how does one eliminate an enemy which is nowhere and everywhere? How is it possible to win a 'war on terror' and how is peace possible in such an environment? The answer to the last two questions is that it is not possible to win a 'war on terror' and peace is not possible in a war without end. These kind of questions, though integral to the 'war on terror' argument, have not been examined or extrapolated by the news media and thus enable the apparent legitimacy of the argument to continue unchallenged.

In the post-9/11 world, the exacerbation of public fear over a possible terrorist attack is an omnipresent news story. But what has become noticeable within this climate is the news media's non-critical stance towards official and elite discourse which seeks to circulate and consolidate the fears being created. As part of America's attempt to overwhelm those states and enemies which fall within the 'axis of evil', pre-emptive action has become a key response and a central tenet of the Bush administration's foreign policy agenda. Passive reporting of the build up towards war in Iraq demonstrated the media's (especially the US media's) importance in supporting the momentum towards invasion and promoting the inevitability of war. That passivity was further reinforced by embedding reporters with military units, which served to perpetuate the military perspective and dramatize the incursion. Once commenced, the news emphasis was about the progress of war rather than examining peace discourse which dealt with the possibility of de-escalation, and just as peace discourse had been marginalized in the build up to war, so it was notable by absence as the war progressed.

For the news media, the war in Iraq, just like the 'war on terrorism', has been about personalization. Bush versus Saddam Hussein, or Bush versus Osama bin Laden, has been the simplistic frame the news media have relied upon to make sense of events. This simplification has not only distorted the conflict issues, but importantly been used to augment the appearance of Bush's leadership skills. If effective leadership is about manipulating fears and reassurances and using ambiguity to further political aims, one can see why Bush was re-elected in 2004. The possibility of terrorist attack has become the constant fear, and the absence of terrorism not so much an indication that fears are misplaced but that political policy is successful in terms of prevention. Superficial claims about a 'civilized' West bringing 'democracy' and 'liberation' to the 'rogue state' have functioned to create the crude dualities and polarizations needed to maintain news narratives, and the 'with us, or against us' scenario forwarded by the Bush administration, has routinely provided the interpretive paradigm by which to read developments and determine potential enemies. When those enemies are invisible, they are planning to strike, and simple polarities move beyond the 'us' and 'them', to, as recently, the 'safety' and 'liberty' debate. The problem for the creation of a peace-oriented approach to debate in this climate is that if war is unwinnable then how can one talk constructively about peace? One potential suggestion here is not to talk about the need for perpetual war in order to maintain perpetual peace, but to talk about perpetual peace in order to avoid perpetual war. Who are the enemies that constitute the need for a 'war on terror', what do they stand for, how can dialogue be developed with them and what fears and anxieties do they have?

What has become increasingly apparent in the post-9/11 world is that militant Islam has been constructed as a threat to world order (a world order which is modelled on a US system of checks and regulations) and that Islamic voices have been repeatedly used to confirm the threat or apologize for it. This representation draws from a history which is all too well described by Edward Said in his book *Covering Islam*, where he observes that: 'Americans have scant opportunity to view the Islamic world except reductively, coercively, oppositionally.' 'Islam', he notes, 'can now have only two possible general meanings, both of them unacceptable and impoverishing. To Westerners and Americans, "Islam" represents a resurgent atavism which suggests not only a threat of return to the Middle Ages but the destruction of what is regularly referred to as the democratic order in the Western world' (1997: 55). This negative representation, which is recycled and intensified in the 'war on terror', has been used not only to exacerbate threats, but also has helped to entrench perceptions of the 'us' which must be defended. Adhering to such simplistic polarities increases fear and feelings of danger and can only serve to augment the potential for conflict.

It is clear that peace is far more complex than war (Howard 2000). For this reason, if the news media is to assist peace, it must embrace complexity. Peace journalism recognizes this necessary change and provides a framework for how to do it. The integration of a range of viewpoints is crucial for overcoming the crude generalities and damaging stereotypes which are perpetuated through the polarities and oppositions which news emphasizes. A growing realization that 'information intervention' can have the same function as 'a soft form of humanitarian intervention' (Metzl 2002: 1) indicates that conflict management in the media age also means maximizing the media's potential to address conflict causes. This includes examining shared as well as divergent interests and discourses. For parties to move towards a position of mutual confidence, it is necessary to develop transparency so trust can be gained. Currently the news media tend to do the opposite, they exacerbate perceived weaknesses, work against transparency and, by focusing on who is winning and losing, obstruct the development of trust. If the media is to humanize opponents to each other, it must discourage the zero-sum game that it promotes. And only when the news media moves towards a process of reporting that increases the potential for peace over the potential for violent conflict can we say that the social and moral responsibility of news has been properly realized.

Bibliography

Abbas, M. *Through Secret Channels* (Reading: Garnet Publishing, 1995).

Adam, G. 'Peace-Building Through the Media', *Crosslines Global Report* (March/April 1997) 47–50.

Adams, G. *Free Ireland: Towards Lasting Peace* (Dingle, Co. Kerry: Brandon, 1995).

Aggestam, K. *'Two-Track Diplomacy: Negotiations Between Israel and the PLO Through Open and Secret Channels*, Davis Papers on Israel's Foreign Policy No. 53 (The Leonard Davis Institute for International Relations: The Hebrew University of Jerusalem, 1996).

Allan, S. 'The Culture of Distance: Online Reporting of the Iraq War', in S. Allan and B. Zelizer (eds) *Reporting War* (London: Routledge, 2004).

Amin, H. Y. 'Social Engineering: Transnational Broadcasting and Its Impact on Peace in the Middle East', *Global Media Journal* 2, 4 (Spring 2004) 1–18.

Arlen, M. J. *Living Room War* (New York: Viking, 1969).

Arno, A. 'The News Media as Third Parties in National and International Conflicts: *Duobus Litigantbus Gaudet'*, in A. Arno and W. Dissanayake (eds) *The News Media in National and International Conflict* (Boulder, CO: Westview Press, 1984).

Arthur, P. *Special Relationships: Britain, Ireland and the Northern Ireland Problem* (Belfast: Blackstaff Press, 2000).

Ashrawi, H. *This Side of Peace: A Personal Account* (New York: Simon & Schuster, 1999).

Avraham, E., G. Wolfsfeld and I. Aburaiya, 'Dynamics in the News Coverage of Minorities: The Case of the Arab Citizens of Israel', *Journal of Communications Inquiry* 24, 2 (2000) 117–33.

Bagdikian, B. H. 'The Media Monopoly', in H. Tumber (ed.) *News: A Reader* (Oxford: Oxford University Press, 1999).

Banks, M., and M. Wolfe Murray, 'Ethnicity and Reports of the 1992–95 Bosnia Conflict', in T. Allen and J. Seaton (eds) *The Media of Conflict* (London: Zed Books, 1999).

Bantz, C. R. 'News Organizations: Conflict as a Crafted Norm', in D. Berkowitz (ed.) *Social Meanings of News* (London: Sage, 1997).

Basic-Hrvatin, S. 'Television and National/Public Memory', in J. Gow, R. Paterson and A. Preston (eds) *Bosnia By Television* (London: BFI, 1996).

Baudrillard, J. *The Gulf War Did Not Take Place* (Bloomington and Indianapolis: Indianapolis University Press, 1995).

Baumann, M., and H. Siebert, 'A Paradigm Shift', *Rhodes Journalism Review* (Online Edition – http:journ.ru.ac.za/review/14/shift.html) 14, 5 (May 1997).

Beilin, Y. *Touching Peace* (London: Weidenfeld & Nicolson, 1999).

Bell, M. 'The Journalism of Attachment', in M. Kieran (ed.) *Media Ethics* (London: Routledge, 1998).

Bell, M. *Through Gates of Fire* (London: Weidenfeld & Nicolson, 2003).

Bennett, L. W. *News: The Politics of Illusion* (London: Longman, 2003).

Benthall, J. *Disasters, Relief and the Media* (London: I. B. Tauris, 1993).

Bew, P., H. Patterson and P. Teague, *Northern Ireland Between War and Peace* (London: Lawrence & Wishart, 1997).

Bew, P., and G. Gillespie, *Northern Ireland: A Chronology of the Troubles* (Dublin: Gill & Macmillan, 1999).

Bildt, C. *Peace Journey* (London: Weidenfeld & Nicolson, 1998).

Bird, S. E. 'Taking It Seriously: Supermarket Tabloids After September 11', in B. Zelizer and S. Allan (eds) *Journalism After September 11* (London: Routledge, 2002).

Blumler, J. G., and M. Gurevitch, *The Crisis of Public Communication* (London: Routledge, 1995).

Bok, S. *Secrets* (Oxford: Oxford University Press, 1982).

Boltanski, L. *Distant Suffering* (Cambridge: Cambridge University Press, 1999).

Boorstin, D. *The Image* (New York: Vintage, 1961).

Bote, J. 'Journalism and Conflict Resolution', *Media Development* 4 (1996) 6–9.

Bourdieu, P. *On Television and Journalism* (London: Pluto Press, 1998).

Brown, R. 'Spinning the War: Political Communications, Information Operations and Public Diplomacy in the War on Terrorism', in D. K. Thussu and D. Freedman (eds) *War and the Media* (London: Sage, 2003).

Bruck, P., and C. Roach, 'Dealing With Reality: The News Media and the Promotion of Peace', in C. Roach (ed.) *Communication and Culture in War and Peace* (London: Sage, 1993).

Burke, J. *Al-Qaeda* (London: Penguin, 2004).

Burkhalter, H. J. 'The Question of Genocide', *World Policy Journal* 11, 4 (1994) 44–54.

Burns, J. 'The Media as Impartial Observers or Protagonists – Conflict Reporting or Conflict Encouragement in Former Yugoslavia', in J. Gow, R. Paterson and A. Preston (eds) *Bosnia By Television* (London: BFI, 1996).

Butler, D. *The Trouble With Reporting Northern Ireland* (Aldershot: Avebury, 1995).

Carruthers, S. *The Media at War* (Basingstoke: Macmillan – now Palgrave Macmillan, 2000).

Carruthers, S. 'Tribalism and Tribulation: Media Constructions of "African Savagery" and "Western Humanitarianism" in the 1990s', in S. Allan and B. Zelizer (eds) *Reporting War* (London: Routledge, 2004).

Carey, R., and J. Shainin, *The Other Israel* (New York: The New Press, 2004).

Castells, M. *The Power of Identity* (Oxford: Blackwell, 2004).

Chandler, D. 'Western Intervention and the Disintegration of Yugoslavia, 1989–1999', in P. Hammond and E. S. Herman (eds) *Degraded Capability: The Media and the Kosovo Crisis* (London: Pluto Press, 2000).

Chomsky, N. 'The Media and the War: What War?', in W. L. Bennett and D. L. Paletz (eds) *Taken By Storm* (Chicago: University of Chicago Press, 1994).

Clapham, C. 'Rwanda: The Perils of Peacemaking', *Journal of Peace Research* 35, 2 (1998) 193–210.

Clotfelter, J. 'Disarmament Movements in the United States', *Journal of Peace Research* 23, 2 (1986) 97–101.

Cohen, R. *International Politics* (Harlow, Essex: Longman, 1981).

Cohen, R. *Theatre of Power: The Art of Diplomatic Signalling* (London: Longman, 1987).

Cohen, R. 'Negotiating Across Cultures', in C. A. Crocker, F. O. Hampson and P. Aall (eds) *Managing Global Chaos* (Washington: US Institute of Peace Press, 1996).

Cohen, S. *States of Denial* (Oxford: Polity Press, 2001).

Collins, J., and R. Glover, *Collatoral Language* (New York: New York University Press, 2002).

Coogan, T. P. *The Troubles* (London: Hutchinson, 1995).

Corbin, J. *Gaza First* (London: Bloomsbury, 1994).

Corcoran, F. 'War Reporting: Collatoral Damage in the European Theater', in W. L. Bennett and D. L. Paletz (eds) *Taken By Storm* (Chicago: University of Chicago Press, 1994).

Cummings, B. *War and Television* (London: Verso, 1992).

Curtis, L. *Ireland: The Propaganda War* (London: Pluto Press, 1984).

Darby, J., and R. MacGinty, *The Management of Peace Processes* (Basingstoke: Macmillan – now Palgrave Macmillan, 2000)

Dayan, D., and E. Katz, *Media Events* (Cambridge, MA: Harvard University Press, 1992).

Delaney, E. *An Accidental Diplomat* (Dublin: New Island, 2001).

De Waal, A. *Famine Crimes* (London: Africa Rights and the International African Institute, 1997).

Des Forges, A. 'Silencing the Voices of Hate in Rwanda', in M. E. Price and M. Thompson (eds) *Forging Peace* (Edinburgh: Edinburgh University Press, 2002).

Destexhe, A. *Rwanda and Genocide in the Twentieh Century* (London: Pluto Press, 1994).

Destexhe, A. 'The Third Genocide', in *Foreign Policy* 97 (Winter 1995) 3–17.

Deutsch, M. *The Resolution of Conflict* (New Haven, CT: Yale University Press, 1973).

Dixon, P. *Northern Ireland: The Politics of War and Peace* (Basingstoke: Palgrave, 2001).

Dorman, W. A., and S. Livingston, 'News and Historical Context', in W. L. Bennett and D. L. Paletz (eds) *Taken By Storm* (Chicago: University of Chicago Press, 1994).

Elderman, M. *The Symbolic Uses of Politics* (Urbana and Chicago: University of Illinois Press, 1967).

Elderman, M. *Constructing the Political Spectacle* (Chicago: Chicago University Press, 1988).

El-Nawawy, M., and A. Iskandar, *Al-Jazeera* (Cambridge, MA: Westview Press, 2003).

Eltringham, N. *Accounting for Horror* (London: Pluto Press, 2004).

Entman, R. M., and B. I. Page, 'The News Before the Storm', in W. L. Bennett and D. Paletz (eds) *Taken By Storm* (Chicago: University of Chicago Press, 1994).

Epstein, E. J. *News From Nowhere* (Chicago: Ivan R. Dee, 2000).

Feeney, B. 'The Peace Process: Who Defines News – The Media or Government Press Offices?', in D. Kiberd (ed.) *Media in Northern Ireland: The Search for Diversity* (Dublin: Open Air, 1997).

Galtung, J., and R. C. Vincent, *Global Glasnost* (Creskill, NJ: Hampton Press, 1995).

Galtung, J. 'The News Values of War Journalism', in *The Peace Journalism Option* (Taplow: Conflict and Peace Forums, 1998).

Galtung, J., and M. Ruge, 'The Stucture of Foreign News', *Journal of Peace Research* 1 (1965) 64–90.

Gans, H. *Deciding What's News* (New York: Random House, 1980).

Gilboa, E. 'Mass Communication and Diplomacy: A Theoretical Framework', *Communication Theory* 10, 3 (2000) 275–309.

Gilboa, E. 'Media Coverage of International Negotiation: A Taxonomy of Levels and Effects', *International Negotiation* 5, 3 (2001) 543–68.

Gilboa, E. 'Global Communication and Foreign Policy', *Journal of Communication* 52, 4 (2002) 731–48.

Gilboa, E. 'Television News and U.S. Foreign Policy', *Harvard International Journal of Press/Politics* 8, 4 (2003) 97–113.

Gitlin, T. *The Whole World is Watching* (California: University of California Press, 1980).

Glenny, M. *The Fall of Yugoslavia* (London: Penguin, 1992).

Glenny, M. *The Balkans* (London: Granta, 1999).

Goffman, E. *The Presentation of the Self in Everyday Life* (London: Penguin, 1969).

Golding, P., and G. Murdock, 'Culture, Communications and Political Economy', in H. Tumber (ed.) *News: A Reader* (Oxford: Oxford University Press, 1999).

Gourevitch, P. *We Wish To Inform You That Tomorrow We Will Be Killed With Our Families* (London: Picador, 1998).

Gowing, N. *Real-Time Television Coverage of Armed Conflicts and Diplomatic Crises: Does it Pressure or Distort Foreign Policy Decisions?*, The Joan Shorenstein Center on the Press, Politics and Public Policy, Working Paper 94-1 (June 1994a).

Gowing, N. 'The One-eyed King of Real-Time News Coverage', *New Perspectives Quarterly* (Fall 1994b) 45–54.

Gowing, N. 'Real-time TV Coverage from War: Does it Make or Break Government Policy?', in J. Gow, R. Paterson and A. Preston (eds) *Bosnia By Television* (London: BFI, 1996).

Grossman, D. *Death As A Way Of Life* (London: Bloomsbury, 2003).

Hall, M. *The Vietnam War* (Harlow, Essex: Pearson Education, 2000).

Hall, S. 'The Social Production of News', in S. Hall, C. Critcher, T. Jefferson, J. Clarke and B. Roberts (eds) *Policing the Crisis* (Basingstoke: Macmillan, 1978).

Hallin, D. *The Uncensored War* (California: University of California Press, 1989).

Hallin, D. *We Keep America on Top of the World* (London: Routledge, 1994).

Hallin. D., and T. Gitlin, 'The Gulf War as Popular Culture', in W. L. Bennett and D. L. Paletz (eds) *Taken By Storm* (Chicago: University of Chicago Press, 1994).

Hammond, P. 'Third Way War: New Labour, The British Media and Kosovo', in P. Hammond and E. S. Herman (eds) *Degraded Capability: The Media and the Kosovo Crisis* (London: Pluto Press, 2000).

Hartmann, F. 'Bosnia', in R. Gutman and D. Rieff (eds) *Crimes of War* (New York: W. W. Norton, 1999).

Hennessey, T. *The Northern Ireland Peace Process* (Dublin: Gill & Macmillan, 2000).

Herman, E. S., and R. McChesney, 'The Global Media in the late 1990s', in H. Mackay and T. O'Sullivan (eds) *The Media Reader: Continuity and Transformation* (London: Sage, 1999).

Herman, E. S., and D. Peterson, 'CNN: Selling Nato's War Globally', in P. Hammond and E. S. Herman (eds) *Degraded Capability: the Media and the Kosovo Crisis* (London: Pluto Press, 2000).

Hoffman, E. *After Such Knowledge* (London: Secker & Warburg, 2004).

Hoge, J. F. 'Media Pervasiveness', *Foreign Affairs* (July/August 1994) 136–44.

Holbrooke, R. *To End a War* (New York: Random House, 1998).

Hollingworth, L. 'A Journalism of Empowerment', in *The Peace Journalism Option* (Taplow: Conflict and Peace Forums, 1998).

Honig, J. W., and N. Both, *Srebrenica* (London: Penguin, 1996).
Howard, M. *The Invention of Peace* (London: Profile Books, 2000).
Ignatieff, M. *The Warrior's Honor* (London: Vintage, 1999).
Iskandar, A., and M. el-Nawawy, 'Al-Jazeera and War Coverage in Iraq', in S. Allan and B. Zelizer (eds) *Reporting War* (London: Routledge, 2004).
Jervis, R. *The Logic of Images in International Relations* (Princeton, NJ: Princeton University Press 1970).
Jones, B. D. ' "Intervention Without Borders": Humanitarian Intervention in Rwanda, 1990–94', *Journal of International Studies* 24, 2 (1995) 225–48.
Jonsson, C. *Communication in International Bargaining* (London: Pinter Publishers, 1990).
Judah, T. *Kosovo* (New Haven, CT: Yale University Press, 2000).
Karim, K. H. 'Making Sense of the "Islamic Peril": Journalism as Cultural Practice', in B. Zelizer and S. Allan (eds) *Journalism After September 11* (London: Routledge, 2002).
Karnow, S. *Vietnam: A History* (London: Pimlico, 1994).
Kattenburg, P. M. *The Vietnam Trauma in American Foreign Policy 1945–75* (New Brunswick, NJ: Transaction Books, 1980).
Keane, F. *Seasons of Blood* (London: Viking, 1995).
Kellner, D. 'The Persian Gulf TV War Revisited', in S. Allan and B. Zelizer (eds) *Reporting War* (London: Routledge, 2004).
Knightley, P. *The First Casualty* (London: Prion Books, 2000).
Kurspahic, K. *Prime Time Crime* (Washington: US Institute of Peace Press, 2003).
Lago, R. 'Interviewing Sinn Fein under the new political environment: A Comparative Analysis of Interviews with Sinn Fein on British Television', *Media, Culture and Society* 20, 4 (1998) 677–85.
Lang, G. E., and K. Lang, 'The Press As Prologue', in W. L. Bennett and D. L. Paletz (eds) *Taken By Storm* (Chicago: University of Chicago Press, 1994).
Lerner, M. *Healing Israel/Palestine* (Berkeley, CA: Tikku/North Atlantic Books, 2003).
Lewis, J., and R. Brookes, 'How British Television News Represented the Case for War in Iraq', in S. Allan and B. Zelizer (eds) *Reporting War* (London: Routledge, 2004).
Livingston, S. 'Beyond the "CNN Effect": The Media-Foreign Policy Dynamic', in P. Norris (ed.) *Politics and the Press* (London: Lynne Rienner Publishers, 1997).
Livingston, S., and T. Eachus, 'Humanitarian Crises and US Foreign Policy: Somalia and the CNN Effect Reconsidered', *Political Communication* 12 (1995) 413–29.
Lynch, J. 'The Conflict in Kosovo – The Lessons from the UK Media', in P. Goff (ed.) *The Kosovo News and Propaganda War* (Vienna: International Press Institute, 1999).
Lynch, J. 'Reporting the World: The Ethical Challenge to International News', in C. Paterson and A. Sreberny (eds) *International News in the Twenty-First Century* (Luton: University of Luton Press, 2004).
Maas, P. *Love Thy Neighbour* (London: Papermac, 1996).
Maladi, N. 'Mapping the Al-Jazeera Phenomenon', in D. K. Thussu and D. Freedman (eds) *War and the Media* (London: Sage, 2003).
Malcolm, N. *Kosovo* (London: Papermac, 1996).
Mallie, E., and D. McKittrick, *The Fight For Peace* (London: Heinemann, 1996).
Mandelbaum, M. 'Vietnam: The Television War', *Daedalus* 3 (1982) 157–69.

Manning, P. *News and News Sources* (London: Sage, 2001).

Manoff, R. 'The Media's Role in Preventing and Moderating Conflict', *Crosslines Global Report* (March/April 1997) 24–7.

Manoff, R. ' "Role Plays": Potential Media Roles in Conflict Prevention and Management', *Track Two* 7, 4 (1998) 11–16.

McChesney, R. *Rich Media, Poor Democracy* (Chicago: University of Illinois Press, 1999).

McDonald, H. *Trimble* (London: Bloomsbury, 2000).

McLaughlin, G. *The War Correspondent* (London: Pluto Press, 2002).

McNair, B. *An Introduction to Political Communication* (London: Routledge, 1995).

McNair, B. *Journalism and Democracy* (London: Routledge, 2000).

McNulty, M. 'Media Ethnicization and the International Response to War and Genocide in Rwanda', in T. Allen and J. Seaton (eds) *The Media of Conflict* (London: Zed Books, 1999).

McNulty, T. J. 'Television's Impact on Executive Decision Making and Diplomacy', *The Fletcher Forum of World Affairs*, 17 (1993) 67–83.

Melody, W. H. 'Communication Policy in the Global Information Economy: Whither the Public Interest', in M. Ferguson (ed.) *Public Communications: The New Imperatives* (London: Sage, 1990).

Melvern, L. R. *A People Betrayed* (London: Zed Books, 2000).

Melvern, L. *Conspiracy to Murder* (London: Verso, 2004).

Merin, J. 'Television News and American Intervention in Somalia: The Myth of a Media Driven Foreign Policy', *Political Science Quarterly* 112, 3 (1997) 385–403.

Merin, J. *Debating War and Peace* (Princeton, NJ: Princeton University Press, 1999).

Mestrovic, S. G. *Genocide After Emotion* (London: Routledge, 1996).

Metzl, J. F. 'Rwandan Genocide and the International Law of Radio Jamming', *The American Journal of International Law* 91, 4 (1997) 628–51.

Metzl, J. 'Defining Information Intervention', in M. E. Price and M. Thompson (eds) *Forging Peace* (Edinburgh: Edinburgh University Press, 2002).

Miall, H., O. Ramsbotham and T. Woodhouse, *Contemporary Conflict Resolution* (Oxford: Polity Press, 2000).

Miles, H. *Al-Jazeera* (London: Abacus, 2005).

Miller, D. *Don't Mention the War* (London: Pluto Press, 1994).

Miller, D., and G. McLaughlin, 'Reporting the Peace in Ireland', in B. Rolston and D. Miller (eds) *War and Words: The Northern Ireland Media Reader* (Belfast: Beyond the Pale Press, 1996).

Mitchell, G. *Making Peace* (London: William Heinemann, 1999).

Moeller, S. *Compassion Fatigue* (London: Routledge, 1999).

Murdock, G. 'Redrawing the Map of the Communications Industries: Concentration and Ownership in the Era of Privatization', in M. Ferguson (ed.) *Public Communications: The New Imperatives* (London: Sage, 1990).

Naimark, N. M. *Fires of Hatred* (Cambridge, MA: Harvard University Press, 2001).

Natsios, A. 'Illusion of Influence: The CNN Effect in Complex Emergencies', in R. I. Rotberg and T. G. Weiss (eds) *From Massacres to Genocide: The Media, Public Policy and Humanitarian Crises* (Cambridge, MA: The World Peace Foundation, 1996).

Naveh, C. 'The Role of the Media in Shaping Public Opinion', in S. Sofer (ed.) *Peacemaking in a Divided Society* (London: Frank Cass, 2001).

Negrine, R. *The Communication of Politics* (London: Sage, 1996).

Neuffer, E. *The Key To My Neighbour's House* (London: Bloomsbury, 2001).

Neuman, J. *Lights, Camera, War* (New York: St Martin's Press – now Palgrave Macmillan, 1996).

O'Brien, B. *The Long War* (Dublin: O'Brien Press, 1995).

O'Heffernan, P. *Mass Media and American Foreign Policy* (Norwood, NJ: Ablex Publishing, 1991).

O'Leary, B. 'The Protection of Human Rights Under The Belfast Agreement', *The Political Quarterly* 72, 3 (2001) 353–65.

O' Shaughnessy, N. J. *Politics and Propaganda* (Manchester: Manchester University Press, 2004).

Oz, A. *Help Us To Divorce* (London: Vintage, 2004).

Pach, C. J. 'And That's The Way It Was: The Vietnam War on the Network Nightly News', in D. Farber (ed.) *The Sixties: From Memory to History* (Chapel Hill, NC: University of North Carolina Press, 1994).

Pach, C. J. 'Tet on TV: US Nightly News Reporting and Presidential Policymaking', in C. Fink, P. Gassert and D. Junker (eds) *1968: The World Transformed* (Cambridge: Cambridge University Press, 1998).

Pach, C. J. 'The War on Television: TV News, The Johnson Administration and Vietnam', in M. B. Young and R. Buzzanco (eds) *A Companion to the Vietnam War* (Oxford: Blackwell, 2002).

Parkinson, A. *Ulster Loyalism and the British Media* (Dublin: Four Courts Press, 1998).

Paterson, C. 'Global Battlefields', in O. Boyd-Barrett and T. Rantanen (eds) *The Globalization of News* (London: Sage, 1998).

Patton, P. 'Introduction', in J. Baudrillard *The Gulf War Did Not Take Place* (Bloomington and Indianapolis: Indianapolis University Press, 1995).

Peterson, S. *Me Against My Brother* (London: Routledge, 2000).

Philo, G., and M. Berry, *Bad News From Israel* (London: Pluto Press, 2004).

Philo, G., and G. McLaughlin, 'The British Media and the Gulf War', in G. Philo (ed.) *Glasgow Media Group Reader Volume 2: Industry, Economy, War and Politics* (London: Routledge, 1995).

Pickering, M. *Stereotyping* (Basingstoke: Palgrave Macmillan, 2001).

Polman, L. *We Did Nothing* (London: Viking, 2003).

Power, S. *A Problem From Hell* (London: Flamingo, 2003).

Preston, A. 'Television News and the Bosnian Conflict: Distance, Proximity, Impact', in J. Gow, R. Paterson and A. Preston (eds) *Bosnia By Television* (London: BFI, 1996).

Prunier, G. *The Rwanda Crisis* (London: Hurst, 1997).

Raban, J. 'The Truth About Terrorism', *The New York Review of Books* (13 January 2005) 22–6.

Rabinovich, I. *Waging Peace* (Princeton, NJ: Princeton University Press, 2004).

Reardon, B. A. 'Towards a Paradigm of Peace', in L. R. Forcey (ed.) *Peace* (Westport, CT: Praeger, 1989).

Reese, S. D. 'Militarized Journalism: Framing Dissent in the Gulf War', in S. Allan and B. Zelizer (eds) *Reporting War* (London: Routledge, 2004).

Reporting The World (Taplow, Bucks: Conflict and Peace Forums, 2002).

Rieff, D. *Slaughterhouse* (London: Vintage, 1995).

Robinson, P. 'The CNN Effect: Can the News Media Drive Foreign Policy?, *Review of International Studies* 25 (1999) 301–9.

Robinson, P. 'The Policy-Interaction Model: Measuring Media Power During Humanitarian Crises', *Journal of Peace Reseach* 37, 5 (2000) 613–33.

Robinson, P. 'Operation Restore Hope and the Illusion of a News Media Driven Intervention', *Political Studies* 49 (2001) 941–56.

Robinson, P. *The CNN Effect: The Myth of News, Foreign Policy and Intervention* (London: Routledge, 2002).

Rohde, A. *A Safe Area* (London: Pocket Books, 1997).

Rolston, B., and D. Miller, *War and Words: The Northern Ireland Media Reader* (Belfast: Beyond the Pale Press, 1996).

Sadkovich, J. J. 'The Response of the American Media to Balkan Neo-Nationalisms', in S. G. Mestrovic (ed.) *Genocide After Emotion* (London: Routledge, 1996).

Said, E. *Covering Islam* (London: Vintage, 1997).

Said, E. *The End of the Peace Process* (London: Granta, 2000).

Said, E. *Orientalism* (London: Penguin 2003 edn).

Schiller, H. I. 'Manipulating Hearts and Minds', in H. Mowlana, G. Gerbner, and H. I. Schiller (eds) *Triumph of the Image* (Boulder, CO: Westeview Press, 1992).

Schlesinger, P. *Putting Reality Together* (London: Methuen, 1987).

Schreiber, E. M. 'Anti-War Demonstrations and American Public Opinion on the War in Vietnam', *British Journal of Sociology* 27, 2 (June 1976) 225–36.

Schudson, M. *The Power of News* (Cambridge, MA: Harvard University Press, 1995).

Seib, P. *Headline Diplomacy: How News Coverage Affects Foreign Policy* (Westport, CT: Praeger, 1997).

Seib, P. *The Global Journalist* (Lanham, MD: Rowman & Littlefield, 2002).

Seib, P. *Beyond the Front Lines* (Basingstoke: Palgrave Macmillan, 2004).

Sharkey, J. 'When Pictures Drive Foreign Policy', *American Journalism Review* (December 1993) 14–19.

Shaw, M. *Civil Society and Media in Global Crises* (London: Pinter, 1996).

Shinar, D. 'Media Diplomacy and 'Peace Talk'", *Gazette* 62, 2 (2000) 83–97.

Simms, B. *Unfinest Hour* (London: Allen Lane, 2001).

Singer, P. *The President of Good and Evil* (London: Granta, 2004).

Sinn Fein. *Setting the Record Straight; A Record of Communication Between Sinn Fein and the British Government, October 1990–November 1993* (Belfast: Sinn Fein, 1994).

Small, M. 'The Impact of the Antiwar Movement on Lyndon Johnson, 1965–8', *Peace and Carnage* 10 (Spring 1984) 1–22.

Small, M. 'Influencing the Decisionmakers: The Vietnam Experience', *Journal of Peace Research* 24, 2 (1987) 185–98.

Small, M. *AntiWarriors: The Vietnam War and the Battle for America's Hearts and Minds* (Wilmington, DE: Scholarly Resources, 2002).

Sparre, K. 'Megaphone Diplomacy in the Northern Irish Peace Process', *Harvard International Journal of Press/Politics* 6, 1 (2001) 88–104.

Spencer, G. *Disturbing the Peace? Politics, Television News and the Northern Ireland Peace Process* (Aldershot: Ashgate, 2000).

Spencer, G. 'Keeping the Peace? Politics, Television News and the Northern Ireland Peace Process', *Irish Journal of Sociology* 10, 2 (2001) 57–76.

Spencer, G. 'Pushing for Peace: The Irish Government, Television News and the Northern Ireland Peace Process', *European Journal of Communication* 18, 1 (2003) 55–80.

Spencer, G. 'The Impact of Television News on the Northern Ireland Peace Negotiations', *Media, Culture and Society* 26, 5 (2004a) 603–23.

Spencer, G. 'Constructing Loyalism: Politics, Communications and Peace in Northern Ireland', *Contemporary Politics* 10, 1 (2004b) 37–55.

Spencer, G. 'Reporting Inclusivity: The Northern Ireland Women's Coalition, the News Media and the Northern Ireland Peace Process', *Irish Journal of Sociology* 13, 2 (2004c) 43–65.

Stech, F. J. 'Winning CNN Wars', *Parameters* 24, 3 (1994) 37–56.

Strobel, W. P. 'The Media and U.S. Policies Towards Intervention: A Closer Look at the "CNN Effect"', in C. A. Crocker, F. O. Hampson and P. Aall (eds) *Managing Global Chaos* (Washington: US Institute of Peace Press, 1996).

Strobel, W. P. *Late-Breaking Foreign Policy: The News Media's Influence on Peace Operations* (Washington: US Institute of Peace Press, 1997).

Tait, R. 'The Conflict in Kosovo – The Lessons from the UK Media', in P. Goff (ed.) *The Kosovo News and Propaganda War* (Vienna: International Press Institute, 1999).

Taylor, P. *Provos: The IRA and Sinn Fein* (London: Bloomsbury, 1997).

Taylor, P. M. *Global Communications, International Affairs and the Media since 1945* (London: Routledge, 1997).

Taylor, P. M. *War and the Media* (Manchester: Manchester University Press, 1998).

Tester, K. *Moral Culture* (London: Sage, 1997).

Tester, K. *Compassion, Morality and the Media* (Buckingham: Open University Press, 2001).

The Peace Journalism Option (Taplow, Buckinghamshire: Conflict and Peace Forums, 1998).

Thompson, M. *Forging War* (Luton: University of Luton Press, 1999).

Thompson M., and D. de Luce, 'Escalating to Success? The Media Intervention in Bosnia and Herzogovina', in M. E. Price and M. Thompson (eds) *Forging Peace* (Edinburgh: Edinburgh University Press, 2002).

Thussu, D. K., and D, Freedman (eds) *War and Media: Reporting Conflict 24/7* (London: Sage, 2003).

Tuchman, G. 'Objectivity as Strategic Ritual: An Examination of Newmen's Notions of Objectivity', in H. Tumber (ed.) *News: A Reader* (Oxford; Oxford University Press, 1999).

Tumber, H. 'Bystander Journalism, or the Journalism of Attachment', *Intermedia* 25, 1 (February 1997) 4–7.

UNESCO. *Many Voices, One World*: the MacBride Report (Paris: UNESCO, 1984).

Vincent, C. 'CNN: Elites talking to Elites', in W. L. Bennettt and D. L. Paletz (eds) *Taken By Storm* (Chicago: University of Chicago Press, 1994).

Volkmer, I. *CNN News in the Global Sphere* (Luton: University of Luton Press, 1999).

Vulliamy, E. *Seasons In Hell* (London: Simon & Schuster, 1994).

Vulliamy, E. ' "Neutrality" and the Absence of Reckoning: A Journalist's Account', *Journal of International Affairs*, 52, 2 (Spring 1999) 603–20.

Ward, S. J. 'An Answer to Martin Bell: Objectivity and Attachment in Journalism', *Harvard International Journal of Press/Politics* 3, 3 (1998) 121–5.

Weber, C. 'The Media, the "War on Terrorism", and the Circulation of Non-Knowledge', in D. K. Thussu and D. Freedman (eds) *War and the Media* (London: Sage, 2003).

Williams, B. A. 'The New Media Environment, Internet Chatrooms and Public Discourse After 9/11', in D. K. Thussu and D. Freedman (eds) *War and the Media* (London: Sage, 2003).

Wolfsfeld, G. *Media and Political Conflict* (Cambridge: Cambridge University Press, 1997).

Wolfsfeld, G. 'Fair Weather Friends: The Varying Role of the News Media in the Arab-Israeli Peace Process', *Political Communication* 14, 1 (1997) 29–48.

Wolfsfeld, G. 'The News Media and the Second Intifada: Some Initial Lessons', *Harvard International Journal of Press/Politics* 6, 4 (2001) 113–18.

Wolfsfeld, G. 'Media, Conflict and Peace', in P. J. Maarek and G. Wolfsfeld (eds) *Political Communication in a New Era* (London: Routledge, 2003).

Wolfsfeld, G. *Media and the Path to Peace* (Cambridge: Cambridge University Press, 2004).

Woodward, S. L. *Balkan Tragedy* (Washington: The Brookings Institute, 1995).

Zartman, I. W., and S. Touval, 'International Mediation: Conflict Resolution and Power Politics', *Journal of Social Issues* 41, 2 (1985) 27–45.

Index